W9-ABF-995

Ward Blanton, Clayton Crockett,
Jeffrey W. Robbins, and Noëlle Vahanian

An Insurrectionist
MANIFESTO

FOUR NEW GOSPELS FOR
A RADICAL POLITICS

Foreword by Peter Rollins

Preface by Creston Davis

Afterword by Catherine Keller

 Columbia University Press   New York

Columbia University Press

Publishers Since 1893

New York   Chichester, West Sussex

cup.columbia.edu

Library of Congress Cataloging-in-Publication Data

Names: Blanton, Ward.

Title: An insurrectionist manifesto : four new gospels for a radical politics
  / Ward Blanton, Clayton Crockett, Jeffrey W. Robbins, and Noëlle Vahanian ; foreword
  by Peter Rollins ; preface by Creston Davis ; afterword by Catherine Keller.

Description: New York : Columbia University Press, 2016. | Series: Insurrections: critical
  studies in religion, politics, and culture | Includes bibliographical references and index.

Identifiers: LCCN 2015034162 | ISBN 9780231176224 (cloth : alk. paper) | ISBN 9780231176231
  (pbk. : alk. paper) | ISBN 9780231541732 (e-book)

Subjects: LCSH: Political theology.

Classification: LCC BT83.59 .I58 2016 | DDC 261.7—dc23

LC record available at http://lccn.loc.gov/2015034162

c 10 9 8 7 6 5 4 3 2 1

p 10 9 8 7 6 5 4 3 2 1

COVER DESIGN: Catherine Casalino

For Zoe and Sophia, Maria and Bryan, Charlie and Rose-Marie,
with a love no diaspora can ever define, nor time ever erase
in this once and for all life.

CONTENTS

FOREWORD

Peter Rollins

In the second century the early Christian ascetic Tatian set himself the task of merging the four gospel narratives into a single coherent whole. By the time he had finished he had crafted a text that merged Matthew, Mark, Luke, and John into one single volume.

The gospels were turned into a Gospel.

The four became one.

While his finished work, the *Diatessaron*, was popular in some circles, it didn't quite gain the support one might expect. Indeed it was mostly used only as a supplement to its source material, and by the fifth century had fallen almost completely out of use.

Given our love of single perspectives it's quite amazing that the four won out over the one—after all the four had themselves won out over a great many more. From today's perspective Tatian's project seems to succinctly express the ultimate dream of religious apologists, taking the messy, conflictual narratives and merging them together in a unified, atomic whole.

Yet there has always been another tradition in theology, one marked by a passion for the Real, a desire for the impossible that is testified to/ produced by conflictual narratives. In opposition to the demand for some clearly defined object believed to be the destination for our ultimate concern, this subversive, insurrectionary theology sets desire in motion by evoking an excitement for what cannot be grasped.

Such a theology does not seek rest in what can be imagined or symbolized, but remains restless, being stirred up in a dialectic of desire that remains open to the future as well as to reimagining the past.

A theology taken up by the Real teaches us to be wary of imaginary claims promising wholeness and harmony and exposes us to the various ways in which we are drawn into creating/serving sovereign powers.

This book brings together four such theorists of the Real, four writers inspired by the impossible. So what better way to present their work than in four separate reflections.

Four testimonies.

Four gospels.

Each one interlinked and intertwined with the others, yet each lacking an ultimate rapport with their neighbor. Each chapter challenging, confusing, and enlightening in equal measure.

Rather than a simple creed, we, the reader, are invited to partake in a multidisciplinary menagerie of ideas that reflect a dynamic, experimental project.

A project underway.

In place of clearly defined dogmas we find in these four essays shared coordinates—coordinates that might help shake us out of old orthodoxies and wake us up to the crisis we are in.

What we find here is a theology against sovereignty, a theology that celebrates the material world in a nonreductive way, a theology in motion that crosses boundaries, takes risks, speaks against the forces of death, and places itself on trial.

In short, we find within these pages a theology in play that refuses the status quo, confronts us with the present state, and unveils new horizons.

Even for those seasoned readers of critical theory, this text is demanding. The writers aren't afraid to cross disciplinary boundaries, requiring us to step into waters that might be unknown to us. At one moment poetic, in the next philosophical, then scientific; readers will find themselves off balance more than once in this journey between earth and sky, mortals and gods.

But this is what makes the work so rich, kinetic, and fertile. If we wrestle with it, we might find that it turns us upside down, inside out, and right side up—though not necessary in that order.

It's no secret that the disparate work done in the name of radical theology suffered somewhat after its moment in the sun around the 1960s. After less than a decade, it appeared to many that this movement had withered and died. But rumors of its demise have been greatly exaggerated, and, after a period of relative latency, it has returned with a renewed vibrancy and urgency, as witnessed in this potent, explosive manifesto.

PREFACE

Creston Davis

In the beginning, the positively charged void of the universe gave birth to the insurrection. Soon Earth revolted against Sky and mortals overthrew the gods, and the world began manifesting itself through an *insurrectionism*, an infinite unfolding of the Good News. This book is the culmination of a faithfulness to the event of insurrection that began in a Philadelphia taxicab in 2005 where we discussed the need for establishing a book series that finally broke from the hegemonic grip of depoliticized "postmodernism." This postmodern "genre" of thinking rendered impossible the ability to name truths. Our theory was that nothing was being said of any significance not just in critical theory but also in continental philosophy, religion, and other subjects because, effectively, scholars were fully inscribed within the neoliberal academic matrix.

This book, these "Gospels" must therefore be read as a true breakout from the dangerous apolitical alignment between postmodernism's apathy to truth and the hijacking of the neoliberal academy in North America. The kernel essence of this book is that the authors show how history isn't determined by a singular commodified event (i.e., Resurrection), which endlessly defers its meaning that never arrives, but rather through materialist immanence that never settles as it tosses and turns in the folds of a materialist struggle configured by the destiny of a cosmically charged revolt!

But one should be careful here, as what this book appears to offer is fundamentally deceptive because, while it ingeniously confronts seminal positions, thinkers, and basic texts of the American "death of God" theological tradition with all its presuppositions, what it ends up revealing is a disavowal truth. That although God is dead, the arguments, symbolic structure, and so forth of this tradition continue to assume a perverse stance that, despite everything, God continues to haunt the discourse. This book finally breaks from this fetishistic onto-theology once and for all not by falling into the trap of poorly paraphrasing their interlocutors only to disguise it by jargon and making some far-reaching conclusions. "The denial of jargon itself," as Slavoj Žižek says, "is today part of the standard jargon, so that, when one reads phrases like 'What I'll say now is not an empty phrase,' one can be sure that what will follow IS an empty phrase."[1] This makes it difficult for me to signal that it is not an empty gesture when we claim that this text completely reframes theology: a theology of a cosmically charged void.

But this "breakout" again shouldn't be read like the "end of ideology" thesis in which a materialist dialectical history is victoriously dispatched to the dustbins of history only to return from the ashes. What this book does is a perfect example of Hegel's strategy of the *Aufhebung* in which what is negated (classical and death of God theologies) is subsumed in its very negation through itself revealing the truth of an ontological insurrectionist moment devoid of time.

So what happens here is that an entirely new resurgence of power is brought to bear from an entirely different point of departure, a point that swallows up all points while perfecting them negatively. And this is the εὐαγγέλιον (Gospel, goodnews, etc.) because it rejects entirely a dead discourse (traditional onto-theology) that will do anything to stay alive long after its object "God" has died. This is done in the following four ways: first, thought as insurrectional force doesn't think about the Real (in Lacanian terms) but *from* the Real as elaborated by Slavoj Žižek and François Laruelle. Second, a Dionysian affirmation of a nonreductive materialism in the wake of Catherine Malabou's work beyond the Derridean obsession with totality on the one hand and infinite deferral of signification on the other. Third, there is here a genuine commitment to a leftist open politics that resists falling back into the dogmatic trap of certitude closed off from a porous externality. This commitment should not be misread as a recapitulation of a politically correct, ecological ideology, but rather seen as a full-frontal assault on the catastrophic effects of neoliberalism and corporate capitalism. Fourth, and finally, what precisely keeps these thinkers out of the trap of the enclosed jailhouse of being at home with itself is the Hegelian dialectical method of experimental openness committed to an unfolding process always under constant evaluation, without assuming a masturbatory self-satisfaction so endemic in today's theory.

It's here, too, where any notion of resurrection is supplanted by thinking the world not from the reductive standpoint of the one, but from a nonrepeatable difference—the world as liberated from resurrection and the demands the Good News that insurrectional theory gives to us today.

An Insurrectionist MANIFESTO

INTRODUCTION
What Is Insurrectionist Theology?

Ward Blanton, Clayton Crockett,
Jeffrey W. Robbins, and Noëlle Vahanian

We believe in the Insurrection, not the Resurrection—whether it be of Jesus Christ or of anyone else. Resurrection generally smacks of simple repetition, whereby the same person is resuscitated, revived, restored to life. Such things are fantasies. We fashion ourselves not as the mythological phoenix, rising from the ashes, but as the salamander, severed and bruised—insurrection as regeneration.

Every genuine creation is an insurrectionary event. *Insurrection* is a political term, and it operates in clear tension with a more individualistic notion of religious resurrection, the idea that each person should be invested in his or her salvation rather than that of anyone else. Insurrection, however, is generally seen in political terms as intrinsically limited, as a failed attempt at change, as change that is destroyed or aborted, change that does not pass to a fully revolutionary action or successful event. No doubt, we have become more skeptical of the possibility and the result of a revolution after the short but intense twentieth century that manifests what Alain Badiou calls a "passion for the Real" and the failure of most of its political revolutions.[1] If a revolution comes full circle, back in some respects to where it began, an insurrection is more of a diagonal line that surges forth without, however, renouncing its passion for the Real beyond imaginary fantasy and the symbolic reality.

The other problem with a political thinking of insurrection is that it is generally seen as reactive, as being an insurrection against a given state of affairs. Just as the Occupy movement was seen as a protest movement without any positive agenda or demands, an insurrection can be viewed solely as a protest against the status quo. But what if we free insurrection from this limited viewpoint and see insurrection as a radically affirmative event, resistance not as reactionary but as constitutive? An insurrection is not primarily against something, but for something: for an idea, a life, a being together whose existence is not given but can only be created through struggle. Insurrection is a *surrection-in-process*, a surging-in that unfurls and surges forth, and it is this vital affirmation that must characterize insurrection and insurrectionary thought today.

Ours is a theological move, to situate insurrection as an alternative to resurrection, just as the radical theologian Peter Rollins names his provocative book *Insurrection* for this very move.[2] But it is, at the same time, a political move, to cross political insurrection with theological insurrection, to form a new kind of political theology that would escape the long shadow cast by the thought of Carl Schmitt.[3] According to Schmitt, "all significant concepts of the modern theory of the state are secularized theological concepts" due to their historical development and their "systematic structure."[4] Schmitt appeals to a conservative politics and a hierarchical theology, however, so, despite his importance for the history of twentieth-century thought, Schmitt's political theology remains a brutal dead end to be circumvented. The question is whether there is or could be a progressive, non-Schmittian political theology. Antonio Negri responds to this question with a forceful no when he writes: "I for my part am acquainted with just one political theology, the one at whose opposite and symmetrical extremes stand Bodin and Stalin, with Carl Schmitt occupying a slot somewhere in between."[5] But why on earth would we declare that it is simply not possible to conceive political theology without sovereignty? Or, if not without sovereignty exactly, then why could we not conceptualize political theology *beyond* the sovereign force of the One of classical logic, monarchy, or monotheism? Indeed, why would we not force a thought of political theology as itself a dispersal and pluralization of sovereign power that outstrips any and every theopolitical logic of the One? Such a political theology would be an insurrectionary political theology, and it would constitute an insurrection not only with theology but also against theology in itself. Theology must free itself from the sovereign One, or God, and this is an insurrectionary task.

Theology names a theoretical discourse about religion, and it is usually understood as a confessional or apologetic discourse. Radical theology, however, means that theology is freed from confessional orthodoxy and opened up to engage genuine and important questions about our lives and our world. In the modern world, religion was generally seen as explainable by or reducible to other terms, other foundations, whether aesthetics, ethics, science, or philosophy. In Kant's famous critiques, religion was appended onto ethics, and there could be therefore no direct critique of religion. Religion seems always to hide in the "depths" of modern discourse and practice during this period, but it never goes away.

We prefer the term *postsecularism* to *postsecular* in order to flag that, for us, the so-called return of religion neither overcomes nor dispenses with the secular. Furthermore, we do not conceive religious and secular in oppositional terms. Postsecularism refers to the fact that modern secularism, which is an ideology of liberal capitalism, fails to be credible, as Schmitt's incisive writings, among others, show. Postsecularism means that any opposition between the secular and the religious falls into oblivion. This event of deconstruction also reverberates in the division of human society between public and private spheres of life and the relegation of religion to the private realm. Religion returns—although it never went away—in explicitly public terms. As Talal Asad argues, the secularization thesis no longer works because "the categories of 'politics' and 'religion' turn out to implicate each other more profoundly than we thought, a discovery that has accompanied our growing understanding of the powers of the modern nation-state. The concept of the secular cannot do without the idea of religion."[6]

In 2005 two of the authors had a conversation with Creston Davis and Slavoj Žižek about a new book series that was proposed to and approved by Columbia University Press. This series was envisioned as a radical series of cutting-edge engagements, which would address theoretically the intersection of religion and politics in the contemporary world in ways that refuse conservatism and complacency in both political and theological terms. At the same time, from that moment we viewed theology not only in radical terms but also as opening up and out in interdisciplinary and transdisciplinary modes that clearly exceed what is today generally counted as theology. When the question arose as to a name for this book series, we brainstormed for a few days, and Jeff Robbins suggested the term *Insurrections,* which we all affirmed. Insurrections has launched books and ideas, original statements and much needed translations in order to become a vital contribution to contemporary academic and intellectual discourse on and around questions of religion and political or cultural life.

Nevertheless, we felt that something was missing, which we were not able to elaborate in 2005. At a subsequent retreat in Western North Carolina in 2011, some of us debated how we could take the next step. That is, how could we articulate the vision behind what we were trying to do with the series, even if of course not every text fully shared that vision, but yet contributed important elements to it? We decided there on the lake to compose a kind of manifesto for insurrectionist theology, not only something that articulates our shared understanding of what is possible, indeed, essential, but also something that, at the same time, does not just articulate but *performs* what we are talking about.

What is insurrection theology? Here we sketch out five elements:

1) A filiation with the tradition of radical theology, which includes a never-ending reflection on the many and multiple "deaths of God" of the inherited traditions.

2) An ontology of the Real that is for us always linked to the theorization of Jacques Lacan and Gilles Deleuze, and elaborated as well by Slavoj Žižek and François Laruelle.

3) A theological materialism that affirms material reality in nonreductive ways, recognizing the valencing effect of ideas that must still be called "vital." This materialism would be a plastic materialism, following Catherine Malabou.

4) A commitment to a leftist political edge that nevertheless eludes dogmatic certainty—ours is the struggle with and within the world for an ethical-ecological vision of Life beyond money, greed, power, and devastation of neoliberalism and corporate capitalism.

5) An experimental theology in which everything is up in the air, staked and at stake, a politico-theological laboratory formulating new tests for a theology that is always *en procès* (in process/on trial, to use a term from Julia Kristeva).

1) *Insurrectionist theology claims a filiation with the tradition of radical theology, including the theologies of the "death of God."* Ours is a complex rather than simple affiliation, and in some respects we find ourselves passing through the "death of the death of God."[7] Above all, our genealogies tend to overload the very "death" of God through the multiplication or serialization of this "death," its comparative explication as always so many deaths, multiple deaths of so many singular Gods, even

if one reads for these passing singularities in Jewish and Christian traditions only. Depending on the text and cultural traffic in question, the God who writes is supplanting, outbidding, and living off the demise of the God who speaks (and vice versa). The God who does flamboyant miracles becomes gauche and passé through the God who deftly refuses such Hollywood flamboyance. With Gods, as much as ourselves, everywhere and always the living live off the consumption of others, living Gods feast for their vibrancy and aura—the very divinity of the divine— off the Gods in decline. The *singular vibrancy* of the Gods in question are viewable in the same moment that our reading takes seriously the profound and also agonistic *differences* in play in these traditions, and no piety is worth the monstrous cover-up operative in the idea that all these agonistic singularities constitute, in the end, a One. Those who follow such a pious path will finally realize that the cost is steep, demanding—eventually—that their own highest values be sacrificed to this One, namely, their *love of a singular deity*. Without difference and multiplicity (which is also to say without death and the passing of singularities) there is no love, and the crusaders for the One and their desperate efforts to synthesize and harmonize these traditions need eventually to become clear about whether they will be true to a Synthetic One or to the Unique One they love.

In any case, this much we want to be clear about: the death of the death of God, if it is conceivable, is not simply a repudiation or renunciation of this death but also an elaboration of it. American death of God theology began in the early 1960s, with the reflection that the idea of God no longer fit with contemporary experience of the world in secular and cultural terms. The theological movement surrounding the expression "Death of God" is multifaceted, and possesses multiple meanings rather than one simple underlying story. Thomas J. J. Altizer is the most famous representative, but other theological thinkers include Gabriel Vahanian, William Hamilton, Richard Rubenstein, Harvey Cox, and Paul van Buren.

We see ourselves as working in the tradition of American death of God theology, even if we want to open it up beyond some of its presentist and provincial assumptions and associations—and even if we also want to link it up to streams of liberationist and process thought. The death of God means the break with the metaphysical presumption of God, rendering belief in God questionable rather than self-evident. It's not that the death of God comes about at some time after the life of God, whether this is understood in terms of divine subjectivity or human projection. The point is that the death of God always accompanies (faith in) God like a lining or a shadow, and it is there from the start, even if this awareness is not evident from the beginning.

In terms of modern genealogy, we can trace a line of descent from Paul Tillich as the alternative to Barthian neo-orthodoxy in the twentieth century. Rather than accepting and endorsing Tillich's system, we affirm Tillich's questioning as well as his insistence that theology is responsive to and shaped by its cultural conditions. Tillich is read in different ways, if he is still read, but we endorse Altizer's affirmation of the "radical Tillich" insofar as his questions open up powerful and transformative reflections that do not correspond to easy answers. As Altizer states in the preface to *The Gospel of Christian Atheism*, "While I have been forced to resist and oppose Tillich's theological conclusions, I do so with the conviction that they are not yet radical enough, and with the memory of Tillich's words to me that the real Tillich is the radical Tillich."[8]

Radical theology means the willingness—the cultivated institutional and intellectual freedom—to challenge and question orthodoxy, rather than to be operate within its constraints or to be predetermined by its implicit threats and promises. The Latin etymology of the word *radical* is *radix*, which means root. Getting to the root means going back to the original experience that is then codified and reified in language, doctrine, and dogma. But what if that original experience is contested—is it possible for theology to be radical anymore? Isn't postmodernism precisely the denial of origins as roots, leaving us hopelessly shallow, displaced, and disempowered in relation to the resources of this *"originary" experience*? As will become increasingly clear, we embrace a different sort of root and a more rhizomatic structure, as Deleuze and Guattari elaborate. A rhizome is a complex knot of connections and affiliations, taken from the description the roots of tuber plants, which they opposed to the conception of radicals and roots. A root structure is tied to a tree metaphor, a metaphor that is linear and hierarchical, while a radical-fascicle implies a principal root that is aborted but nonetheless stubbornly remains in a truncated form. Deleuze and Guattari argue that "a rhizome as subterranean stem is absolutely different from roots and radicles. Bulbs and tubers are rhizomes."[9] Radical theology passes over into rhizomatic theology when it becomes postmodern. In any case, it is a passage we do not lament, buzzy as we get on the question of new networks, new solidarities, new sites of linkage and transformation.

Postmodern theology emerges in the late 1970s and early 1980s when the insights and questions of death of God theology are crossed with French poststructuralism and deconstruction. Here theology is seen explicitly as a type of language or discourse formation. It's less about theology's supposed referent and more about what theological discourse does, including how it interacts with other discourses. Here theology is caught up in the linguistic turn. Mark C. Taylor is the most celebrated postmodern theologian, and his 1984 *Erring: A Postmodern A/theology* sets an agenda with its four themes: the death of God, the disappearance of the self, the end of history, and the closure of the book. Other representatives of postmodern theology include Carl Raschke, Charles Winquist, and to a lesser extent Edith Wyschogrod and Robert Scharlemann. As Raschke puts it in an essay on "The Deconstruction of God," "deconstruction, which must be considered the interior drive of twentieth-century theology rather than an alien agenda, is in the final analysis *the death of God put into writing*, the subsumption of the 'Word' by the 'flesh,' the deluge of immanence."[10] Deconstruction, associated primarily with the poststructuralist philosophy of Derrida, is here identified as the death of God put into writing in the writing of a postmodern theology of the death of God.

The interests and themes of postmodern theology were less explicitly political and more epistemological, aesthetic, linguistic, and, in the case of Wyschogrod's powerful engagement with Emmanuel Levinas, ethical. There was a radicality to this thought in theological terms, but a lack of radicality in political terms. In some ways both postmodernism and the death of God could be read, precisely, as buffers from—or neutralizations of—leftist and liberationist theological and political struggles. Certainly the death of God was controversial when it was emblazoned so fashionably on the cover of *Time* magazine. But in a predominantly secular and increasingly consumerist culture, the "devaluation of the highest values" could just as easily make latter-day men and women yawn and look for new things to purchase.

In the 1990s, postmodern theology took a more conservative theological turn in the work of Jean-Luc Marion and the Radical Orthodoxy movement primarily associated with John Milbank. At the same time, however, the powerful social critique of contemporary capitalism represented by Radical Orthodoxy resonated with many readers, whether or not they embraced the solutions offered by Milbank, Graham Ward, Catherine Pickstock, Phillip Blond, Daniel Bell, and others. Around the same time, during the 1990s a continental philosophy of religion took shape, largely inspired by attention to the religious interests of Derrida and Levinas as well as Marion. This movement, associated with philosophers of religion like John D. Caputo, Merold Westphal, and Richard Kearney, was more explicitly philosophical and tended to view the term *theology* with suspicion.[11] Many of these debates concerned questions of phenomenology and followed in the wake of the Heideggerian rejection of metaphysics.

As we approached the twenty-first century, American postmodern theology had dissipated, Radical Orthodoxy was widely read, and there was a strong interest in thinking through the theoretical implications of contemporary continental philosophy in an increasingly globalized and pluralistic world. *Incipit 9–11*. It was not simply the event itself, but the reaction on the part of the Bush administration—including the Patriot Act, the surveillance and restrictions of civil rights of Americans, as well as the wars unleashed against Afghanistan and Iraq on the part of an emboldened neoconservativism, with its justification of torture— that shook many complacent liberals to the core. Perhaps it is Jeffrey W. Robbins's essay on "Terror and the Postmodern Condition" that best encapsulates the political critique of postmodern theology along with the call for a radical political vision expressed in the subtitle, "Toward a Radical Political Theology." Robbins argues that a radical politics is needed due to "the vacuity in the prevailing political order" and, at the same time, that radical theology "provides a model for the revitalization of theological thinking without setting the religious in opposition to the secular."[12] Here a vision of radical theology is joined to a vision of radical politics, and this was the seed for an insurrectionist theology that is committed not just to social reality but to the Real.

2) *Insurrectionist theology expresses an ontology of the Real that is tied to the theorization of Jacques Lacan and Gilles Deleuze, which is further elaborated by Slavoj Žižek and François Laruelle.* What is the Real? In his early seminars Lacan was more interested in the distinction between the imaginary and the symbolic. Here the category of the real refers mainly to a presymbolized brute existence that is foreclosed and inaccessible once a person enters the symbolic order of language and desire. Later, and in a way that remains important to us, Lacan shifts to wrestle more powerfully with the ways in which desire is a failure and the symbolic

is fractured by the Thing or the just-barely-symbolized Real. The Real returns in language to mark a limit of language, an irreducible excess that cannot be overcome.

Most of the time our thinking about God takes place in what Lacan calls the imaginary register. We invoke God as a fantasy for the providential benevolence of the universe, as the idea that there is a meaning behind irrational and traumatic events, or as the comforting notion that somebody cares about me as an individual and will preserve my essence after I die. In more symbolic terms, God functions to guarantee ethics or the social order. Here God is identified with what Lacan calls the Other, who is the crystallization of a symbolic field of which we are usually unconscious. But what is God in the Real? Many theologians do not approach a true reflection of God in terms of the Real, which lies beyond the symbolic and imaginary orders while remaining implicated in both of them. As the Real, God is not omnipotent, does not love us, and is not conscious in any recognizable way. Here God is what Tillich calls being-itself, and the statement that God is being-itself is the only nonsymbolic statement one can make about God without slipping back into an imaginary view of divinity (even if Tillich himself tried to take this claim back).

According to Žižek, Lacan's later thinking about the Real is decisive for his philosophy and its cultural and political implications. In seminar 20, Lacan contrasts a "feminine" logic of non-All with a "masculine" logic of exception. What is the significance of this distinction? According to the stereotypical "masculine" logic, the Real is taken to constitute an exception to the symbolic order. So, anything that takes place in our finite worldly existence would be seen as contradicted when applied to God in and as the Real. For example, our social symbolic existence is finite, but we might posit the Real as outside the symbolic, imagining that the Real is infinite in opposition to finite experience. This Lacan reads as a masculine logic of exception—the Real is the exception to the universal order of things. God, and anything divine, becomes an exception to the rule. On the other hand, the "feminine" logic of not or non-All refers instead to a lack of closure of the symbolic order itself, its internal inconsistency. The Real, in this logic, becomes the not-All of the symbolic itself. Here the Real does not take place outside or beyond the symbolic, but rather curls up within the symbolic as the "logic" that, precisely, *prevents* the symbolic from achieving totality, completion, or groundedness. This curled-up Real is the "source" of insurrection.

As Žižek tends to explicate it, the Thing—as a name for the Real—is first posited outside our shared reality in a masculine way. But, as a kind of moment of maturation, when we shift to a Lacan's "feminine" logic, we realize that the Thing is actually intrinsic to our own experiential logic itself. This is a very subtle shift, and one that could no doubt operate perfectly well without reference to sexuality at all. But it is nevertheless a crucial distinction. By positing the Thing in the Real out there, we suppose that it is inaccessible. But, when we shift our focus, we realize that the Thing is not "out there," or a sphere to which one might "break through," so much as what distorts our focus in such a way that we would never attain a god's-eye field of vision in the first place. As Žižek explains, "the Real is *simultaneously* the Thing to which direct access is not possible [masculine] and the obstacle that prevents this direct access [feminine]; the Thing that eludes our grasp [masculine] and the distorting screen that makes us miss the Thing [feminine]." We think the Real is that which lies beyond our ability to access, but when we work progress through the dialectic we discover that the Real is better understood as the irreducible distortion of our knowing, which makes it impossible to simply grasp the Thing in itself. As this shrewd Hegelian often does, here Žižek goes on to explain his peculiar synthesis of these options by saying that "the Real is ultimately the very shift in perspective from the first standpoint [masculine] to the second [feminine]."[13] The Real is a shift in perspective, which Žižek later designates a central category for his larger philosophical and political project, the Real becoming what he calls a "parallax view."

In ways that become increasingly clear, it is important to note that insurrectionist theology is a commitment to thinking the Real, despite the fact that the Real cannot be accessed directly. For Gilles Deleuze, who is often unhelpfully read over against Lacan and psychoanalysis in a simple sense, the Real is not inaccessible beyond the symbolic but produced in conjunction with the imagination. Despite important tensions between Deleuzean and Lacanian perspectives, we take them to be more complementary here than many recognize. (Indeed, one characteristic style of insurrectionist theology so far is often a profound disinterest in the repetition of standardized, even ready-made distinctions between various schools of thought. We hardly think it less than comical to abandon one orthodoxy to its anxious guardians and caretakers in order to repeat the same anxious gesture elsewhere. Rhizomatic thought is not simply an openness to aleatory networks; it is a disciplined refusal to allow our thinking to function as a mere repetition of the same. That we leave to others, a job for which there seem, these days more than ever, to be many applicants).

Deleuze was working on similar theoretical issues as Lacan in the late 1960s and early 1970s, and Lacan highly praised both *Difference and Repetition* and *The Logic of Sense*. It was the uncompromising polemical nature of *Anti-Oedipus*, matched with Lacan's interest in consolidating his own role on the French intellectual stage, that introduced an irreparable break, despite the fact that Lacan was already moving in similar directions in the 1970s.[14] For Deleuze and Guattari, the two-volume *Capitalism and Schizophrenia* project involved an effort to produce the Real as a deterritorializing event that cannot be reterritorialized by capitalism. The production of the Real as an event constitutes a very different logic than the subtraction of the Real from symbolic reality in more conventional Lacanian terms, but we prefer to view these processes as more complementary than contradictory.

As already mentioned, even if we cannot produce the Real in a straightforward manner, we can still participate in the creation of the Real with and beyond symbolic and imaginary forces. As a patchwork discourse with a massive history of thinking about aleatory (or chance) participations without productive ownership, theology is more interesting when it attends to the Real, to its implication in the Real, and to the creation of Real energies and ideas, rather than when it reflects the status quo symbolic order or participates in whatever fantastic wish fulfillment. The Real can be articulated and expressed in different ways, but it is the *insistence* of the Real that we affirm.

Finally, we want to add Laruelle to our list of Lacan, Žižek, and Deleuze as thinkers of the Real. Laruelle uses the term *Real* in a way similar to Lacan, as that which we can never fully reach or express. For Laruelle, philosophy totalizes experience in trying to reach the Real and to think the One. The problem is that philosophy can never reach its goal despite its presupposition of its own sufficiency or "the principle of sufficient philosophy."[15] The shift to what Laruelle calls nonphilosophy occurs when we stop trying to think *to* the Real and start to think *from* it. This produces what Laruelle calls a "vision-in-One." A vision-in-One is our positing of the One or the Real, from which we think, from the Real to our own existence.

To think from the Real to our experience of thinking only goes one way. We cannot think to the Real; we can only think from it. The thinking from the Real to our existence constitutes what Laruelle calls a "unilateral duality": because it is unilateral, and in its line from the Real to us, it draws a line that divides the dual halves of what lie on either side. According to Laruelle, "everything is processed through a duality (of problems) that does not constitute a two or a pair, and through an identity (of problems, and hence of solution) that does not constitute a unity or synthesis."[16] In theological terms this means that we cannot proceed from our own experience to God. In attempting to reach God, we always presume our own theological sufficiency to think and comprehend God. The only way for a genuine theology or non-theology to proceed is to think God as Real or as a vision-in-One and to go from God to the world.[17] This thinking *from* God sets up what Laruelle calls a unilateral duality in its movement from the Real to us. Unilateral duality means that it only goes one way; it is unilateral and it works with and makes use of dualities that are never reified into oppositions.

Laruelle, like Lacan, Deleuze, and many other French theorists, is difficult to read and has his own idiosyncratic terminology. Some theologically interested readers may wonder if the punch lines are worth the entry fee. But the challenge is not just to read and comprehend cutting-edge theory; it is the task of an insurrectionist theology to take on leading philosophical writing and to work through it rather than refuse it or shrink from it. All of thinking remains at stake, and the best interlocutors need to be gathered in order to continue a collective struggle of knowing what it means to think and seeing what the stakes of thinking are today in a world that seems so effectively to banish profound intellectual work even from schools, colleges, universities. These days, as ever, we cannot afford not to think, and we cannot afford not to think the Real, a Real that is material in nature.

3) *Insurrectionist theology is committed to a theological materialism that affirms material reality in nonreductive ways and recognizes the importance of vital ideas.* The *new materialism* is a phrase coined in the late 1990s to describe the work of theorists such as Manuel DeLanda, Elizabeth Grosz, William Connolly, Jane Bennett, Diana Coole, and Rosi Braidotti, most of whom are influenced by the ontological work of Deleuze and Guattari. The new materialism is a materialism based on agency, vitality, and energy transformation rather than on a reductionist atomic materialism.[18] The new materialism is a vital materialism, and it is linked to cutting-edge work going on in the natural sciences, including chaos and complexity theory in physics, genetics and epigenetics in

biology, and the work being done on the frontier of neurology and brain sciences. Rather than simply mining these sciences for results, theorists and philosophers are attending to the processes at work and marking how these processes also work in the humanities and social sciences.

The new materialism is a plastic materialism, following the philosophy of Catherine Malabou. In her book *Plasticity at the Dusk of Writing*, plasticity is offered as a new motor scheme to replace writing, which has reigned in continental philosophy under the sign of poststructuralism. Malabou argues that writing driven by "the power of the linguistic-graphic scheme is diminishing and that it has entered a twilight for some time already. It now seems that plasticity is slowly but surely establishing itself as the paradigmatic figure of organization in general."[19] Plasticity as a phenomenon and motor scheme means that matter is not simply inert stuff, but dynamic form, with the ability to generate as well as receive form, together with the crucial third element of plasticity, the capacity to explode form itself in a moment of auto-annihilation.[20]

As Malabou affirms in the conclusion to her book *The New Wounded*, "I continue to suggest that the only valid philosophical path today lies in the elaboration of a new materialism that would precisely refuse to envisage the least separation, not only between brain and thought but also between the brain and the unconscious."[21] For Malabou, this plastic materialism is "the basis for *a new philosophy of spirit*," and we would agree.[22] Plasticity means there is no dualistic separation of mind and body, matter and spirit, and, ultimately, form and energy.

In terms of insurrectionist theology, we embrace the term *materialism* for two main reasons. First, an emphasis on material reality works against the location of meaning and value elsewhere than the world in which we live. There is an immanence to theological thinking and practice that resists redirection to a Platonic *eidos* or a heavenly afterlife. For Rollins, "Christianity can be described as a theological materialism; it is that which transforms our material existence."[23] We want to direct or redirect our religious and spiritual energies into this-worldly transformation rather than denying or fleeing our material existence. And, whereas classical materialism tends to dismiss and denigrate religion and religious practice, we do not see material and spiritual ideas and practices as opposed. There is no dualism and consequently there is no reductionism. Being is energy transformation, and energy is fully material and fully spiritual at once. We do not want to reduce thoughts to bodies but to embrace both in their materiality. Thinking is a practice;

language and writing are material practices. The tedious repetition of stale dualisms and stable oppositional figures of thought seem to us useless—almost willfully stupid.

The other reason we embrace, with real affection, the term *materialism* is for its political charge. Materialism does not mean the reification of matter, but the deployment of it. In the first decade of the twenty-first century, Slavoj Žižek scandalized many leftists, not to mention Christians, by his affirmation of a materialist Christianity and his identification as a Christian atheist. In his famous confrontation with John Milbank, *The Monstrosity of Christ*, Žižek claims that "it is Milbank who is in effect guilty of heterodoxy, ultimately a regression to paganism: in my atheism, I am more Christian than Milbank."[24]

Žižek's thought is complex, influenced by G. W. F. Hegel and Lacan as well as Karl Marx, so it is not materialist in a conventional or classical sense, but rather in an importantly paradoxical or dialectical way. For Žižek, the death of Jesus Christ, identified as Son of God and as God, manifests the actual death of God. The cry of Jesus on the cross: "Father, why have you forsaken me?," indicates an irreducible gap or split within divinity, which is the same gap within both humanity and nature itself. This gap opens up a parallax, which drives radical and revolutionary political activity.

4) *Insurrection theology affirms a leftist political edge without any dogmatic certainty—it's about the struggle with and within the world for an ethical-ecological vision of Life beyond money, greed, power, and the devastation of neoliberalism and corporate capitalism.* There is no neutrality—we have to take sides. As the great historian of American labor Howard Zinn claims, "You can't be neutral on a moving train," especially one that is quickly going off the tracks. We side with life, with vitality, with affirmation, and with compassion, empathy, love, and care for others and ourselves. Life is complicated and paradoxical, and it is complicit with the worst forms of suffering, torture, and murder, but we do not have to affirm these aspects and we do not have to numb ourselves to them. Consumerist capitalism isolates and impoverishes us; it is destroying our lives by burying them in banality, violence, and enslaving debts.[25]

Capitalism has never been just; it has been accompanied by brutality, racism, and war. At the same time, there is something powerful and liberating about capitalism, its capacities to harness and to promote growth, progress, and material development. Now, however, the practice of neoliberal corporate capitalism threatens to destroy human civilization in new modes. Imperatives of growth are colliding with real limits of material resources and producing a global ecological crisis. You cannot have infinite growth given a finite resource base, and we have forgotten the material reality of Earth in our fantasies of technological progress. Insurrectionist theology is *against* contemporary neoliberal capitalism and *for* a radical posthumanist ecological vision of life beyond its capture in quantitative monetary values. Posthumanism is not antihumanism any more than postmodern is antimodern. We face, however, the possibility of the extinction of human and many other forms of life on Earth. The urgency of our material-ecological-economic-political situation requires us to experiment with critical theories and liberationist practices.

5) *An insurrectionist theology is an experimental theology in which the most important elements are up in the air or at stake, a kind of testing in which theology is always* en procès *(in process/on trial, to use a term from Julia Kristeva).* Theology is not settled or finished. It does not live off of a long-past event. We view theology as inventive and experimental, as a testing of itself in a continual process of transformation as well as a testing ground of and for other discourses, ideas, energies, and practices. Theology does live off itself, or its own traditions and histories, which can be stifling—and in that case should be treated as Martin Luther wanted to treat the book of James, namely, by chucking it into the fireplace. Much of the time, when we think theologically (or otherwise), we substitute catchphrases for ideas, once more mining historical archives for predetermined conclusions, words degenerating into platitudes and clichés. Theology is necessarily parasitical of other discourses and experiences, which is how creative or generative thinking works. It crosses boundaries and breaks rules, connecting and disconnecting channels to produce intensity and novelty if we let it. We should not resist this as temptation but embrace it as an opportunity.

In *Revolution in Poetic Language* Julia Kristeva writes about subjectivity as always *en procès*, where *en procès* means both "in process" and also "on trial." She says that there is something about the "dialectical notion of the signifying process as a whole" that "puts the subject in process/on trial [*en procès*]."[26] For Kristeva, this discussion of the formation of subjectivity concerns her distinction between the semiotic and the symbolic, which loosely follows Lacan's terminology of real and symbolic, although the semiotic is not precisely what Lacan understands by the real. In any case, the semiotic for Kristeva references a presymbolic semiotic *chōra* in which a person resides prior to her entrance into symbolic language. Once a person becomes a symbolic being, however, her identity is continually affected by the return of the semiotic in both disturbing and liberating ways. A subject becomes a subject by entering into a "thetic phase," where the thetic phase "marks the threshold between two heterogeneous realms: the semiotic and the symbolic."[27]

Drawing on Kristeva's formulation, and recognizing its proximity to Lacan, we want to affirm a kind of subjectivity for theology that is always *en procès*, both in process and on trial. Theological subjectivity is thetic, and it is caught between the drives of the symbolic and what Kristeva calls the semiotic, which constitutes what Bracha Ettinger calls a "matrixial borderspace."[28] Theology is divided internally by its commitment to the real, its need for symbolic consistency, and its desire for fantastic imaginations. Theology should be viewed as *en procès*, always in process and always on trial, internally and externally, subject to its internal demands as well as the claims of the world, perhaps especially the cultured despisers of religion.

Theology must be willing to lose itself to find itself. To do this, theology must be willing to risk not only the content or object of theological thinking, including God, but even the form of theology itself as a language. Theology is insurrectionist with and against theology as well as insurrectionist with and against the world in which theology takes place. Theology is for nothing else but the word and the world, and you cannot have one without the other. And you cannot have theology without both. Theology attends to how the "world worlds," as Martin Heidegger expresses it, a turn of phrase of more than a little significant for the four kerygmata of this book, these proclamations, gospels, which emerged from the intensities and intuitions of our mountain retreat years before.

In his introduction to *Being and Event*, Badiou starts by saying: "let's premise the analysis of the current global state of philosophy on the following three assumptions." The first assumption is that "Heidegger is the last universally recognizable philosopher."[29] Following Badiou, we affirm Heidegger as the last universally recognizable great philosopher, although it is likely that Deleuze and perhaps even Badiou himself will be recognized in this way in the future. From the start, in thinking about how to structure our book, we decided that our insurrectionist theology must take the form of a set of gospels. Moreover, given our philosophical desires and our commitment to philosophy as a central touchstone for any political thought worthy of the name, we decided that our fourfold repetition of gospels must strongly echo the structure of Heidegger's famous "fourfold": Earth, Sky, Mortals, and Gods.

Before we discuss the fourfold, we should register that our writing—in our own names in this case—new gospels is nothing like the laughable hubris we are all taught from childhood that it must necessarily be. On the contrary, our decision to play in the production of new news is much more in keeping with the production of the four originals (so to speak, as if there were only four!) than those who seem to want always and everywhere to urge obedience, docility, and mere consumption of the inventiveness of others would ever acknowledge. Such desires invent fantasies of Christian origins that have little to do with the contingencies, agonistic contest, and retroactive justifications of the "original" moment.

As nineteenth-century biblical scholarship already realized, perhaps the most striking thing about the production of the New Testament Gospels was the shift in attention they solicited from "the gospel" (as a *kerygma* only vaguely rooted in reference to an original "great teacher," e.g., as in Paul) to "a Gospel" as a quasi-biographical narrative about the Galilean Jesus. The invention of "a Gospel" from "the gospel" was, as the form critics liked to say, the invention of a new cultural form that necessarily signaled new modes of community organization, new modes of agency and consciousness, leaving the modern European biblical scholars to wonder in turn what their form-critical reconstructions of early Christian consciousness were, in turn, becoming, yielding, producing. There is no sense in playing shy as we participate in events of the emergence of new forms, as no humility can shield us from the audacity of the event of becoming running right through our labor.

We note, too, that these texts originally circulated without a title like "Gospel of Matthew," a fact that brings with it the striking likelihood that later efforts to nail down "authorship"—and especially to locate the projected authors to arborescent root structures of legitimation (Jesus speaks to Peter who speaks in front of Mark who writes a Gospel, etc.)—were more about early Christian struggles for hierarchy, control, and ownership over the great becoming than they were about passively receptive *repetitions* of a given history or a certified, authenticated narration of divine authority. Eusebius of Caesarea, the apologist of Constantine who wrote the *Ecclesiastical Histories*, is for us perhaps the most ingenious architect of such an arborescent Christian tradition, blending inherited Augustan rhetoric of imperial domination with Constantinian rhetoric of legitimation, integrating the mix without difficulty with biblical and ecclesiastical narratives of divine participation in his elaborate legitimation-and-control machine.

These are only snippets of tales in a much more elaborate epic. But, truth be told, the only hubris there ever was in relation to the invention of early Christian gospels (so many gospels in fact!) was that dire and scandalous suggestion that only *some* of these productions had the legitimacy to be born into the world. In all seriousness, rather than worrying about the transgression of proper limits, insurrectionist thinkers of all sorts should rather read more biblical history . . . and to invite others—anyone and everyone—to participate in the production of new forms of news worthy of the name "good." So it is with laughter that we read that beloved old trout Irenaeus, whose ad hoc justification of why there must be four (and only four) canonical Gospels referred to the fact of "four winds" blowing from four corners of the earth. The caretaker needs to spin around in place six times fast and then receive from us a little lesson in counting. But, why not?—perhaps we like his four, although we reserve the need to play around with his concepts and categories. We certainly like Heidegger's, and the game of analogies to the fourfold newsies strikes us as more useful, namely, the intertwining of Earth, Sky, Mortals, and Gods.

Heidegger's fourfold can be stretched broadly enough to incorporate what we want to express in and with our insurrectionist theology. Drawing on Gianni Vattimo and Santiago Zabala, we invoke Heidegger's thought with the confidence that it may be, must be, liberated from the shackles of Nazism by crossing his thought with that of Marx.[30] For us, therefore, the fourfold names four sites of transformative and insurrectionary struggle, four zones of political and theological intersection that can be articulated in a new synthetic *nomos*. This *nomos*, if it is one, is not fully worked out in this book, but it is announced, even prophesied.

In chapter 1 Crockett offers a new materialist depiction of Earth by crossing Hegel with Deleuze and suggesting what it would mean to think Earth in Hegelian terms, as substance becoming subject, along with an analysis of Deleuze and Guattari's "geology of morals." The becoming-subject of Earth is a theological transformation, because theology for itself is energy rather than simply language. We need to think from the Earth, not just about the Earth, and to articulate a radical theology of Earth that thinks about Earth in terms of the Real, rather than the imaginary fantasy of a natural harmony or the symbolic practical prescriptions of stewardship or utilitarianism. Deleuze's and Deleuze and Guattari's philosophy, Lacan's psychoanalytic theory, as well as non-equilibrium thermodynamics contribute to this new materialist theological vision.

In chapter 2 Blanton takes up Heidegger's gesture toward Sky in the guise of a Gospel-and-Acts form in order to sift for good news in some of the shifting structures of transcendence that characterize our everyday lives. He argues that we are stuck with a strange and occasionally horrifying world in which we all seem individually and collectively to birth forms of transcendence or agencies of transcendence that, in turn, feed off us like so many vampires from our own excessive dreaming. We live, move, and have our being today in the structure of the incessant production, consumption, and being-consumed by transcendent vampirisms of our militarized and economized skies. Without giving in (to vampirism) or giving up (on our ecstasies), his good news consists in distinguishing the excessive or sur-real aura of divinity from the monotonous and brutal project of the New Divinity Managers who seem, like the insurrectionist, to have understood very well the permanency of our theologico-political predicament.

In chapter 3 Robbins articulates a theory of insurrection that reads David Mitchell's *Cloud Atlas* and its film adaptation by way of James Cone, Antonio Negri, and Catherine Malabou. It is situated in the zone of the mortals insofar as it is concerned with mortality—or more precisely, the mortal logic of consumption by which we misconstrue human nature by a Darwinian economy of survival of the fittest, of life predicated on death. Once we predicate our nature on this deadly logic of "eat or be eaten," we then are perpetually confined to the fate of the cross and the lynching tree. But what if, Robbins asks, resistance to this mortal logic is not reactionary but constitutive? What if nature bespeaks more than struggle in striving? What if we could actually change our nature? Indeed, what if nature was change? Then insurrection would not be seen as quixotic, but as fundamental as the earth we inhabit, the air we breathe, and the gods by which we continue to give name to our striving. Insurrection, so conceived, is an affirmation of life before death.

In chapter 4, Vahanian's "Gospel of the Word Made Flesh: Insurrection from Within the Heart of Divinity" is a deliberate effort to subvert the Heideggerian fourfold even while employing it. Here a theology of insurrection is a secular theology of language that, on the one hand, is anchored in a radical materialism developed from the new materialism of Catherine Malabou. On the other hand, the insurrectionist viability of a theology of language finds expression here as it is put in question by the decolonial thought of Aimé Césaire and the critical race theory of George Yancy, among others. Vahanian proposes that the logic of language is a logic of conversion, where both are predicated on some form of denial—where, for instance, the Christian denies the failure of the messianic in the profession of her faith and, likewise, the child must learn to deny the difference between a word and its referent in order to enter into language. Because this logic is penultimate in the interpellation of a subject and in the subsequent formation of a so-called identity, Vahanian proposes that insurrection from within begin with the avowal of this logic, in the materiality of one's flesh, the plasticity of one's being, and the porosity of an intra-active identity or subjectivity *en procès*. Back to the Heideggerian fourfold, this means that while there is no escape from the violence of civilization or from the dwelling that turns out to be an inhospitable building, the means to resist this violence or this building that betrays a disappointing caring and thinking are nowhere to be found but among us mortals.

This is our radical theology for today.

1

EARTH
What Can a Planet Do?

Clayton Crockett

I was certainly scared when I recently saw the photographs of the earth taken from the moon. We don't need an atom bomb at all; the uprooting of human beings is already taking place. We only have purely technological conditions left. It is no longer an earth on which human beings live today.

—Martin Heidegger, "Only a God Can Save Us,"
Der Spiegel interview (1976)

Why is Heidegger so afraid? We still live on planet Earth, don't we? In another essay, "The Thing," Heidegger writes affirmatively, even nostalgically, about the Earth, saying that "Earth is the building bearer, nourishing with its fruits, tending water and rock, plant and animal."[1] We get our nourishment from our planet, which is the only one we know of that supports and sustains organic life.

Earth is a very special planet. But human activities have so encompassed and transformed the planet that many people follow Heidegger and argue that it's no longer the same planet or soon will not be. Bill McKibben, for example, has renamed it *Eaarth*.[2] McKibben says that, largely as a result of human activity, our future existence on the planet will be much more difficult than what we have grown accustomed to. Many ecologists and naturalists claim that we live in a new geological era, the Anthropocene, a name coined by Eugene Stoermer in the 1980s to indicate that, due to our own actions and their effect on the planet, our world is completely different than it used to be. Ecology is important because we recognize that we live in an era of radical transformation, which has resulted in a state of crisis in our relationship with the Earth.

I.

I will briefly lay out three aspects of this contemporary crisis before turning toward a deeper theoretical and theological understanding of Earth: the ecological crisis, which is often viewed primarily in terms of global warming; the energy crisis, which involves peak oil and the limits of our ability to extract and exploit the cheap energy of fossil fuels; and finally the financial crisis, which involves the deleveraging and destruction of massive amounts of money and credit. Each of these problems is interrelated, because money is dependent upon energy, and energy is a product of finite and diminishing natural physical resources. In a larger geological perspective, we may be accelerating what Elizabeth Kolbert and others call a sixth mass extinction event.[3] There have been five massive extinction events in the history of Earth, and we are currently undergoing a sixth. The difference is that this extinction event appears to be primarily connected to the actions of human beings on the planet. According to Vandana Shiva, humans are undertaking numerous planetary wars against the Earth, with the result that "humans have driven 75 percent of agricultural biodiversity to extinction because of industrial farming, and between three to 300 species are being pushed to extinction every day."[4] The irony of this situation is that humans may themselves undergo extinction in a worst-case scenario as a result of ecological and environmental devastation.

First we can consider global warming. Large-scale climate change with unpredictable and irreversible effects has been caused by human activity over the past couple of centuries, with the increase of carbon, methane, and other emissions in the earth's atmosphere. Scientists disagree on the extent and the timing, but not on the fact of human-caused climate change; however, corporations invested in denying and obscuring these facts have sponsored numerous studies intended to cloud the issue, to raise enough doubt in the public mind so that present practices can continue. In *Heat: How to Stop the Planet from Burning*, George Monbiot offers a radical and desperate plan to cut carbon emissions by 90 percent in 2030. He explains that "carbon dioxide levels have been rising over the past century faster than at any time over the past 20,000 years," and the only way to account for this increase is human activity.

"Carbon dioxide is produced by burning oil, coal and gas and by clearing forests, while methane is released from farms and coal mines and landfill sites."[5] The increase of greenhouse gases is heating the atmosphere and the planet, especially the oceans, which is melting polar ice and raising sea levels.

Monbiot's book was published in 2007, and the failure to reach any agreement at the United Nations Climate Change conference in Copenhagen in 2009 proves that the global community of nations is unable or unwilling to seriously address this problem. Global warming, and the chaotic climate change that it creates, is already affecting the planet, with extreme weather events including storms, droughts, floods, fires, and heat waves across the world.[6] We fiddle around making money while Earth burns. As climate scientists are becoming more alarmed, they are making insurrectionary demands. For example, Kevin Anderson, deputy director of the Tyndale Centre for Climate Change Research in the UK, argues that the only way to avoid catastrophic warming of 2 degrees Celsius or more requires "revolutionary change to the political and economic hegemony."[7] The most recent fifth assessment report of the Intergovernmental Panel on Climate Change (IPCC) claims that the best-case scenario is 2 degrees C, if we act quickly and effectively to reduce carbon emissions. This best-case scenario will likely increase sea levels between .25 and .5 meters across the globe. If we continue not to act in any significant way to address this situation, then the rise is likely to be 4 degrees C and sea levels will rise almost a meter.[8]

Climate change is the major focus of this debate, although we are seeing many signs of resource depletion and species extinction that all attest to the indisputable footprint of humanity upon the earth. Basically, humans are overpopulating and overexploiting the resources of the world at an unsustainable rate, and we cannot continue with our present wealthy (especially if living in the Western or English-speaking world) lifestyle for much longer. We are using up what Thom Hartmann calls "the last hours of ancient sunlight," which means the compressed and stored energy of fossil fuels.[9] As Michael T. Klare explains, "the era of readily accessible oil and gas has come to an end; from now on, vital energy supplies will have to be drawn from remote and forbidding locations, at a coast far exceeding anything experienced in the past."[10] This situation does not only affect energy; raw minerals including rare earth elements are becoming scarcer and more expensive, even as demand for them grows. The demand for energy resources also competes with the demand for arable land, and agricultural production to feed over seven billion people and growing requires massive amounts of water, petroleum, and nitrogren-based fertilizers. "To guard against inevitable food shortages, government-backed agricultural firms in China, South Korea, Saudi Arabia, and the United Arab Emirates are already buying vast tracts of arable land in Africa and elsewhere to produce food for consumption at home," according to Klare.[11] This inexorable depletion of our resources will also be "profoundly affected by the accelerated global warming of the planet and associated climate effects."[12]

In his book *Carbon Democracy* Timothy Mitchell sums up the situation: "The ecosystem appears to be approaching two limits simultaneously: an end to the easy availability of fossil fuel, whose avoidance allowed the development of modern, mechanized life; and the loss of an ability to regulate global temperatures within the range that allowed human sociality to develop."[13] The worst part of this problem is how difficult it is develop a politics adequate to confronting it as opposed to a politics determined to obscure, dismiss, and deny it. Our inability to confront these limits is connected to our inability to adequately understand to what extent our modern and contemporary world is shaped by the extraction of fossil fuels, including coal and oil. Mitchell details the connections between energy extraction and the forms of politics to which they give rise in Europe, North America, and the rest of the world.

How did our extraordinary technological civilization come about? Many explanations trace the origin of the industrial revolution to the cleverness of the human (or Western European) mind, but it has more to do with the discovery and exploitation of cheap energy in the form of fossil fuels. Coal, natural gas, and, above all, oil are tremendous sources of energy, and burning them has generated the enormous power and material wealth that we possess in the early twenty-first century. We could not have built the global civilization that we have, as flawed as it is, without a seemingly limitless amount of cheap energy. Oil fuels our automobiles and planes, it produces electricity, it allows us to construct computers and the Internet, and in the form of plastics these hydrocarbons pervade almost every aspect of our lives. As Allen Stoekl points out in his provocative study of Georges Bataille, *Bataille's Peak: Energy, Religion, and Postsustainability* the concentrated power of energy in carbon forms provides "energy slaves" for those of us who are able to make use of it due to our extraction of and consumption of these fossil fuels.[14]

The American century was generated by its discovery and exploitation of oil, and when oil supplies started to become scarce the United States allied closely with Saudi Arabia, the country with the largest oil reserves in the world by far. Oil production in the United States peaked in 1970, and many people, including, most famously, Shell geologist M. K. Hubbert, have predicted world oil production to peak during the first decade of the twenty-first century, a decade that is now past. The geologist Kenneth Deffeyes predicted that oil would peak in 2005, and this year has been confirmed in a 2012 article in the journal *Nature*.[15] Peak oil does not mean that we run out of oil; it means that we have used up approximately half of the oil that can be extracted, and the other half is more difficult and more expensive to extract, which causes declining rates of production. As far as oil production can be measured, world oil production has leveled out along a plateau, although it has not yet severely declined.[16]

One reason peak oil has been masked has been the financial meltdown that occurred in September 2008, which actually started in August 2007 when the credit markets froze up due to the unsustainable accumulation of debt. The world recession that resulted in 2008 initially sparked higher oil prices, which rose to record levels approaching $150 a barrel in summer 2008, before plummeting along with the weakening economy that then recovered somewhat in spring and summer 2009. Although many people predicted a recovery by summer 2009, this recovery is still faltering in 2015 due to lack of employment and the European debt crisis that is affecting sovereign nations like Ireland, Spain, Portugal, and in particular Greece.

There is no way to simply recover from this recession, because we lack the availability of cheap energy that would fuel such a recovery. In fact, it is likely that peak oil touched off the downturn of the housing market, which in turn led to the seizing up of credit markets in 2007. Despite the lowering of oil and gas prices at the end of 2014, Timothy Mitchell points out that "the sudden abundance of oil in the United States in fact reflects a global scarcity. The shale boom has been used to dismiss the evidence of peak oil; in fact, the boom is its latest symptom."[17] The U.S. has been able to develop technologies to extract oil shale and natural gas, but these technologies are energy intensive and expensive. They represent a short-term boon, but in the long term do nothing to alleviate the reality of energy scarcity.

Money is based on energy, and money can be created as more and more energy is produced, but when available energy peaks and declines, money declines as well. Despite the perception of steady growth, the history of capitalist economy is more accurately the creation and bursting of a series of financial bubbles, starting with the Dutch tulip bubble in the early 1600s.[18] The unprecedented growth between 1945 and 1970 in large parts of the world is due to the exploitation of oil and the financialization of the oil economy that was established by the Bretton Woods Accords in 1944 toward the end of World War II. As the United States started to reach limits in oil production, super-giant oil fields were discovered and developed in Saudi Arabia, and the United States' alliance with Saudi Arabia "won" the cold war by flooding the market with cheap Saudi oil in the 1980s, destroying the Soviet economy.

A key year is 1970 when worldwide growth began to slow, as the United States reached a limit in domestic oil production, and the world reached a limit in the global cost of energy per capita, which required a new transformation of global capitalism. These events initiated an ongoing transformation from a Keynesian capitalism that established safety nets and guaranteed nearly full employment to first-world workers to a more efficient but invidious corporate capitalism that began in the 1970s. Although she does not make the connection with energy, Naomi Klein traces the political and economic aspects of this new corporatism in her book *The Shock Doctrine*. The shock doctrine is actually a response to a shock to the world economy by the first impacts of ecological limits on cheap energy. United States oil production peaked in 1970, and in 1971 Richard Nixon was forced to abandon the gold standard, which marked the end of the Bretton Woods arrangement. Interest rates floated free, and a de facto oil standard was established after the shocks of the OPEC oil embargo. The early 1970s also saw the first real flowerings of a planetary ecological awareness, with the Club of Rome's famous book *The Limits to Growth*, published in 1972, and the founding of the first Green movements and parties.

The new economy that emerged in the 1970s, at the same time as the Chicago Boys were wreaking havoc in Latin America, was the start of a financial economy, where the stock market was detached from the real economy and it spiraled off into stratospheric heights even as the productive economy sputtered. As Christian Marazzi explains in *The Violence of Financial Capitalism*, this new "mobility of capital, its orientation towards developing countries with high rates of profit and company delocalization are all processes that have contributed to increasing profits, without, however, triggering a new wave of general prosperity, rather an extreme polarization of incomes."[19] Basically, as energy became scarcer and more expensive, the only way that corporations could grow was in relative as opposed to absolute terms, which meant that capitalism had to transform itself into a more efficient and powerful machine to reallocate wealth, primarily by means of money and debt.

The incredible concentration of wealth in richer nations, corporations, and peoples since the 1970s can only occur at the expense of the impoverishment of more and more people and countries that are not rich and will never become wealthy. In our desperate struggle for more and more growth in the face of increasing resource scarcity, we are creating what Mike Davis calls a "Planet of Slums." Davis details the situation of this surplus humanity, which has been forced into enormous urban slums around the world. He explains that in large part the cause of the growth of these slums are the "policies of agricultural deregulation and financial discipline enforced by the IMF and World Bank [that] continued to generate an exodus of surplus rural labor to urban slums even as cities ceased to be job machines."[20] Cities cease to generate jobs because of the reality of energy scarcity and subsequent limits to growth. As corporate industrial agriculture forces more and more people off the land, they migrate to the cities, but there are no jobs in the cities. So they squat and form slums, living in what seem to most of us subhuman conditions of desperate survival. This planet of slums is the material underside of the neon lights and shiny hotels that are the product of the powerful draw of investment capital to "develop" countries and cities.

You cannot have infinite or indefinite growth given a finite resource base. Global capitalism has come up against real ecological limits. This is basic, and everything has to change, not because we have the will to do things differently, which we largely do not, but because we will no longer grow in material, economic, and financial terms. We will have to make do with less, and the transition from more to less will in all likelihood not be pleasant, because capitalism does not really work in reverse. According to Kojin Karatani, "the enormous scale of industrial development in India and China has resulted in depletion of natural resources and accelerating environmental destruction," which creates a fatal situation for capitalism.[21] Karatani, a Marxist philosopher, shifts Marx's emphasis from modes of economic production to modes of exchange, and he acknowledges that human labor is not the ultimate source of value; he focuses on the material metabolic exchanges between humanity and nature.[22] Economic theories of capitalism tend to mask this material metabolic exchange.

Capital, according to David Harvey, "is a working and evolving ecological system within which both nature and capital are constantly being produced and reproduced," but this ecological system is pressing up against real limits.[23] Capitalism seems to work when you have abundant resources and significant growth, even if this growth is inherently unequal and tends to accentuate inequalities. But capitalism does not continue to function in an environment of decline; rather, it shreds apart as it desperately attempts to squeeze more and more production out of already strained resources.

So where are we, with the triumph of global capitalism colliding with the strains of overpopulation, resource depletion, and the specter (and, in some respects, the dawning reality) of global warming? Why is an insurrectionist theology necessarily concerned with the Earth? To repeat the question of Gilles Deleuze and Félix Guattari: "Who Does the Earth Think It Is?" To undertake a serious thinking of Earth in its critical state, we advocate a new materialism that would also be a materialist theology.[24] Theology usually opposes materialism in a dualistic way, but an insurrectionist theology allows a thinking of material reality that avoids consumer materialism, reductionist atomic materialism, and the denial of material reality in favor of a spiritual reality that supersedes it.

II.

I suggest that this terminal crisis of global capitalism, which affects human civilization in its entirety, could provide an opening for a new kind of orientation to thinking and acting, a new way of being in and of the Earth. This opening is an opening onto a new materialism that is neither a consumerist materialism nor a reductive atomic materialism but a materialism that takes seriously the material and physical world in which we live. This new materialism is a theological materialism based on energy transformation, because theology for itself is energy, as I will explain in the conclusion of this chapter. Energy itself is not reductive matter, but resonates with "spirit" and "life." Energy is never static, but always dynamic, and being itself is energy conversion.

Here is a radical theological vision of Earth, even though it stretches what is usually understood by theology almost beyond recognition. What we need is not another reformation of theology or religion; what we need is a deformation of theology. Religion is universal at the level of human being, although most people like to think that only some humans are religious and argue whether that is a good or a bad phenomenon. Religion is coextensive with human thinking and life, whether in the form of an organized religion or church or simply a "religion without religion," as Jacques Derrida and John D. Caputo suggest.[25] Theology as a form of discourse indicates what Paul Tillich calls "ultimate concern," the fact of being ultimately concerned about something, whether in terms of form or content. In the introduction to the first volume of his *Systematic Theology*, Tillich offers two formal criteria of every theology. The first formal criterion of theology states: "*The object of theology is what concerns us ultimately. Only those propositions are theological in so far as it can become a matter of ultimate concern for us.*"[26] According to the second formal criterion, "*our ultimate concern is that which determines our being or not-being.*"[27] Our ultimate concern is with the world, which Ludwig Wittgenstein says is all that is the case. Our being and not-being as a species is tied to the fate of the earth. The challenge for all forms of theology and philosophy over the past few centuries has been to take account of how our concerns are implicated in our material reality in an undeniable way without succumbing to a reductionist and deterministic materialism. We need a theology that genuinely takes account of the earth without lapsing into wishful thinking about what it means to live in harmony with nature or New Age platitudes about Gaia that produce a false spirituality.

Traditional theology locates value and meaning outside of, and far beyond, the earth in a transcendent realm of heaven. Plato coined the Greek word *theology*, but Aristotle goes the furthest in defining it in his *Metaphysics*, which concerns "first things." Here unity is the essence or substance of being, and being is grounded in a "first mover" that "exists of necessity."[28] God is a substance both unmovable and eternal, separated from all the things we experience that change and grow and die.

Christianity takes over and modifies this conception of God, giving God a personality and positing a stronger link between divinity and humanity by way of the incarnation of Jesus as the Christ, the Son of God. Here, drawing on Israelite and Jewish traditions, God is the absolute creator of the world, but God also intervenes within human affairs. Unfortunately, often the affirmation of the goodness of creation attested in Genesis 1:31 is lost after the Fall of Adam and Eve. This fall of humanity into sin entails a sinful state of nature and sets up a hierarchy where humans lie between a transcendent divinity that Christ invites us to reacquire and a sinful nature from which Christ redeems us. The apocalyptic strains of Second Temple Judaism inflect Christian scenarios of the end of the world to such an extent that early Christians imagined the complete destruction of the world and the creation of a new heaven and a new earth, most famously in the book of Revelation that closes the New Testament.

According to a seminal article by Lynn White Jr., "The Historical Roots of Our Ecologic Crisis," many of these Greek, Jewish, and Christian attitudes toward nature are perpetuated and amplified in the views and practices of modern Western science and technology. He claims that "modern technology is at least partly to be explained as an Occidental, voluntarist realization of the Christian dogma of man's transcendence of, and rightful mastery over, nature."[29] At the same time, White evokes the counterexample of St. Francis of Assisi, who believed that animals have souls and "tried to depose man from his monarchy over creation and set up a democracy of all God's creatures."[30] White argues that if we could change our orientation to religion, it would have positive practical effects on our world.

According to Ludwig Feuerbach's famous modern reversal, theology is anthropology, which means that our ideas and concepts of divinity arise out of a projection of the ideal qualities of human being. At the end of his book *The Essence of Christianity*, Feuerbach claims that "we have shown that divine wisdom is human wisdom, that the secret of theology is anthropology; that the absolute mind is the so-called subjective mind."[31] Our ideas of humanity, divinity, animality, and technology are all interrelated, and how we think about one of these affects the others. Furthermore, Earth is the ground of all of our ideas, insofar as the earth serves as our ground, as literally ground, and gives us the idea of ground. Do we stand on solid ground? Is there a strong foundation for our actions and beliefs?

For most of human history, Earth was the center of the universe, even if it was not the most valuable or important part of it. Up and down, along with the four cardinal directions, oriented humans in space. Cosmology, religion, and metaphysics coincided to a great extent. But the

Copernican Revolution changed everything, tearing away the notion of Earth as center and as foundation. During the modern era, scientists and intellectuals have been continuing to grapple with the expansion of space and time, as we learned more and more about the age and extent of the universe and the Earth.

One of the most influential intellectual works of the twentieth century is Thomas Kuhn's book *The Structure of Scientific Revolutions.* Kuhn describes a scientific revolution as a paradigm shift that leads to a new worldview. He contrasts normal science, which works within a given paradigm, with revolutionary science, which occurs once a number of anomalies emerge that contest the reigning paradigm. Eventually the accumulation of anomalies precipitates a crisis, and a scientific revolution takes place. He compares a scientific revolution to a political revolution, arguing that both share certain fundamental qualities.[32]

Many intellectuals have conceived of science as a cumulative and gradualist process, with experiments and inventions adding to the existing state of knowledge of the world in a linear, progressive sense. But, largely due to the result of the revolutions in physics in the early twentieth century associated with relativity theory and quantum physics, Kuhn argues that we need to view scientific transformation in more radical and revolutionary terms. He says that "the normal-scientific tradition that emerges from a scientific revolution is not only incompatible but often actually incommensurable with that which has gone before."[33] So successive understandings of the world are not simply developmental, but involve revolutionary paradigm changes in response to a crisis that affects the normal state of scientific practice.

What is interesting about this view of science is how, in retrospect, the revolutionary transformation is assimilated into a new paradigm, and this new paradigm becomes the new normal worldview. The new paradigm may exaggerate or ameliorate its differences from the previous one, but it quickly becomes accepted and taken for granted. We know that our cosmology is radically different from that of early modern Europe, ancient Greece, or medieval China, but this does not prevent us from importing and assimilating large portions of these other worldviews into our own without much concern. We think that we know what is essentially the same and what is different about these other worldviews, and we unconsciously revise our understandings of the world based on new information, whether or not it is logically consistent with our previous worldview.

As Nietzsche says in his preface to *The Genealogy of Morals*, "we knowers are unknown to ourselves, and for a good reason: how can we ever hope to find what we have never looked for?"[34] This statement is later complexified by former Secretary of Defense Donald Rumsfeld in his explanation of the logic of the Iraq War. "There are known knowns. These are the things we know that we know. There are known unknowns. That is to say, there are things that we know we don't know. But there are also unknown unknowns. There are things we don't know we don't know." And Slavoj Žižek, who made Rumsfeld's amateur philosophizing famous, adds the final piece that Rumsfeld leaves out: "What he forgot to add was the crucial fourth term, the 'unknown knowns,' the things we don't know that we know—which is precisely, the Freudian unconscious."[35] For many traditionalist religious believers, science is something that functions as an unknown known or a strange attractor. We know it, but we do not want to know that we know it. And we do not want to know to what extent our science affects and warps our theology.

The religion and science debate is often facile, precisely because it treats science and religion as two separate entities or forces, whether they compete for the same territory or are simply incommensurable with each other. For instance, the title of one of Ian Barbour's books is *When Science Meets Religion: Enemies, Strangers, or Partners?* Barbour is a leading scholar of the interaction between religion and science, but this meeting is staged in such a way as to reduce the known to the unknown and vice versa. In the book he sets out four possible models of interaction—conflict, independence, dialogue, and integration.[36] Ultimately Barbour supports an integration of the two, which seems reasonable, but the problem is the supposition that they are not already integrated, and we can pretend that we do not know this so that we can introduce them to each other and they can meet and come together in a productive fashion. It's like an old married couple who pretend that they are meeting again for the first time so that they can overcome their conflict and estrangement by recognizing anew how connected they are to each other.

A more integrated contemporary approach is ecotheology, which sees intrinsic spiritual value in the earth. Ecotheology responds to White's critique by drawing on resources in the Jewish and Christian traditions as well as other religious traditions, including pagan orientations, that offer more affirmative views of nature and the natural world. The traditions, resources, and formulations are sophisticated, but many boil down to a similar basic critique. Although Christianity and the West have done great harm to the natural world by treating it as a resource to be exploited—and this fundamental attitude is related to the treatment of nonhuman animals, women, and non-Western colonial others—nevertheless, if we can liberate the true essence of Christianity, sometimes purged of its Greek overlay, we can restore harmony between men and men, men and women, and man and nature. Christianity is here what Plato calls a *pharmakon*, a gift that is both the poison of the world as well as potentially its cure.

In Christian ecotheology we can see a shift from a theology based primarily on the crucifixion to a theology based on Christ as the human incarnation of God. In his book *Finding God in the Singing River*, Mark I. Wallace claims that "God is carnal, God is earthen, God is flesh," precisely because God takes human form in the incarnation, and the Holy Spirit then repeats this move, incarnating itself in the world. The spirit as the third person of the divine Trinity "has been persistently infusing the natural world with divine presence."[37] The incarnation of God in Jesus and the descent and continuing presence of the Holy Spirit affirms the presence of the divine in and to some extent as the world. Wallace and other ecotheologians extend the incarnational Christ beyond Jesus to include other humans as well as the natural world as a whole. He claims that "it is theologically proper to say, therefore, that the world is the 'form' God takes among us, that the earth is the 'body' of the Spirit we encounter daily."[38] If God takes form as earth, then the violence that humans do to the earth, as well as each other, is a violation of God.

God gives up godself to our will, our technology, our domination and brutalization, and this is also kind of crucifixion. Wallace calls it a "cruciform spirit." He says that "if God's body . . . continues to suffer and bleed, then does not God, in some sense real but still unknowable and mysterious to us, also suffer and bleed?"[39] As Margaret Atwood puts it in her novel *Surfacing*, "anything that suffers and dies instead of us is Christ," whether it suffers and dies voluntarily or not. "The animals that die that we may live, they are substitute people, hunters in the fall killing deer, that is Christ also."[40] We live in a sacrificial world, where the death of one form of life sustains the live of another, in a web of life that is based on death understood in exchangeable and sacrificial terms. Traditional religious transcendence tends to place humanity outside this sacrificial order, along with God, and exempts human beings from this process. Ecotheology wants to retain God as a source of meaning and transcendent value that infuses the entire natural world so that humans and other animals can participate in this spiritual play.

Ecotheology offers a radical critique of both traditional theology and modern technological and economic practices. Wallace argues that "politically applied deep ecology . . . is a bearer of green spirituality to a culture that hungers for authentic religion in an age of corporate development and the degradation of our fragile earth community."[41] Ecotheology combines a scientific and naturalist perspective on the environment as a complex ecosystem enriched by biodiversity with a spirituality that values these natural entities and processes beyond their instrumental value for human needs and ends.

There are two basic problems with this ecotheological approach, despite its significance and importance. First, there is an ambivalence between the location of value in the natural world and the invocation of religious and theological models of transcendence, however modified. If something beyond the world is needed to provide value to the world, then that devalues the world, because the world is not all that is the case. Why care about the ultimate value of the earth if the earth is not ultimate? And if the theological aspects of ecotheology are marginalized or deemphasized, then the problem is that ecotheology as *theology* becomes instrumental and instills cynicism. Why appeal to religious and spiritual values if a naturalistic and nonreligious understanding of the world is sufficient? If it is mainly designed to appeal to religious people because so many humans are Christian, then it necessarily fails as a solution, because religious practitioners are perceptive enough to see through the facade.

The other basic problem with many varieties of ecotheology is the appeal to a kind of natural and spiritual harmony. The assumption is that humans existed in a harmonious state of nature up to a certain point, after which transcendence and technology took over, producing a state of alienation from the natural world. But we know that nature is not in a state of harmony; it does not exist or persist at equilibrium. Humans cannot, even as a part of nature, exist in a perpetual sustainable relationship with their environment. A view of nature that exists in a state of natural harmony is imaginary; it is the product of nostalgia produced by the aftereffect of human technology. We romanticize earlier states in light of the conditions of later ones.

As Slavoj Žižek explains in his book on Schelling, *The Indivisible Remainder*, the ecological crisis exists due to the splitting of humans into natural and spiritual being. This separation is what allows humans the potentiality for good and for evil, as Schelling articulates it in his philosophy. According to Žižek: "As part of nature, man would be an organism living in symbiosis with his environment, a predator exploiting other animals and plants yet, for that very reason, included in nature's circuit and unable to pose a fundamental threat to it; as a spiritual being, man would entertain towards nature a relationship of contemplative comprehension with no need to intervene actively in it for the purpose of material exploitation."[42] The problem is not this basic conflict, but the notion that it could have a simple resolution for human being, because humans come into existence as subjects based on this twofold identity. Later Žižek explains that the term *ecology* is necessarily an empty signifier. He says that "every attempt to define a substantial core of ecology, the minimal content with which every ecologist has to agree, is necessarily doomed to fail, since this very core shifts in the struggle for ideological hegemony."[43] We emerge as ecological subjects precisely by positing the central signifier, ecology, as empty. This is why radical ecophilosophers such as Tim Morton have come to oppose the concept of nature itself. In his book *Ecology Without Nature* Morton critiques the intrinsically ideological status of the concept of nature and develops a more critical "dark ecology."[44]

In *The Indivisible Remainder* Žižek appeals to the uncertainty, complementarity, and entanglement of subatomic particles in quantum physics as a breakthrough that "compels us to question the ultimate and most resilient philosophical myth . . . that of the absolute gap that separates nature from man."[45] Over against our desire to overcome or fill in the gap between animals and humans, or humanity and nature, "quantum physics opens up a totally different path: what it calls into question is not the specificity of man, his exceptional position with regard to nature, but, rather, the very notion of nature implied by the New Age assertion of a deeper harmony between nature and man."[46] The fundamental duality of quantum physics, where quantum phenomena are not simply waves or particles but in some way both, is irreducible. We cannot overcome the split between wave and particle at the subatomic level. In the same way, we cannot overcome the split between humanity as alienated from and at the same time as belonging to the natural world. The split is fundamental.

Ecotheology, like most ecological thinking, attempts to address and overcome the split between human culture and the natural world by reenvisioning how we think about God. But, for Žižek, what Christianity properly shows is not the overcoming of the split between God and humanity; rather, the true lesson of Christianity is that it shows how the irreducible gap at the heart of the human being also affects God. The incarnation and crucifixion of Christ overcomes the separation between humans and God not by healing it but by demonstrating that the same gap exists in both divinity and humanity, just as it also exists in nature. In *The Puppet and the Dwarf* Žižek explains that "we are one with God only when God is no longer one with Himself, but abandons Himself, 'internalizes' the radical distance that separates us from Him. Our radical experience of separation from God is the very feature which unites us with him."[47] God, humanity, and nature are not harmonious in themselves, but all three exist in a state of radical separation, which is what they have in common.

This radical separation or splitting testifies to an irreducible excess of nature, humanity, and divinity that refuses to allow them to close in on themselves, refuses to unite any or all of the three together in harmony. Žižek says that "what makes life 'worth living' is the very *excess of life*."[48]

III.

What is this excess of life that makes everything nonidentical with itself? I argue that it is energy, drawing on newer scientific understandings of nonequilibrium thermodynamics as well as the philosophy of Gilles Deleuze. Thermodynamics is the science of how energy works, and it developed in the wake of the industrial revolution in the 1800s. Most nontechnical accounts of thermodynamics are based on this nineteenth-century perspective, which studies the way that machines work productively and how they give off heat as a byproduct. Thermodynamics generally explains how systems tend to approach a state of equilibrium, which means that they eventually achieve a stable steady state. In an equilibrium situation, energy is dissipated and dissolved, and entropy takes over. Entropy is the loss of productive energy, usually in the form of heat. From this nineteenth-century viewpoint, all systems progress from a state of lower entropy to a state of higher entropy. Low entropy coincides with structure and organization, while high energy and equilibrium is associated with disorder and chaos. I am suggesting that this view of thermodynamics is limited, based on the findings of nonequilibrium thermodynamics and the philosophy of Deleuze.

Nonequilibrium thermodynamics is a relatively new theoretical account of how energy works, but it is grounded in developments that took place during the twentieth century. Energy is dynamic; it is always in transformation. Energy is productive, but there is always a cost, and the cost is named entropy. Entropy is seen as the loss of energy from the standpoint of usable work, but we can also see how the generation of entropy is an intrinsic part of the process of energy becoming itself. As stated earlier, we generally view entropy as disorder from the standpoint of nineteenth-century thermodynamics and mechanical engines, but twentieth-century views of thermodynamics make entropy a much more complex phenomenon. Energy flows, and it produces what we call entropy as a result of gradient reduction. A gradient is a difference that is set up between two things, for example a temperature difference between a hot room and a cold one. The flow of molecules from the hot room into the cold one reduces the temperature gradient and eventually it produces a state of equilibrium, or mild temperature.

Most of the time this reduction of gradient differentials appears destructive as it produces a homogeneous equilibrium. However, in special cases, in systems that are not in a state of equilibrium, the flow of energy and the reduction of gradients produces and sustains patterns, forms, and structures. In order to explain how this works, I have to go into more detail about entropy and its connection to the flow of energy. Entropy is the term coined by Rudolf Clausius to formulate the famous Second Law of Thermodynamics. The Second Law of Thermodynamics asserts that you can never build a machine of perpetual motion, because you cannot get more work out of a system than you put into it, at least in the form of usable energy. Clausius was developing the consequences of Sadi Carnot's experiments with steam engines in the early 1800s, and he proved mathematically that you can never get more productive energy out of a system than you put into it. Entropy comes from a Greek word that means transformation, or "turning toward," and it suggests that thermodynamic systems always transform from an ordered toward a disordered state. The First Law of Thermodynamics states that energy is infinite; it is always conserved. The practical problem with this conservation of energy is the Second Law, which states that all organized systems of energy tend toward a state of less order or organization. Energy is always conserved, but it changes form; it goes from a more structured to a less structured state, and it gives off heat (or information) as a byproduct. We usually view entropy in negative terms, as a constraint or a limit. Closed systems at rest tend toward equilibrium, which involves a progressive loss of structure. But nonequilibrium systems, or what Ilya Prigogine calls dissipative structures, actually produce elaborate structures.

What is a nonequilibrium system? A system is a means of talking about organic and inorganic processes without making a strong division or dualism between the two. A system that is not at equilibrium means that there is a continuous source of energy flow into the system. Another way to say this is to state that a nonequilibrium system is an open system, whereas a system that is in or tends toward a state of equilibrium is a closed system. In a closed system, thermodynamics and entropy leads to a state of disorder, homogeneity, and "heat death." But in an open system, with constant inputs of energy, things look very different. Living organisms are open systems, and they require continuous sources of nutrition, air, and water to survive. They also possess the ability to evolve into states of greater complexity, higher structure, and lower entropy.

The two great scientific discoveries of the nineteenth century are thermodynamics and evolution. The problem is that they appear on the surface to be at odds with each other. On the one hand, the theory of evolution offers a mechanism, natural selection, for the variation and complexification of forms of life. On the other hand, thermodynamics suggests that complex systems inexorably lose their complexity and become simple states at equilibrium. How can we reconcile these two viewpoints? Does biological evolution offer a special exception to the general laws of physics? As the ecologist Rod Swenson explains, this apparent incompatibility gives the impression of "two incommensurable rivers—the river of physics that flows downhill, and the river of biology, psychology and culture that flows uphill."[49] In his famous book *What Is Life?* Erwin Schroedinger coins the term *negative entropy* to characterize the increasing complexity of biological evolution, and some scientists use the term *negentropy* to mean the opposite of entropy.

But what if they are the same river? What if what Schroedinger and others call negative entropy is actually entropy, but better understood? Most nonscientists assume a nineteenth-century view of entropy and thermodynamics and ignore the newer understandings of nonequilibrium thermodynamics that have developed in the twentieth century. Swenson builds on the work of Ilya Prigogine and Ludwig von Bertalanffy, and he argues that nonequilibrium open systems are self-organizing—Swenson uses the technical term *autocatakinetic,* which means a self-organizing system. Swenson claims that when an open, self-organizing system encounters a gradient differential, it will select the path or paths "that minimize potential or maximize the entropy at the fastest rate given the constraints."[50] This is what Swenson calls the law of maximum entropy production, because it maximizes the efficiency of reducing a gradient. Given a temperature or pressure differential, a difference forming a gradient between two levels of pressure or temperature, the flow of energy that occurs will work to reduce this gradient differential as quickly and efficiently as possible. Swenson gives the example of a warm cabin in cold woods. In a closed cabin the trapped heat escapes into the surrounding environment relatively slowly, but if a window is opened the rate of heat dissipation increases in order to maximize the entropy as quickly as possible. The opening of the window allows nature to reduce the temperature gradient more efficiently.

Organized flow through the window is more efficient at reducing gradient differentials than disordered flow, and this is most clearly seen in a rotating vortex, where organized air or water flow empties a container much more quickly than a slow, disorganized system. One way to imagine this process is to think of a "storm in a bottle," where two plastic soda bottles are taped together with one side filled with a liquid. Turn the bottle over and the liquid will slowly and inefficiently fill the other bottle. But a bottle that is rotated will produce a vortex that organizes the liquid and allows it to empty at a much faster rate. Swenson draws the conclusion: "the world can be expected to produce order whenever it gets the chance—the world is in the order-production business because ordered flow produces entropy faster than disordered flow."[51] If Swenson is correct, then the production of order is not an exception to the Second Law, but a consequence of it. The functioning of self-organized systems have been analyzed as exceptional structures, but what if these structures are the rule rather than the exception?

Swenson restates the Second Law of Thermodynamics as the law of maximum entropy production. The law of maximum entropy production means that maximum entropy is the most efficient means of reducing any gradient differential, whether it is a temperature, pressure, or a chemical gradient. In their book *Into the Cool,* Eric D. Schneider and Dorion Sagan provide an overview of nonequilibrium thermodynamics. Schneider, an environmental scientist, and Sagan, a science writer and the son of Carl Sagan and Lynn Margulis, restate the Second Law of Thermodynamics as saying that "nature abhors a gradient."[52] Entropy is gradient reduction, not the inevitable triumph of disorder over order. Usually, what we perceive as order is the establishment and maintenance of gradient differentials, whereas the reduction of gradients leads to random equilibrium. However, in open self-organizing systems that are not in a state of equilibrium, the flow of energy can take the form of organization, structure, or pattern.

Energy flow organizes a system, maintaining large-scale gradients even while working to reduce smaller-scale gradients more effectively and efficiently. Entropy can produce form in certain situations, even as it works to undermine and destroy forms in other cases. Because entropy gives a direction to the flow of energy, it constitutes a general sense of time, a before and after, or a movement from a low entropy to a high entropy state. Thermodynamics provides an arrow of time, and nonequilibrium thermodynamics helps us understand the arrow of time that organizes life and prevents it from closing in on itself. This nonequilibrium thermodynamics is the *excess* that Žižek identifies at both the subatomic and the existential/philosophical level. Life is not an exception to the universe, just as humanity is not an exception to nature. Both are special forms of energetic-entropic production.

In their book Schneider and Sagan detail the many scientific advances in understanding entropy and thermodynamics over the course of the twentieth century. They explain how French physicist Henri Bénard, early in the twentieth-century, used a steep temperature gradient to organize sperm whale oil into "completely nonliving, honeycomb-like 'cells.'"[53] Fueled by the temperature gradient of heat, the oil organized into symmetrical hexagons that endured as long as the gradient remained in place. Bénard observed that "when these systems bifurcate from conduction to convection, from random to organized, the system's heat flow—its entropy production—goes up."[54]

Complex systems like Bénard cells and, later, the self-organizing vortices studied by G. I. Taylor do not emerge out of nowhere, or from some mysterious spiritual potential, but they occur in specific contexts of continuous energy flows. Furthermore, while these systems are not totally unpredictable, "no absolute predictability is possible because nature's tendency to organize complex degradation systems, creative destroyers, may be restrained by inadequate materials, inadequate quantities of energy, or insufficient systemic organization to use the energy and materials."[55] The specific situation, including energy flow and gradient differential, leads to the emergence of temporary states and patterns of complex organization. This organization is a self-organization that is made possible by a persistence of thermodynamic flows of energy. There is no self that precedes the organization; the self emerges out of the intrinsic organization of the system.

Another striking quality of these thermodynamic states, discovered by fluid dynamicist David Coles, is that they contain an implicit memory of previous states. Although, initially, "nature displays no intrinsic preference for one rather than another gradient-breaking solution," once an organized system of vortices is established, "in their cyclicity they embody past modes of seeking equilibrium."[56] The past history of a system affects future behavior, because the system demonstrates that it will follow the same pattern once a pattern is established.

This is a somewhat technical description, but the basic idea is that the physical system "remembers" its previous states and is much more likely to repeat the pattern that it previously followed. This memory is called hysteresis, which is a retardation or lagging induced by tendency to repeat previous patterns of organization. Hysteresis is a kind of implicit memory that is expressed by physical systems; it is not conscious, but it demonstrates that previous states contribute to future states based on their organization and history.

The reduction of gradient differentials, differences between gradients in the form of temperature, pressure, and other kinds of forces including chemical gradients, explains how thermodynamic energy works. Energy is the excess of being that seeks equilibrium in the form of gradient reduction. In its tendency to reduce gradients, these systems can produce new forms of organization in highly specific situations that occur in systems that are not at equilibrium—or near the edge of chaos—but are sustained by flows of energy. Energy flow produces structures or patterns that degrade differences more quickly, and these structures are maintained so long as energy flow persists.

The reduction of gradient differences is the same as the production of entropy. Entropy is produced as the most efficient way to overcome a gradient differential. Entropy usually produces equilibrium, and it always does so in closed systems. The key, however, is that the flow of energy organizes a pattern or structure that in special cases is even more efficient at degrading gradients and producing entropy.

Finally, and even more strikingly, I am claiming that this thermodynamic entropy production of energy is theological, in a way, because it is the becoming-organized of energy, that is both material and spiritual at once. We do not need to dualize matter and spirit; Albert Einstein showed us that energy and matter are convertible at the speed of light. Energy is matter or the mass of matter multiplied by the speed of light squared. What we call spirit is a manifestation of this energy transformation, not an illusion or its precondition. Spirit is inherent in matter as energy. Energy is material form in dynamic transformation. Being is energy-in-transformation. And one of the tasks of theology is to attend to what is being itself. Before turning to the theological implications of this understanding of energy, I want to show how Gilles Deleuze expresses an understanding of philosophy and ontology that is compatible with this understanding of energy and thermodynamics.

IV.

In *Difference and Repetition* Gilles Deleuze articulates a very similar view to the nonequilibrium thermodynamics that I have sketched out in the language of physics. Deleuze's philosophy explains energy transformation as the repetition of difference. Here Deleuze uses the term *intensity* to indicate his understanding of energy. *Difference and Repetition* is extremely complex, drawing on the entire history of philosophy as well as mathematics and physics. Although the book was published in French in 1968, it was not translated into English until 1994. Scholars increasingly recognize the central significance of *Difference and Repetition* for Deleuze's philosophy. However, many readers focus on difference as the pivotal concept of the book and neglect the concept of repetition. I argue, however, that repetition is the key to understanding the book and to appreciating that repetition is a repetition of difference. Repetition of difference occurs based on an energetic intensity, a force that repeats everything differently. What Deleuze calls repetition of difference in *Difference and Repetition* resembles the way that energy flow reduces gradient differentials in nonequilibrium thermodynamics.

The fundamental question of *Difference and Repetition* is how repetition can be understood as a repetition of difference rather than identity. If something repeats, there has to be something that persists in its identity through the repetition in order to repeat. At a basic level of logical sense, Deleuze's claim that difference repeats appears incoherent. How can difference be repeated? Deleuze addresses this problem at the end of chapter 2 of *Difference and Repetition*. Drawing on Heidegger, Deleuze asserts that it is not enough to assert empirical differences. There must be some way to "relate different to different without any mediation whatsoever by the identical, the similar, the analogous or the opposed."[57] This relation of different to different is accomplished by a *differenciator*. What is a differenciator? Deleuze says that the only way a differenciator can function as an in-itself to difference is if a system is organized into a series, "each series being defined by the differences between the terms which compose it."[58] Series are defined by the differences among their members, and therefore a differenciator is what allows us to compare two series together and see that identity emerges out of difference, rather than vice versa. The differenciator is a second-degree difference because it relates the first-degree differences to one another.

The result of this process of relating differences together is similar to what physicists call a diffraction pattern or a moiré, where two waves are superimposed and the result is generated by the difference between them.[59] Deleuze calls the differenciator a dark precursor; he explains that "given two series of differences, the precursor plays the part of the differenciator of these differences."[60] So identities emerge out of differences based on the operation of a differenciator or dark precursor. This identification of a differenciator, however, is not sufficient to explain repetition, because something must actively relate the series together. The force that propels a series of differences together and makes them interact is called intensity. Intensity is what drives repetition. Deleuze says that "there are intensities, the peculiarity of intensities being to be constituted by a difference which itself refers to other differences" (117). Intensity is energy flow. Intensity is the force that relates difference to difference that enables the convergence or overlay of two series so that they can be compared and something new can emerge as the product of their differences. This is genuine repetition, as opposed to the false repetition that presumes the replication of a prior identity.

Deleuze calls the intensive relation of difference to difference that "resonates to infinity *disparity*" (222). He develops this thread appearing at the end of chapter 2 more fully at the beginning of chapter 5, which is the least well-understood part of the entire book. Here intensity is more directly correlated with energy and contrasted with extensity, which means the extensive surface on which differences are canceled out. Extensity is the level on which we perceive identity and lack of apparent difference, while intensity is the hidden force that produces difference and the extensity that appears to cancel it out. The problem, according to Deleuze, is that "we only know forms of energy which are already localized and distributed in extensity, or extensities already qualified by forms of energy" (223). Energy in itself is intensity, a repetition of difference, but it manifests itself in forms of extensity.

Drawing on the work of Léon Selme, a French theorist who critiqued Clausius's formulation of the Second Law of Thermodynamics as being a kind of transcendental illusion, Deleuze criticizes our general idea of entropy. Intensity is difference, but this difference is hidden underneath and canceled out in extensity. In nineteenth-century thermodynamics, "intensity defines an objective sense for a series of irreversible states which pass, like an 'arrow of time,' from more to less differenciated, from a productive to a reduced difference, and ultimately to a cancelled difference" (223). Here intensity is correlated with order, extensity with disorder, and the arrow of time runs inexorably from one to the other. But this notion of thermodynamics is outdated, even if it persists in the popular imagination. Energy is the force of intensity, which is the differentiation of differences. Entropic intensity is the force that reduces gradients in the quickest and most efficient way possible. The result in most cases appears to be a loss of organization, but the intensity that drives the process not only destroys structure, it creates it in specific circumstances, as we have seen. According to Deleuze, in classical thermodynamics "intensity is suspect only because it seems to rush headlong into suicide," but that is an incorrect interpretation of intensity (224). The explication of difference cancels out difference; "to be explicated is to be cancelled or to dispel the inequality which constitutes it" (228). Difference drawn outside itself cancels itself out in extensity, which is how we ordinarily conceive of thermodynamics. But this view is incomplete because "difference of intensity is cancelled or tends to be cancelled in this system, but it creates the system by explicating itself" (228).

As cited by Deleuze, Selme points out that entropy cannot be measured by any "procedure independent of energetics." This means that entropy is paradoxical. On the one hand, it is an extension or explication of a system and the inevitable canceling out of difference as intensity. On the other hand, entropy can only exist as implicated, "because it has the function of *making possible* the general movement by which that which is implicated explicates itself or is extended" (229). The intensity of energy flow makes explication possible, and this revised view of thermodynamics is the result of an expansion of entropy from a specific measure of extensive effects to a more general economy that incorporates intensive difference. Intensive difference cancels itself out, but it reserves itself and persists in driving further repetition. There is always a remainder, and that is what Deleuze calls intensity or intensive difference.

In his provocative book *Nihil Unbound*, Ray Brassier offers an interpretation of chapter 5 of *Difference and Repetition*, but he misunderstands Deleuze insofar as he associates this productive intensity with a psychic vitalism. Brassier claims that Deleuze introduces an idealist, psychic principle that is ultimately negentropic to overcome "the transcendental illusion of entropy." He says that Deleuze privileges the psychic realm because "psychic life escapes from the entropic domain of physical death."[61] Due to his commitment to vitalism, Brassier says, Deleuze privileges "psychic expression" over "its bio-physical location."[62] Although Deleuze is influenced by the vitalism of Henri Bergson, it is an overreading to equate Deleuze's critique of classical thermodynamics with an embrace of psychic life. Schneider and Sagan's treatment of nonequilibrium thermodynamics allows us to view Deleuze's work from a different perspective, one that is entirely physical and material. We do not require life or consciousness to have intensity or to understand how energetic intensity informs entropy as gradient reduction. Life and mind are themselves extensive forms that are produced by intensive difference.

Intensity is a force, which is why Deleuze says that it is a kind of affirmation. He says that "since intensity is already difference, it refers to a series of other differences that it affirms by affirming itself."[63] Sensible form is a product of an asymmetrical synthesis. The title of chapter 5 of *Difference and Repetition* is "Asymmetrical Synthesis of the Sensible," and it refers to the working of energetic intensity. Intensity is the name for the result of this sensible synthesis, and it is an asymmetrical because it is based on gradient reduction. Gradient reduction is directional; if referring to temperature gradients, it proceeds from the hot *into the cool*. The reduction of gradient differentials goes only one way, from the more highly structured, less entropic state to the higher entropy state of equilibrium. This directionality is what Deleuze means by asymmetrical. Gradient reduction is an asymmetrical synthesis.

Gradients are differential forces, like an atmospheric gradient where a high pressure mass of air meets a lower pressure zone. The gradient is reduced as efficiently as possible, which means from the state of higher pressure toward the state of lower pressure. And this example usually results in a dramatic thunderstorm.

Deleuze casts this relation in metaphorical terms of height and depth when he says that gradient reduction, or asymmetrical intensity, goes from high to low. The descent is the reduction of the gradient differential, which is reduced in the most efficient way. This reduction, however, harbors an intensity that can contribute to the setting up and maintaining of other gradients, given the right conditions and the continuous flow of energy. Deleuze says that "intensity affirms even the *lowest*; it makes the lowest an object of affirmation."[64] High and low are not terms of moral value, but serve to contrast the gradient differential. Entropy as gradient reduction means that existence goes in one asymmetrical direction; there is no simple symmetry between past and future states. This directionality, however, is not itself simple, because it proceeds along the path of whatever gradients are established, which are the result of previous gradients and their reduction. Here is the path of the dark precursor. "Everything goes from high to low, and by that movement affirms the lowest: asymmetrical synthesis."[65] The affirmation of the low is the force of energetic intensity that is thermodynamic in non-static or nonequilibrium terms. The intensity cancels itself out in extensity, where differences are reduced and equilibrium is achieved, but there is also a remainder of intensive difference. This vital remainder of intensity is hidden underneath the extensive quantitative field, but it contributes to the generation of further differences. A symmetrical synthesis cancels out all of the terms, while an asymmetrical synthesis preserves intensive difference as an energetic remainder. This remainder means that our laws and systems are neither closed nor static—they evolve.

In terms of cosmology, the theoretical physicist Lee Smolin draws upon thermodynamics to argue that scientific laws themselves evolve in time, in entropic terms. In his book *Time Reborn*, Smolin argues that contemporary physics needs to more fully appreciate the reality of time. In the physics of Sir Isaac Newton, the relativity theory of Einstein, and even the equations of quantum mechanics, we can imagine a block universe where time is an illusion. Smolin contrasts the philosophy of Gottfried Wilhelm Leibniz with that of Newton, arguing that Leibniz's understanding of space and time is dynamic and evolving. Although

Smolin does not cite Deleuze, I think that there is a general compat-
ibility between Smolin's cosmology and Deleuze's ontology in *Difference
and Repetition*.

The conventional understanding of the Second Law of Thermodynamics as implying a movement from order to disorder only applies
to isolated systems "enclosed in a box," but, as we have seen, "no
living system is an isolated system." Smolin argues that "the steady
flow of energy through a system can result in complex patterns and
structure, evidence that systems are far from thermodynamic equilibrium."[66] We all ride flows of matter and energy—"flows ultimately
driven by energy from the sun."[67] According to Smolin, in our universe gravity works as a force to slow the dissolution of energy to
form stars, and these stars then function as nonequilibrium systems
that generate structure and, at least on Earth, life. Smolin claims that
not only objects evolve and change, but the very scientific laws we
discover also change over time.

The point of Smolin's cosmology and Schneider and Sagan's nonequilibrium thermodynamics is that all of existence is thermodynamic, but
we need to understand thermodynamics in a twenty-first century way,
rather than in terms of the nineteenth-century formulations in which it
arose. Energy works thermodynamically to reduce gradients in dynamic systems that do not exist at equilibrium or in a box. Smolin argues
that we need a better understanding of how philosophy and physics interact, and he collaborates with a Brazilian political philosopher,
Roberto Mangabeira Unger, in *The Singular Universe and the Reality of
Time*, to develop a natural philosophy in which scientific laws evolve.[68]

Energy transformation is what is most real about reality, from the Big
Bang to stars to planets to ecosystems to humans. Energy is material,
but it is not atomic; it cannot simply be reduced to tiny building blocks
that make up larger objects. Organization only works with energy flow.
Energy flows generate and sustain organization. We need a new cognitive understanding of the world to appreciate this situation, which the
philosophy of Deleuze helps us to achieve.

V.

Deleuze's philosophy and the physics of nonequilibrium thermodynamics suggest a new view of energy and its relation to entropy. Entropy is
less the inexorable move from order to disorder and more the efficient

reduction of gradient differentials. We cannot adequately comprehend Earth as a nonlinear system unless we understand something essential about the nature of physical reality, which I have presented in terms of energy, entropy, intensity, and difference, drawing on Deleuze as well as Schneider and Sagan. Earth is only possible given energy flows that reduce gradients in an extraordinary way.

How do you assemble an Earth? We cannot say exactly, because we have no way to simply repeat the process in experimental form. We have to speculate based on indirect evidence and retroactive extension of current processes. Here is part of Schneider and Sagan's description of the cosmological processes that produced Earth: "On scales far vaster than the everyday, gravity produces gradients. Even before life emerged on a thermodynamically grounded process of replication and expansion—feeding on ambient gradients—gradients helped form the stuff from which life was made. Temperature and pressure gradients inside massive stars formed the setting for the production of the elements—the carbon, oxygen, iron, and other atoms—that compose our bodies."[69] Stars transmute elements from hydrogen into heavier ones by means nuclear reactions, and supernovas shoot these elements out into space. Gradients organized these elements and compounds formed from them in what became our solar system. "Earth formed with the other planets and sun from a rotating disk of ice, gas, and dust."[70] The protosolar nebula or solar accretion disk coalesced into a star, our sun, with the heavier elements drawn by gravity toward the center that formed the inner rocky planets. Schneider and Sagan explain that "lighter materials with hydrogen in them . . . congregated around the massive gas giants Jupiter, Saturn, Uranus, and Neptune along with their moons."[71] From about 4.6 to 4 billion years ago, these early planets were bombarded with meteorites as the particles of the solar disk compacted into stable planets with relatively stable orbits. The Earth's moon was formed about 4.5 billion years ago when a glancing collision with a planet (Theia) the size of Mars sheared off part of the crust and this material settled into orbit and eventually clumped together under the force of gravity.

As far scientists can tell, cellular life on earth began almost four billion years ago, which is extremely close to the earliest time that life could form as the planet began to stabilize and cool at the end of the Hadean eon. As Schneider and Sagan say, "the oldest rocks on Earth are not much older than the oldest with traces of life," which means that "scientific dates for the oldest bacteria are now nearly coincident with Earth's cooling to the point where it had a solid crust."[72] Life emerged incredibly early in Earth's history, even though most of the larger organisms that we associate with complex life emerged over three billion years later with the Cambrian explosion. Life occurred when it could, given the appropriate energetic and thermodynamic conditions.

A recent theory of life proposed by an MIT physicist involves the application of thermodynamic principles. According to Jeremy England, life evolves as a specific case of a more general physical system. An article states that England has "derived a generalization of the second law of thermodynamics that holds for systems of particles with certain characteristics: The systems are strongly driven by an external energy source such as an electromagnetic wave, and they can dump heat into a surrounding bath. This class of systems includes all living things."[73] The key is how these systems replicate and dissipate entropy into their surrounding environments. England's theory is too new to be scientifically established as valid, but it is an interesting hypothesis that awaits further experimentation and it shows how thermodynamic energy is intrinsic to the formation of life.[74]

Why is Earth the only planet we know of that currently supports life? We now know that Mars used to have water and possibly life, but not anymore. Its magnetosphere ran out and its atmosphere was pinched away into space.[75] Without an atmosphere, which functions like a protective coating or envelope to filter solar radiation, you cannot sustain life. But, in order to maintain an atmosphere, you have to have a magnetosphere or magnetic and therefore electrical fields that function as a force field to keep the atmosphere in place. A magnetosphere is similar to what Deleuze and Guattari call a "Body without Organs" in *Anti-Oedipus* and *A Thousand Plateaus*. The problem is, we do not exactly know why we have a magnetosphere. How is the earth's anomalously strong magnetic field produced?

Even though we do not understand the entire process, we should appreciate that Earth got extremely lucky. It formed at just the right distance from the sun and received the lion's share of the heavier nuclear elements that could fuel the reactions that produced and continue to produce the magnetosphere and atmosphere. Mars, the next planet out, got enough to produce a magnetosphere, atmosphere, liquid water, and therefore life for a little while, but then ran out of fuel. Still, the question is, how was this magnetosphere produced in the first place?

In *Difference and Repetition* Deleuze references Pierre Curie, and it is Curie's temperature that creates the main difficulty in understanding how a magnetic field is generated. According to basic physics, as theorized and formulated by James Clerk Maxwell and Einstein, an electrical field generates a magnetic field that then propagates another electrical field and so on, and this occurs at the speed of light. But there is no known source of electricity within the core of the Earth that could propagate a magnetic field, so the magnetic field has to be generated another way. The sun, along with the gas giants, have enormous magnetic fields, because they are so large they contain compressed plasma gases that generate and conduct electricity, but these magnetic fields are unable to sustain an atmosphere conducive to life as we know it since they are too far away from the sun and their atmosphere is mostly hydrogen. For Earth, Curie's temperature is important because it sets a limit on the ability to conduct electricity and magnetism. If heated above the Curie temperature, a magnet will lose its magnetism. The Curie temperature differs for different elements, but this temperature is generally exceeded in the Earth's core and mantle.

The Curie temperature means that the Earth should not be able to sustain an electrical or magnetic field, although it does. The reason it does has everything to do with gradients, but not just temperature gradients. You need temperature gradients, but you also need pressure gradients and nuclear reactions in the Earth's core and mantle to generate a magnetic field. The pressure and temperature gradients combined with the movements inside the Earth to produce the magnetism we require for an atmosphere and for life, even if we do not yet understand exactly how this process works.[76]

This is one hypothetical scenario for how Earth makes for itself a magnetic field or a Body without Organs (BwO). Technically the BwO is the energy field that produces the magnetosphere because of the production and reduction of gradients. According to Deleuze and Guattari in *A Thousand Plateaus*, a body without organs—they borrow this phrase from Antonin Artaud—is a smooth, completely idealized plane of consistency that refers to the matrix of gradient change.[77]

Deleuze and Guattari claim that that the BwO "is not space, nor is it in space; it is matter that occupies space to a given degree." Furthermore, "it is nonstratified, unformed, intense matter, the matrix of intensity, intensity = o; but there is nothing negative about that zero, there are no negative or opposite intensities."[78] They declare that they treat the

BwO as "the full egg before the extension of the organism and the organization of the organs, before the formation of the strata; as the intense egg defined by axes and vectors, gradients and thresholds, by dynamic tendencies involving energy transformation."[79] The strata are the layers of materials in the earth, while the BwO is the intensive energy that informs the strata, operating below and between geological strata as well as stratified individual organisms. In some ways, the term *egg* is metaphorical insofar as it relies on an organic model, but at the same time we should view the entire Earth as an egg, one that is cracking and hatching. Ontogeny, the generation of an organism, recapitulates phylogeny, the evolution of a phylum or group of species, but phylogeny also recapitulates a geology.

Deleuze and Guattari's complicated analysis in *A Thousand Plateaus* works on many different levels at once. These levels are all plateaus, which means that they are not organized hierarchically. Deleuze and Guattari are setting forth an ontology, a geology, a biology, a philosophy, a metaphysics, and an epistemology. This is an extremely experimental work, but we can also read it from the standpoint of energy and Earth as well as based on an understanding of intensity from *Difference and Repetition*. We should read this extraordinary book as a book about Earth and as contributing to an insurrectionist theology of Earth, because they take Earth as the subject of their work.

In *Anti-Oedipus* and *A Thousand Plateaus*, which are both subtitled "Capitalism and Schizophrenia," Deleuze and Guattari develop their analysis of two terms, *territorialization* and *deterritorialization*. Basically, territorialization is an understanding of life, politics, and philosophy based on territory, on conquering, occupying, living in, and defending a piece of ground. Deterritorialization is a breaking up of territory, which can lead to a reterritorialization in different terms. These notions of territory and territorialization refer to the earth and to how humans occupy and live on Earth. For example, traditional wealth has always been tied to ownership and production of land. But with capitalism you have a deterritorialization, where money as capital replaces the original value of land as territory. Land is no longer primary, but wealth has been deterritorialized as land and reterritorialized as capital. In *Capitalism and Schizophrenia*, Deleuze and Guattari make a desperate attempt not only to theorize contemporary capitalism but to push it to its limits by pairing it and contrasting it with schizophrenia. Schizophrenia is not simply the medical condition of psychosis, but a broader phenomenon of splitting that pushes deterritorialization so far that it cannot be reterritorialized. This absolute deterritorialization is also associated with their treatise on nomadology, or the war machine, in *A Thousand Plateaus*. The war machine works against the territorializing of the state and serves to open up spaces and lines of flight that function as new becomings. Deleuze and Guattari do not endorse the literal violence of the war machine, but valorize its opposition to the state form of territory. They attempt to push deterritorialization as far as it can go and wager that it may not be able to be reterritorialized in state or capitalist terms.

The problem with the nomadology is that it runs into the apparatuses of capture by the state. The state is capable of capturing, appropriating, and reterritorializing the nomadic elements of the war machine for the purposes of capitalist production and wealth formation. Deleuze and Guattari imagine, but cannot quite see how to arrive at, a process of absolute deterritorialization. At the end of *A Thousand Plateaus*, they assert that an absolute deterritorialization belongs to the Earth. The earth "is deterritorialization par excellence; that is why it belongs to the Cosmos, and presents itself as the material through which human beings tap cosmic forces" (509). Perceiving the earth as deterritorialized allows us to glimpse this absolute deterritorialization that operates under and against superficial global corporate capitalism. To extend deterritorialization to its maximum limit is to reach the point where deterritorialization "can be called the creator of the earth—of a new land, a new universe, not just a reterritorialization" (509). Deleuze and Guattari envision the creation of a new world which is a creation of Earth. Not another Earth or a different Earth, but the creation of Earth itself as subject of its own events and humans and other territorial creatures as individuations of this new comprehension of Earth.[80]

Here is a new theological ecology, rather than an ecotheology that maintains the same theological and environmental categories and simply remaps them onto each other. A theological ecology stages an insurrectionist encounter between theology and ecology that distorts and transforms both based on the gradients of their energy transformation. The constructive thinking of a new Earth, the composition of a perspective of Earth as a whole, is the positive side of this theological ecology. This positive vision is the flip side of the segmentation, destruction, and expropriation of all the territories, material resources, and populations of Earth. In all this cataclysmic destruction and extinction, we are bringing something new into being, but not us, not as us. We, signifying beings, are not the goal of evolution, but we are a kind of witness and we can therefore testify to the sublime beauty of this creation.

Earlier in *A Thousand Plateaus* Deleuze and Guattari famously claim that "God is a lobster, or a double pincer, or a double bind" (40), because the conventional understanding of divinity represents a blueprint for a double articulation. Double articulation refers to the symmetry that exists in the universe, on Earth, and on most organisms. This symmetry of course is never exact; it is symmetrical only in virtual terms. In actual fact existence is asymmetrical, as Deleuze states in *Difference and Repetition*. In *A Thousand Plateaus* Deleuze and Guattari contrast the BwO, the deterritorialized Earth, with the inevitable stratification into layers and belts that takes place in and on the earth.

Deleuze and Guattari assert that strata "consist of giving form to matters, of imprisoning intensities or locking singularities into systems of resonance and redundancies, or producing upon the body of the earth molecules large and small and organizing them into molar aggregates" (40). Strata capture by coding and territorializing the deterritorialized body without organs. Strata always come in pairs, which is why God is a lobster, organizing the entire grid of stratification. "Each stratum exhibits phenomena constitutive of *double articulation*" (40). The first articulation "chooses or deducts, from unstable particle flows, metastable molecular or quasi-molecular units (*substances*) on which is imposes a statistical order of connections and successions (*forms;* 40). The first articulation establishes a process of sedimentation, which distributes substances in an arrangement. The second articulation takes these forms established by the first articulation and produces substances or structures out of them. This second articulation "is the 'folding' that sets up a stable functional structure and effects the passage from sediment to sedimentary rock" (41).

What does this mean? In both epistemological and ontological terms, we solidify the processes of the first articulation into the second. The first articulation is the tentative establishing of form, but the second articulation takes these forms and substantializes them. There are always at least two levels of strata, and one serves as a substratum for the other, which gives us the illusion that it is well-grounded. We take the Earth for a thing, a preformed, pregiven object of our experience, there for our use and appropriation of it.

If God is a lobster, then He is the God of the strata. Most versions of theology are ossified stratifications, resistant to any probing of the sedimentary process of theology itself. Many understanding of contemporary science operate the same way, taking proclamations and pronouncements on faith with very little understanding of the process of how scientific investigation works. Deleuze and Guattari loosen this up, with the result that they risk incomprehension and incoherence due to the mixing of levels or strata of discourse. We have a tendency to dualize the strata, but there are never just two, always at least two. And, furthermore, when we only pay attention to the strata, we lose sight of the body without organs, the assemblage that operates between the strata: "the assemblage is between two layers, between two strata" (40). The BwO is the plane of consistency or differenciator that individuates as an entropic intensity—"becomes compact or thickens at the level of the strata" (40).

Deleuze and Guattari replace their theorization of machines in *Anti-Oedipus* with a theory of assemblages in *A Thousand Plateaus*. An assemblage is an abstract machine that refers to the work of intensities and singularities to generate differences. The assemblage contains the miminal amount of form necessary to function, and it works because it stays in contact with the body without organs, the plane of consistency that allows for creation, differentiation, and individuation. An entire Earth conceived in terms of assemblages rather than strata correlates with an absolute deterritorialization; it is a "Mechanoshere" (514). I am suggesting, in more literal terms, that Earth's magnetosphere operates somewhat like what Deleuze and Guattari call a body without organs, because Earth's magnetic field emerges from the nuclear and thermodynamic energy processes of gradient reduction that produce geological sedimentation. Insofar as Earth is an egg, composed of deterritorialized potentialities that generate magnetism, electricity, and life, the magnetosphere functions as an abstract machine to generate magnetic and electric fields, which are spatiotemporal dynamisms required for life on Earth.

The evolution of cellular life is not about simply genetic replications and reproductions; it is also driven by thermodynamic and metabolic gradient differentials. The first key component to the generation of life is the creation of a cellular wall, a lipid layer that separates an inside from an outside. Life is a fundamentally metabolic process, as H. J. Morowitz explains in *The Beginnings of Cellular Life*.[81] Next, there is the incredible transition from prokaryotic cells to eukaryotic cells, and with it the possibility of multicellular, complex organisms. These organisms need not only genetic material but energy, which is generated by mito-chondria, the genetic components of the original methadon cell before it swallowed up a protobacterium, according to the hydrogen hypoth-esis as explained by Nick Lane in his book *Power, Sex, Suicide*.[82] Respira-tion occurs in cells due to the formation of ATP, and this occurs when electron flows in mitochondria pump protons across a membrane.

There is an inherent plasticity of biological evolution, to draw on the philosophy of Catherine Malabou. For Malabou, plasticity is the abil-ity to give form, the capacity to receive form, and finally "the capacity to annihilate the very form it is able to receive or create."[83] Biological plasticity is not simply passive adaptability, but the resilience of organ-ic life that transforms, persists, and dies in the creation of new species. Malabou claims that "plasticity situates itself effectively at the heart of the theory of evolution" because it establishes "a fundamental connec-tion that preserves at once the variability of individuals among the same species and the natural selection between these same individuals."[84] Evolution is not only a neo-Darwinian punctuated equilibrium, as the-orized by Stephen Jay Gould, but it is also a neo-Lamarckian swapping of genetic materials via bacteriological symbiogenesis, as originally sug-gested by Lynn Margolis and developed by contemporary epigenetics.

In *Evolution in Four Dimensions* Eva Jablonka and Marion J. Lamb sketch out a new biological synthesis that argues that "there is more to heredity than genes; some heredity variations are nonrandom in origin; some acquired information is inherited; and evolutionary change can result from instruction as well as selection."[85] Epigenetics means that experiences in utero and after birth can affect methylation-marking pat-terns of proteins in the DNA of cells, and these patterns form epigenetic inheritance systems that can be passed on to offspring.[86] Here evolution is not solely genetic, since epigenetic variations can be inherited as well. Epigenetics is more complex than genetic determinism, and it acknowl-edges how evolution is a complex organizing system that itself evolves or changes over time. It's not just organisms that evolve; what we call evolution as a complex system evolves as well.

Sometimes nonscientists fall into the trap of supposing that science gives theorists, philosophers, and theologians positive results, but does not itself reflect or think. This is a prejudice against the best and most cutting-edge science, and it also reifies scientific investigation in a way that precludes creative cross-fertilization. Theologians need to stop wasting time and energy on absurd debates about intelligent design that merely react positively or negatively to scientific determinations that are appropriated as ready-made. An insurrectionist theology delves into the theoretical process of scientific invention itself and is informed by the best theoretical thinking about science, including scholars like Deleuze, Malabou, Badiou, Michel Serres, Isabelle Stengers, Bruno Latour, Donna Haraway, François Laruelle, and Karen Barad.

VI.

What does this theoretical perspective on Earth mean for theological thinking? I argue that theology is entangled with energy, and this needs to be more fully appreciated. Energy as entropic production avoids the extremes of teleological vitalism, on the one hand, whether in its crude creationist guises or more sophisticated idealistic interpretations, and completely random chance, on the other. Both alternatives are as insipid as the stereotypical opposition between theism and atheism, and an insurrectionist theology of Earth cuts across both. Energetic repetition organizes life. In hindsight we can identify some crucial transformations, including the formation of a cell wall out of lipids, the development of eukaryotes out of prokaryotes, the emergence of life out of water onto land with organisms carrying their own water inside them, massive extinction events, and finally the development in bipedal large-brained homo sapiens of abstract thought, logic, philosophy, art, mathematics, and religion. These are all profound repetitions of difference that exhibit tremendous complexity in the effects of their transformations, but they do not proceed in any straight line or upward ascent. The teleological view of evolution as leading to humans is a story about evolution as *for us* but not as evolution for itself.

James Lovelock has given Earth a proper name, Gaia. He means by this that Earth is a complex self-organizing system.[87] Gaia has accrued a mystical connotation, but Lovelock does not intend it as such, and I don't think we need to take it as such for it to be a good name. Recently Bruno Latour and Catherine Keller have endorsed this name. As Latour claims, "by facing Gaia, that wholly secularized and earthbound set of processes, . . . there is a dim possibility that we could 'let the Spirit renew the Face of the Earth.'"[88] We could also think about Earth or Gaia as the subject of an impossible encounter or a queer crossing between the philosophy of Hegel and that of Deleuze (and Deleuze and Guattari). Earth is here Substance becoming Subject, which is the answer of sorts to the question of the Geology of Morals: "Who Does the Earth Think It Is?"[89]

An insurrectionist theology of Earth is a spiritual repetition in Deleuzean terms. In *Difference and Repetition* Deleuze contrasts a bare, material repetition of the same with a masked, spiritual repetition of difference. The second occurs inside the first: "one is material, the other spiritual, even in nature and in the earth."[90] Repetition leads to complexity, articulation, and reproduction. It also leads to depletion, devastation, destruction, and death. And this is the Good News. As Stoekl writes about some of the implications of Bataille's philosophy, "when we recognize that human labor is not the sole source of value, and that energy slaves are indispensable to all the cultural, not of mention industrial, production we associate with modernity, then we confront the fact that *everything must be rethought.*"[91] Insurrectionist theology affirms that everything must be rethought, everything is unsettled, even the Earth we stand on and take for solid foundation.

In conclusion, being is energy transformation, and I claim that, counter to most intuitions and expectations, theology is energy. Theology is energy when thought according to an insurrectionist theology. Theology is not energy in itself, to borrow Hegel's famous terminology. According to Hegel, something in itself or *in sich* is an object *for us.* Theology in itself is an instrumentalized version of theology that serves human needs, wishes, and desires. Most varieties of theology consist of wishful thinking, even if we are sincere in our devotion to and appropriation of it. Theology in itself serves as ideology because it helps us domesticate and control ourselves and others. Theology in itself is pure ideology, precisely because we do not recognize it as ideology. We can only recognize theology as ideology from a standpoint outside or beyond it. But we do not simply leave theology behind.[92]

I am suggesting here that theology for itself is energy. For Hegel, something that is for itself or *für sich* is aware or conscious of its being. Based on my understanding of Deleuze and thermodynamics, I claim that consciousness is not the most decisive category here. Energy is an intensity that generates self-organization even as it destroys gradients. Self-organization is a better term than consciousness for an entity that is for itself. Theology is not simply a discourse but rather a process that self-organizes entities in its working and by its effects.

Energy is the best name we have for the real as real. Theology, when it is not self-serving ideology, concerns the real. Therefore, theology *for itself* is energy or entropic production. An understanding of theology as energy offers a new vision of Earth. Theology as energy for itself articulates the intensive body-without-organs of an abstract machine that generates Earth as subject rather than just substance. A theological ecology inspired by Deleuze, Hegel and others is an insurrectionist theology that is neither nostalgic nor orthodox in political or theological terms.

If theology in itself is ideology, and theology for itself is energy, then what is theology in and for itself? Hegel claims that Spirit is *an und für sich*; it becomes self-conscious and manifest through thinking human beings. We need to follow Marx and set Hegel back on his feet, where spirit is material and energetic rather than the subsumption of matter and energy into a higher principle. Or maybe, as Žižek suggests, Hegel is already theorizing spirit in energetic and material terms, and the dialectical *Aufhebung* or sublation is not a subsuming or an accumulation but instead an opening, a subtraction, or a contraction. Spirit thought in "absolute" terms is radically split, divided in itself. We are split too, in our self-consciousness, but that does not mean that other animals, organisms, being, or God are not also split in their very essence. I claim that theology in and for itself is a kind of reflective perspective on conscious life that can also be given the name of psychoanalysis. Psychoanalysis in general, rather than the more specific doctrine and practice attached to Freud, is a kind of philosophical and reflexive taking into account of the human condition as irreducibly split between thought and action, between inside and outside, between a particular embodied situation and a more abstract and universal perspective. This split takes that form of what Žižek calls a parallax, which is a "constantly shifting perspective between two points between which no synthesis is possible."[93]

Throughout his career, Paul Tillich was profoundly interested in depth psychology and the depth aspects of being. In *Difference and Repetition* Deleuze locates the intensity that drives differential repetition in the depths. But later he and other poststruturalists came to complicate any simple opposition between depth and surface. The depth lies precisely on the surface, not beneath it. As Jacques Derrida claims in his famous essay "Différance," "there is no maintaining, and no depth to, this bottomless chessboard upon which Being is put into play."[94] Depth is on the surface, or rather depth and surface form a parallax, expressed theologically in Catherine Keller's extraordinary repetition of the Genesis story in *Face of the Deep*. Keller attends and gives voice to the Hebrew *tehom*, the deep that forms the "face" of existence, and she redefines creation *ex nihilo* to mean a creation *ex profundis*, a creation (out) of profound depth that "lets creation itself emerge from *the topos of the Deep.*"[95] Keller traces the production of order out of chaos, but this chaos is not absolute nothingness. Chaos is rather "the disruptive, randomizing element of chance, which can only be probabilistically measured in fluctuations."[96]

As Deleuze argues, in order to think about chaos you require a screen to imagine it and to filter it: "we require just a little order to protect us from chaos."[97] Chaos theory and complexity theory offer scientific tools to articulate chaos in ways that are compatible with Deleuze's philosophy and Keller's theology. Earth is what Ilya Prigogine calls a dissipative system, and we can think about this in terms of contemporary thermodynamics, systems theory, and chaotic complexity, but *we are also included in this system.* This inclusion is paradoxical, or parallaxical, because we want to think of ourselves as outside the system as well, as not implicated in and subject to its conditions. But what if we stop thinking about ourselves as subjects and Earth as an object, but turn it around and view Earth as subject and humans as objects, but of a very special kind? We are a kind of *objet petit a* for Earth, expressing its own desire, but also its neurosis and, more recently, its pathology, a psychopathology that is generating a new convulsion, and perhaps a new creation, that may happen with or without us.

Keller's theology constitutes an insurrectionary analytic intervention into the process of creation of world and Earth. Insurrectionist theology is a form of psychoanalysis, in a broad and less technical sense, because it is necessarily split between the critique of theology in itself as ideology and the affirmation of theology for itself as energy. Insurrectionist theology is ungrounded in Earth and always already swept up in Sky.

2

SATELLITE SKIES; OR, THE GOSPEL AND ACTS OF THE VAMPIRISM OF TRANSCENDENCE

Ward Blanton

It should be clear that the plane of immanence, the plane of Nature that distributes affects, does not make any distinction at all between things that might be called natural and things that might be called artificial. Artifice is fully a part of Nature, since each thing, on the immanent plane of Nature, is defined by the arrangements of motions and affects into which it enters, whether these arrangements are artificial or natural. Long after Spinoza, biologists and naturalists will try to describe animal worlds defined by affects and capacities for affecting and being affected. For example, J. von Uexküll will do this for the tick, an animal that sucks the blood of mammals. He will define this animal by three affects: the first has to do with light (climb to the top of a branch); the second is olfactive (let yourself fall onto the mammal that passes beneath the branch); and the third is thermal (seek the area without fur, the warmest spot). A world with only three affects, in the midst of all that goes on in the immense forest. . . . Such studies as this, which define bodies, animals, or humans by the affects they are capable of, founded what is today called ethology. The approach is no less valid for us, for human beings, than for animals, because no one knows ahead of time the affects one is capable of; it is a long affair of experimentation, requiring a lasting prudence, a Spinozan wisdom that implies the construction of a plane of immanence or consistency. Spinoza's ethics has nothing to do with a morality; he conceives it as an ethology, that is, as a composition of fast and slow speeds, of capacities for affecting and being affected on this plane of immanence. That is why Spinoza calls out to us in the way he does: you do not know beforehand what good or bad you are capable of; you do not know beforehand what

a body or a mind can do, in a given encounter, a given arrangement, a
given combination.

—Gilles Deleuze, *Spinoza: Practical Philosophy*

God is a lobster, or a double pincer, or a double bind . . . "overcoding"
the aggregate.

—Gilles Deleuze and Félix Guattari, *A Thousand Plateaus:*
Capitalism and Schizophrenia

Insurrection is above all an invitation, an *euangelion* or a *protrepsis* to a form of political experimentation without which we find ourselves unhelpfully lost and hopelessly asleep, awash in compulsive repetitions without significance or orientation—repetitions without the vibrancy of a solidarity-in-becoming. Redemption, effective soul therapy, or spiritual exercise within the insurrectionists' experimental atmosphere tends to spark up therefore around the textures and styles—the zest and zeal—of instances of solidarity, shareability, and common property, all those instances that can be wrested from the forgotten, unthinkable, and illegitimate of our everyday existence.

In keeping with Deleuze's wonder about animal worlds, insurrectionist experimentation sifts through ethologies as archives, archives as ethologies, all the while testing how those passingly effective names of God have indicated or might indicate new models—an organology— of new solidarities. Archivists of insurrection, we suggest that the many divine names be broken down into a strange new science that maps these names as so many singular passages of resonance into repetition, repetitions consistent enough to become regularized affective zones until they come to constitute organs bearing designations and functions, subjects and objects, insides and outsides, worlds present and worlds to come. That our archival Gods along with their proper names have passed into oblivion or have become emptied of the vibrant life they once radiated, resonated, organized, and repeated is for us not at all a problem, certainly not something we hold against any of the mothballed deities on our overflowing shelves, our dusty card catalogues, our searchable databases. On the contrary, our new science of singular solidarities has a genuine fondness for these dear departed in their very slipping out of consciousness into a kind of death or their entry into the mere museum of religions. Even (and perhaps especially) when these souls are on ice, they function as bearers of the life of instances of solidarity that may yet become significant for a tinkering together of new solidarities. In fact, for the archivist of insurrection, the point of deity certainly isn't to live forever (only other Gods, Gods always and ever "on the way," live forever, never the ones that have shown up, never the ones that have housed us).

Rather than as indications about how to live forever or how to desingularize ourselves, archivist activists look to the archival Gods in search of those organs of solidarity, which often live slower, longer, even vestigially within and through the deity in question. The life of God and the genealogy of organs of solidarity are always related topics, both of central interest—but they remain distinct, even stuck into temporalities and geological strata that intersect only in fits and starts. Here, in the fits and starts, is where new gospels start, the affirmation of or seizing on a chance, a movement of involution in order to take up life-giving residence inside the corpse of the old. No gospel, no good news, without the grasping at a chance opportunity, which is also to say that it is through the fits and starts of a flickering *kairos* or opportune chance that the archivists of insurrection approach the issue of the political. No politics worthy of the name without risk, chance, and an affirmation that looks like *pistis* or trust organizing itself into an amalgam of dangerous solidarities that cut right through the laughably predictable animosities and strong-arming instrumentalities of the reigning identity politics. Critical theory, critical stances, critical gestures are all completely pointless if they do not lose themselves in a fit of laughter that is indistinguishable from an irruption of solidarity, a politics of friendship. We call to everyone and no one and we laugh to find real friends with whom we live and die.[1]

The politics of *pistis* was (and not just in the ancient apostle Paul but also in his Hellenistic philosophical contemporaries) a mode of forcing an inoperability, a break, a death, within the order of *nomos*, law—within the nomological ordering of the social. It was a utopian enterprise in the most aggressively "critical" sense, and no scoffing from the order of a Realpolitik can protect us from the test of a utopian *kairos* of friendship, its problematic demand or the very *krisis* of a harsh judgment which curls up necessarily inside promise and utopian affirmation of the affirmed chance itself. This gospel and its *pistis* of a chance solidarity is not at all the same as those currently reigning gospels of free markets and their call for a trust in a universal friendship of potential business partners, all those gospels without singular difficulty, without inherent *krisis*. Our news affirms, it is something we all must bear, that there is a kind of ineluctable violence and awkward new discipline demanded of every chance affirmation. There are no solidarities worthy of the name without the grounding force of trust which loves to struggle for the satisfaction of the other.

This structural issue we bear also into our archive of often deceased singularities. After all, that the sustaining economies and communicative worlds of our dear departed deities have fallen into chaos or oblivion is often clear enough. The question of whether *our* solidarities—all our organs of solidarity that pass into a now that (we spontaneously assume) must be the time of living—indicate a living worthy of the name is the difficult one, the question that, as we say, remains to be seen. For the insurrectionist archivist of the dead and dying Gods, there is never anything more questionable than the obvious distinction between *their death and our life.*

Put differently, as odd archivists of the step back into insurrection, our sifting through the archive of religion for the emergence and maintenance of these regularized, affective, or organ-ized zones necessarily brings with it a plague of fantasies for a chaotic ethology without ready-made artifice, nature, animal, human, or God. This fantasy attends our every effort to register—as if by catching a fugitive glimpse—these divine and earthly beasties in their eventalness, in their happening as a coming into their own, into their worlds as identities in relation to each other. Insurrection, as a phantasmatic "step back" into the organizing of affective zones, the constitution of old and new ethologies, is an experimental science *sometimes* indicated by that great philosophical anarch of the scientific tradition, Martin Heidegger. Ever prescient in his catastrophic life, we feel Heidegger was onto more than he could say when, in "The Onto-Theological Nature of Metaphysics," he attempted to invent a machine for the binding of ontology and theology within the philosophical tradition he called Occidental.[2] This machine, ironically tinkered together by the would-be-peasant-thinker, was an automatic response system of a sort, a communicative system that points toward Thomas Alva Edison's mechanizations of the living voice of interiority as much as toward Heidegger's much beloved ever laconic peasant farmers.[3] To press a Heidegger toward an Edison, we might say that Heidegger's "onto-theology" machine is one in which the presence of an addressee is given only by the mode in which this addressee is able to send messages or, rather (just consider your inbox at work today), to send messages that effectively produce claims and demands in the other addressees, so much passing around of a debt. In this communicative looping of identity and presence, which we tend to gloss as Heidegger's theses on "onto-theology," being and existence or category and instantiation message each other as if eternally. Incorporated users in the frame of "onto-theology" may of course be awakened from the game, but perhaps as if only to wonder whether this messaging in which one participates is generated from, or received by, some virtual "bot" whose reality emerges only as a mirroring program to another's messaging.

Heidegger's tales of the onto-theological are of much more interest than have tended to be acknowledged by the caretakers and underwriters of religion or theology in relation to philosophy, and our new science of the dead and dying Gods attempts to develop some of these issues. Like that ingenious old curmudgeon Marshall McLuhan, for example, in spite of himself Heidegger would have made a useful ontologist of the love of wisdom in an age of digital romance. One can change the name of the game and switch its passwords (Googling for matchmaking sites rather than networking for business partners), but the basic rules of Heidegger's "onto-theology" machine remain, namely, deferring or presencing through a relational displacement. Telos or ground (causal beginning or causal end, whether common reality or the sur-real), it is the mechanism or operation of deferring and relational displacement that finds itself whirring away in Heidegger's story, and this whether it occurs under the headings of *onto-* or *theo-*. It is in this respect that, whatever their carefully managed self-understandings, these two sciences are selected for pairing by Heidegger's great matchmaking machine. Consider it as an online communicative match, as if made in heaven:

> Because being appears as ground, existence is that which is authenticated. However, existence *par excellence* is that which understands in the sense of being the First Cause. If metaphysics thinks Existence with an eye toward its basis which is common to every individual existent as such, then metaphysics is logic in the form of onto-logic. If metaphysics thinks existence as such in terms of the whole, that is, with an eye toward the highest all-understanding existence, then metaphysics becomes logic in the form of theo-logic.[4]

With a move that foreshadows Deleuze's later fascination with a Lobster God or our own archival fascination with the specific communal *organs* of the passingly effective instances of vibrant solidarities, Heidegger concludes: "Because metaphysical thinking remains imbedded in difference which as such is not the object of thought, metaphysics is at one and the same time uniquely ontology and theology by virtue of the unifying oneness of the issue."[5] More than commenting on the intertwined history of two discrete enterprises, Heidegger is inviting us, as it were, to consider ontology and theology in light of von von Uexküll's tick that drops down onto the yummy mammal. More than a comment on philosophy or theology, it is a call rather to imagine theology and ontology as tales akin to maps of the various stimuli that set the Lobster to pinch mode, that make the tick take the leap of faith, or indeed the stimuli, the ethos, of those games that solicit us *as* lovers, as business partners, as e-mail hacks of one type or another. For us, it is Deleuze who hits—for philosophy or theology—the relevant tone in his wonder about the tick (which is also our wonder about our online lovers, our business partners, and our archival Gods): a "world with only three affects, in the midst of all that goes on in the immense forest"!

In Heidegger's automated response system, we are ever players bearing what he calls the particular "stamp" or "authentication" pressed or passworded by a unification machine whose rules are merely exemplified by the specific machine term *ontotheology*. A crucial point for an insurrectionist science of the dead and dying Gods, we might say that the important point in Heidegger's text is not that the *onto-* or the *theo-* both vie for supremacy as "the One,," that unity which, in Heidegger's philosophy of difference, becomes always an *effect* of a singular communicative machinery of unifying-*as*. *The more important issue in this text is that, in any case, it is the autoresponse machine that oddly gives us the roles we play even as it necessarily forecloses our direct habitation of access to the same.* Put differently, the more important issue than the relation between ontology and philosophy is that we are all—in Heidegger's difference machine—stranded, *the hyphen* where all actants live (cf. *onto-logy," theo-logy,," onto-theology*). This is an important insight for us, key to our proclamation—good news in bad—of a vampiric transcendence.

Troll for lovers or bankers or wait around for the return of a God no doubt about to buy his ticket to Earth, the endgames here are variations of a return to a One that must, after Heidegger's intervention, increasingly take responsibility for itself, bear its own load, rather than remain unthought and unremarked. The "One" is the space of the "world" of the tick, but also the "pinch" of the lobster, or that rendezvous in person to confirm online pictures (with a new lover or an old God). This is the recursive machinery operative in a mode Heidegger can *also* designate as "onto-theology." You draw near to or embrace the game you are playing, and this particularly as you negotiate the passwords and protocols of "authentication" that give the game its revelatory actuality, its real buzz. In performing our passcodes, pinching when we divinities do so, we are always and ever discovering, testing, how we play the game that is playing us.

Revelation in the Age of Consumptive Presence

For us and our interest in a new science of all our unconscious or Lobster Gods, it is Heidegger who saw it coming—an age of a relentless, everyday, as if eternal experience of consumable spiritualities, sexual experiences, humanitarianisms, religions, niche-market irreligiosities, professions, confessions, carefully nurtured apathies, any one of which emerges as a niche market, an online association, a society with its own epicures pressing their cohort to ever greater heights of achievement on the attainment of exquisite taste in their requisite delicacy. When we say these *bioi* or avatars of the living are consumable, we mean only that the solidarities and our enactments of them consume each other, yield themselves in the other as if through a mimetic dance or play of mirrors. Here again, Heidegger was more correct than he realized.

In each case, the setting up of mirrors or the facing off of mimetic dancers occurs as if through a miraculous irruption of a gesture, a glance, a catchphrase. Suddenly new tics are falling on new animals, new aggregates find themselves new Lobsters by virtue of their recent defensive pinching. In the gesture is discovered the miracle of new being. Heidegger perhaps did not say this clearly enough, but the game's clearing of space for the players appears most directly only by an indirect focus on the specific form of passcodes (for authentication) or the emergence of new exemplars as "types" (for the maintenance of the given solidarity in question). Heidegger's sometimes counterintuitive effort to think difference and singularity without preexisting models implies that, in every case, my ecstasy is an excessive intensity, which, far from escaping or transgressing a system-game that would appropriate it, *is itself* the gesture nourishing the game. Our intensities are not transgressive. They are rather investive (if we may say so), ingressive into a new game that appears nevertheless, and not without warrant, to feed off our "excess." Heidegger's problematic here is a profound challenge to a great deal of what passes as critical theory, not to mention our usual jeremiads about the abuse that is a capitalism without orientation and limits. It is also this problematic that shapes our different insurrectionist interests in staying "with" theology as an archive of dead and dying Gods, something I hope will become clearer as we proceed.

Others should therefore hesitate before taking Heidegger to point in his discussions of onto-theology primarily to a tale of the received past (wherein, say, the thought of God and the thought of being have been more intertwined than current disciplinary regimes acknowledge). Even less are we interested in a script about how we might *save* a theology now chastened of ontological pretensions, that flat conservativism which marks so many recent praises of finitude, and a "postsecular" whose passcode and buzz seem above all to revolve around an affection for the bended knee. Rather, the *binding* of theology and ontology happens in their mutual occurrence within the machinery of a hyphenated identity that both gives and takes away the ground or endgame at stake in its enactment.

Ever a fascinating reader of Heidegger and ever an inspiration for our new archival science of the dead and dying Gods, Peter Sloterdijk suggests that we develop a new sort of bestiary of an "immanently transferrable transcendence." Sloterdijk's bestiary would attempt to articulate all those modes of thought—and practices of messaging—that escape what Sloterdijk calls a "metaphysics of the strong sender."[6] As Sloterdijk narrates in a nicely Heideggerian way:

> Viewed from this perspective, the concept of revelation unmistakably belongs to the world of *Homo Hierarchicus*. It sets up an analogy between the feudal relationship of lord and vassal and the cognitive relationship of object and subject, with a clear emphasis on the primacy of the lord and the object. According to this model, the receipt of a revelation corresponds to the extreme of vassalic passivity. It marks a case in which listening and obeying coincide; in other contexts one would speak of an offer that cannot be refused. It is immediately clear why this model loses its plausibility, both socially and epistemologically, in cultures characterized by devassalization. The notion of purely receptive subjects transpires as logically and empirically untenable. The subject could not reply to the angel of the object: "May it be as you have said"; on the contrary, as it knows that it impresses its own "frame of possibilities" upon all the objects

it experiences. For this and other reasons, the idea of a revelation that can be dictated and passively accepted reaches a point of crisis.[7]

For us, Sloterdijk says much too much when he seems to differentiate Mary's weak performative gesture in the Gospel of Luke from the post-metaphysical communicative relay of the weak sender. After all, Mary's deflationary gesture is perhaps precisely what we are left with in the present age, a little "let it be" or "OK"—the merest strength of a mere affirmation, even a kind of shrug of acquiescence. Indeed, isn't the relevant comparative point that this weak gesture ("OK," "so be it," "as you say") is all that the transcendence game seems to need to ground itself through us? This is a crucial issue for any effort to imagine an "immanently transferrable transcendence." After all, forget the imagined weak gesture of Luke's poor Mary promised her little lamb by a youth claiming to be an angel; daily ten thousand people flinch without any acquiescing words at all, flinching as a gesture with only a barely measurable jerk of an index finger, and this to the barest suggestion of a message. Miraculously, as these things go, there is an Advent, and suddenly "fat kid on a roller coaster" proliferates via YouTube new modes of vibrancy. So many flinches and through the clicks there emerges soon a Lobster's pinch, the buzz of spectacle and the organization of new satellite organs of collective attention. New organs appear, feeding off the buzz in question: "fat kid falls"; "fat kid fails"; the whole deliciously malevolent genre of "fails" and "falls."

Click. "Let it be," as the earlier Gospel writer imagines Mary, quite retro now, as yet needing *to speak* to the messaging angel. Moreover, with the radiation of acquiescing clicks, new Lobsters of all sorts invariably evolve *to make a claim to the pinching effect.* New genres crystallize to organize the flinch-as-clicks, to incorporate them into more complex associations. Soon arrives a kind of New Testament collection expounding on the founding miracle, the Ultimate Fails Compilation, updated yearly, then monthly, now weekly. With a new flinch a new genre and a new game has—as Heidegger says it perfectly—"cleared" itself, clearing, in this case, the annunciation of good news, a little pleasure in meticulously documented pain. And, as all gospels do, this little annunciation, this little revelation of a new way of seeing, soon enough solicits others to go forth, cameras in hand always ready to expand the revelation to the ends of the earth. This is indeed good news, and perhaps the disciples will be ready for you, or for me, the next time we fall or fail or frighten ourselves into the miraculously operational categories of the new genre or consumptive revelation. When it happens, angelic clearing will exult. The Lobster will pinch, the tic will fall, the lover will reply in kind. In an economy of "weak senders" our weakest affirmations will begin to give buoyancy to a transcendent life which ever needs to feed back upon us for more. In our excessively festive "off hours" we play soccer by the sea. Kids are running wild, and I decide to kick the ball to kingdom come, running, reaching back with a foot now become a canon. The muddy field likewise transforms said feet into ice skates, and Dad flies, flies until feet miraculously above head, soon crashing back down to gasp for the breath so effectively knocked out of him. Children scream in carnivalesque joy, immediately lamenting that the fall had not been recorded, a prize entry no doubt on YouTube or *You've Been Framed*. The minuscule is mirrored in the massive, and these small moments of the everyday, mere tick bites, are not without a home in the expropriating—vampiric—mirror play of our new satellite skies.

Vampiric Sky: From Bram Stoker's Dracula to Philo's Abraham

It is in just this sense, in fact, that Heidegger's brilliant expansions of the deferring mirror plays across the difference of an ultimate ground, cause, or height of enthusiasm always leave us flat when he speaks of "sky" the way he does. Indeed, to be workable at all for a kind of baseline "everyday" that could inform contemporary thought, here as elsewhere we need to force Heidegger's texts to do more than he might have wanted them to do. Heidegger's "sky" often enough appears in one of his frequent Greco-peasant fantasies, that amalgam of fantasies which were always strong enough to get him chopping his own wood at his mountain hut, but alas never so strong as to keep him there when he had a chance to become the Nazi rector of his university. For example, of the sky, that excessive sphere to which we ever "look up," Heidegger posed a kind of philosophical hymn to the "shipping merchants" of Bremen.[8] "The sky is the path of the sun, the course of the moon, the gleam of the stars, the seasons of the year, the light and twilight of day, the dark and bright of the night, the favour and inclemency of the weather, drifting clouds, and blue depths of the ether."[9] Beautiful, perhaps, but Heidegger's sky is not yet populated enough to be for us more than a soporific fourth in the mirror play of earth, sky, divinities, and mortals.

Sky is not here, for example, the site of that gaze which made the world an image, the famous "blue marble" shot which indicates indirectly sky as now the *subject* of a gaze that scrutinizes earth and, increasingly, the elect of its inhabitants. Yes, yes, sky as path of the sun, moon, but Heidegger's sky was not yet a new sea to be crisscrossed by proliferating bands of revolving satellites, satellites eventually no longer even owned by nation-states, that shift which indicates that the mirror image of mortals on earth these satellites beam back are less and less about the measurable surfaces of most physical or political geographies we know.

Compared to Heidegger's skies, ours will be skies wherein the regularities and harmonics of these transcendently synthesizing "ethers" are, as it were, hacked by optical proxies as virtual corporations manufacture artificial sensoria to instantiate and promote a buzz of intensity that operates, as it were, between the satellite and the mortals on earth "below" (a spatializing term that orients worldhood only when we forget our apparatuses of orientation, all our global positioning devices). The times and seasons and patterns of Sky as overarchingly and persistently determining backdrop for mortal life must for us, against Heidegger, merge more completely into a different image of *economy* as a vampirically transcendent site for the passage of trends, enforced transformations of habit and routine. In his excellent *Vampire Lectures*, Laurence Rickels cites a line of Chris Braddick that would have been useful for Heidegger to remember as well: "Dracula is feudalism's death warmed up."[10] Heidegger was living in a moment when, in a more than incidental sense, the territories of transcendence were becoming ever more a zone of surveillance, speculation, and control. Significantly, in that spate of post-WWII lectures in which Heidegger's comments appear, he would eventually find himself lecturing about the openness of sky, transcendence as the violent opening of the open itself, and this in the year 1957 . . . the same year the Soviets launched Sputnik. The annunciation of Sputnik's orbit was met with panic in the United States, which hurled itself into the development of fiber optic cables and the Internet as so many efforts to hang nuclear-strength garlic above the threshold of their sense of national sovereignty.[11]

Heidegger, prophet-like, perhaps saw some things coming, but without fully working through his ongoing mourning for a receding world of peasant farmers laboring under an autumn sky. In his important lectures on *die Ereignis* or "event," Heidegger produces poetry (read it and weep) that expresses the central category of openness as "errancy," as a moment when "the human being" forgets that it has become the "satellite of the devastation and . . . the [mere] "guarantor" of the truthlessness" of such a situation.[12] Heidegger's nostalgic poetry says more than he could know in an age in which, very soon, indeed by the time he was done lecturing in Freiburg, there would be no security for rootedness on the earth without a capacity to trace the territory of earth through the gaze of a satellite view. In 1957 Heidegger's discourse was still oriented around images of a secret sharing between mortals and the divinities of the sky, a sharing that would be the "violence" (as he liked to say) of the opening of thought itself. Still rehearsing the older Gospels for the 1957 audience in Freiburg, Heidegger still fantasized a version of the old Judeo-pagano-Christian complex of avant-garde mortals leading the way by becoming-stars, ascending to become the errant courses of stars—the very mystery of transcendence as a divine-human traffic of ascent into the sky. That year when, like Christ, the vision of the Soviets would ascend to the heights, the result would be all the more mundane than even Heidegger's ostensibly secularized ascent narratives recognized.

In fact, one even wonders in relation to the earlier presatellite lectures whether (as Graham Harman calls them) the "shipping merchants" constituting Heidegger's benefactors in Bremen would have already found Heidegger's "sky" strangely retro compared to what they knew of openly piratical seas, lawless competition in circulations of capital between the proprietorial delimitations imagined by physical borders of land. For this, one need not wait for the space race or the proliferation of satellites which, by the beginning of our twenty-first century, would see a sky dotted with some eight thousand satellites.[13] A decade earlier than Heidegger's lecture on the fourfold of earth, sky, mortals, and divinities, Carl Schmitt would put important insights into bad hands, pointing out in his *Grossraum* essay (which Heidegger knew) that the seventeenth century was "the period in which there reigned a wonderful harmony between, on the one hand, the political and economic interests of the British world empire and, on the other hand, the recognized rules of international law."[14] Schmitt continues with a riff on the "open" seas which seems already to be more than a little relevant to the "open sky" of Heidegger's lecture a decade (and a second world war) later:

> In the politically decisive case, "freedom" means a rewriting of the conceptual, specifically British global imperial interest as concerns the great traffic routes of the world. "Freedom of the seas," in other words, means,

according to a formulation of Wheaton-Dana's that became famous through its citation in the Miramichi case [which enabled Britain to seize goods carried in British vessels during wartime]: "the sea is *res omnium*, the common field of war, as well as of commerce." As long as England had dominance on the seas, the freedom of the seas received its borders, indeed, even its content, through the right and the freedom of war-conducting states to police the commerce of neutrals.[15]

The very deterritorialized openness of the sea as the extraterritorial space for the flow of vessels, circulating behind the scenes like so many stars in our sky, was itself the openness to seizure. Legally, proprietorially ambiguous, sea was nevertheless the site of so many ticks falling, so many lobsters pinching. Deterritorialized space of emerging proprietorial worlds, the free sea was in this way an odd umbilical union between openness, commerce, and warfare, a tie Schmitt refers to as "the unavoidable link between ways of thinking about international law and a certain kind of political existence."[16]

Another text with which Heidegger was no doubt familiar, but whose ethos is repressed amidst his Greco-peasant fantasies, was the sky of the first world war, memorialized by Ernst Junger as the open visual space soldiers must attain the most of in order to be the best protected from the fusillades of the enemy: "During those instants of waiting, you had to try to get a place where you could see as much of the sky as possible, because it was only against its pale backdrop that it was possible to see the black jagged iron of those deadly balls with sufficient clarity. Then you hurled your own bomb, and leaped forward."[17] We think already the shipbuilders of Bremen would have found something clunky in the symbolic rather than automated function of sky in Heidegger's fourfold. Schmitt and Junger are here, as it were, good readers of that other great if often unrecognized thinker of modern transcendence, Bram Stoker. Like Junger in the trenches, Stoker urged us to see that one mistakes at one's own peril the "nature" of sky for instances of its many life-taking vampires and satellite or piratical overseers.

Heidegger, obsessed with modes of transcendence to the end, would have philosophized better were he to have more closely followed the practice of Doctor Seward, who—despite himself—learned to hand himself over to following the gaze of his psychotic patient Renfield in his own visual tracing of the sky: "When he saw me he became furious, and had not the attendants seized him in time, he would have tried to kill me. As we were holding him, a strange thing happened. He suddenly redoubled his efforts [to escape], and then as suddenly became calm. I looked round instinctively, but could see nothing. Then I caught the patient's eye, but could trace nothing as it looked into the moonlight sky, except a big bat, which was flapping its silent and ghostly way to the west."[18] Pioneering seafarers of a sky open for new commerce and new seizures of deterritorialized property, Heidegger, too, should have looked up to realize the arrival of all the bats, satellite stars, and new surveillance stealth planes in order to wonder how his romantic categories of transcendence were colonized by more lurking vampires than would seem to be the case. Renfield was definitionally psychotic, but he was not misleading.

These stories we have not yet begun to trace, and their ongoing inscription onto the necks and psyches of the religious will be dramatic. In a comparative moment more relevant for us than we tend to imagine, Philo of Alexandria's *On the Migration of Abraham*, the philosophical genealogist imagines religion as the tale of the founding of a people, and he does so in the following way. The man eventually named Abraham dwelt in Ur of the Chaldees (a place eventually to be called Iraq). This founding "outsider" is called by the globalized One to a new land, but, Philo asserts, this was a revolutionary emigration and founding that one could have foreseen or predicted. After all, Philo writes, it was in Iraq that Abraham was first exposed to the open of Sky as a processing of regularized motions and harmonic rotations. Philo's Abraham looked up, in Heidegger's lingo, and sensed himself to be an interface *between* the hurly-burly of earth (and, in fact, its cacophony of plural deities) and the Sky as regularized, organized, and therefore stable transcendence. In Philo's philosophical and scriptural reshuffling, Abraham's travels were a kind of earthly analogue to a heavenly ascent, a quest on earth for a kingdom of the One-God, that implied Regularizer in the regularized Sky.

Rather than rejection as an obfuscating myth of origins, the tale of the revolutionary founding of the Abrahamic needs rather updating in the bright light of our more populated vampiric skies. Among the many figures we could select, we wonder about the young Iraquis, future leaders of lastingly significant theologico-political movements, whose look up to the skies is a flinch of recognition of the distinct buzz of a U.S. "drone," perhaps just surveilling from the sky above, perhaps approaching for a not-so-precise precision attack. Heidegger and Philo wrote of regularized skies that, because underpopulated, have little to do with ours, but they were both correct to wonder about what new Gods might violently and transformatively tear through the Sky as the vampirically susceptible gaze of the mortal looks upward. "Immanently transferrable transcendence" indeed. The vampiric skies are not simply obstructions in the generation of the new, not simply a kind of cynical self-reflexivity. On the contrary, we need to prepare ourselves for the writing of a new emigration of outsiders ready to found, once more, a people from the resonance they intuit in the regularized Skies and errant satellite stars under which they stand. The new sensorium with Sky as its backdrop will yield new Iraquis, new Abrahams as surprising solidarities founded on foreign lands. How could it be otherwise? New skies, new divinities, new excessive/transcendent missives and missions, none of which will have much to do with Heidegger's rooted peasant farmers.

Expropriating Sky and the Genealogy of Insurrection

With a kind of satellite retuning of Heidegger's imaginary fourfold, however, we feel better the force of his exceedingly important nomenclature when he suggests that the "fold" of the sky into its mirror selves as earth, Gods, and mortals is precisely the folding-into-unity about which one can only say that "each of the four within this bringing into ownership (or simple unity) is much more expropriated to what is its own."[19] Here Heidegger's prescience as a thinker of the event as spectacle and mysteriously miraculous buzz is awkwardly illuminating for what has become our current regimes of consumable identities or, indeed, our "sold" spiritualities (as Jeremy Carrette and Richard King have it).[20] The "play" (as Heidegger also named it) of the fourfold isn't so much just a happy "ringdance" of Heidegger's fantasized Greco-peasant totality as much as something suggesting, more darkly, a "being played" by spheres which are agencies always susceptible of becoming "agencies" of a ploddingly different sort: new markets, objects of speculative investment, and finally brutally enforceable economic demands on mortal workers hacking away at the earth to maintain these vampiric divinities alive. The event or happening of the emergence of the fourfold—replete with that excess of sky to which we look up (now as if gripped by the throat)—is itself the fly constituting this holistic ointment, that very expropriation of all the empassioned or ecstatic players from the very fold of the game in which they find themselves.

As he sometimes is despite his own protestations, for us Heidegger is a kind of intensified Marx inasmuch as the fourfold names our being expropriated from the modes of production whereby we manufacture ourselves. To be sure, Heidegger's intensification of the Marxist tale borders more perilously on a story of the irreparable, certainly beyond the (relatively easy) fantasy of a new movement of factory takeover. It was to be in the year of Sputnik that Heidegger would effectively try to "update" and save a concept of dialectical materialism by radicalizing "labor" as the activity grounded only within the expropriating fourfold, this move effectively allowing a vision of Marx as merely technical, tactical, or calculating production of human being to offer itself to a more radical Hegelianism, which, in these lectures, Heidegger will valorize as "thought" itself.

> Many will repudiate this [Marxist] construal of world history and its underlying conception of the essence of the human. But no one can deny that today technology, industry, and economy authoritatively determine all actuality of the actual to be the labor of the self-production of the human. Yet with this assessment we already fall out of that dimension of thinking in which Marx's expression just cited concerning world history as the "labor of the self-production of the human" moves about. For the word "labor" here does not mean mere activity and performance. The word speaks in the sense of Hegel's concept of labor, which is thought as the basic trait of the dialectical process, by which the becoming of the actual unfolds and completes its actuality.[21]

Saving Marx from the Marx he became in the hands of his followers, Heidegger becomes the philosopher of a dialectical materialism without hope of natural or emancipatory ground outside the expropriating echo chamber of his fourfold happening of being. It is in this sense that we are in all seriousness tempted to rebuke most of the would-be Heideggerian theologians for having forgotten their Abraham van Helsing in order to find in Heidegger's Greco-peasant fantasies a future for a postmetaphysical redemptive ringdance. As the fictive philosophical physician van Helsing urged on those in need of his particular therapeutic wares:

> Before we do anything, let me tell you this; it is out of the lore and experience of the ancients and of all those who have studied the powers of

the Un-Dead. When they become such, there comes with the change the curse of immortality; they cannot die, but must go on age after age adding new victims and multiplying the evils of the world; for all that die from the preying of the Un-Dead become themselves Un-Dead, and prey on their kind. And *so the circle goes on ever widening*, like as the ripples from a stone thrown in the water.[22]

Expropriating ringdance, which gives and takes away life as the very nature of the "event" of being, these days we find van Helsing's vampiric transcendence more illuminating than the skies in view from the Black Forest peasant sage.

Heidegger's undeadening of the Marxist story is of supreme helpfulness, and here we should not be afraid to describe Heidegger's fourfold, grounded in dispropriation, as a kind of hyper-Marxism, a Marxism with another turn of the century's worth of insight to intensify the earlier insights. Heidegger's Marxism—effectively becoming a "dialectical materialism" indistinguishable from the violent openness of thought itself—was a Marxism in which the "vampire" elements of Marx's earlier analyses were, as if read back through Van Helsing, generalized, opened out. Indeed, if we read Heidegger here as repeating his earlier and career-making gestures against metaphysical certainties grounding and explaining behavior (which is necessarily reduced to calculation), then what we have is a kind of vampiric-Paulinist movement beyond the "dead letter" of Marx's own undead. Heidegger, with a tried and true gesture, gets to the real revelation of Marx's vampirism by liberating the "spirit" of the undead over against the undead's otherwise prescripted vampirisms.

If we remain intrigued by transcendence, therefore, it is only because it is a name for the surplus value constituting the capitalization driving our most banal everyday experiences. The transcendence that intrigues us is a vampiric transcendence naming ongoing and often brutal expropriations constitutive of the unplaceable play constituting our irreparably dispersed worldhoods. Here one must hold fast to the image of Heidegger's satellite skies, radicalizing Marx, against a panoply of "postsecular" theologians who seem always and ever keen to submit before institutional, professional, and political borders what, precisely, we generally do want to refuse, defuse, make public and common. In reading these sections of Heidegger, one could get along well here with theologians who were always keen to find in sky a kind of transcendence, that to which humanity "looks up" (as per Heidegger's echo of Augustine and Calvin throughout *Being and Time*).[23] Fair enough, but one must be clear here against the (equally) soporific theologians, sticking up for, precisely, the way the folding into unity of the fourfold is effectively a story of ex-propriation, that Mr. Jekyll who overshadows for us the good Peasant Doctor Heidegger. For us, Sky is indeed the sphere of an excess that transcends but draws the desire of the mortals looking "up" from the Earth, effectively rendering Sky a place swarming with spy satellites, fusillades, and vampire bats, as Junger and Stoker knew even better than the philosopher. One must forever refuse the ringdances and bucolic scenes that foreclose our by-now everyday experiences of Sky as the *operation whereby the excessive ecstasies of the mortals as such are syphoned off into a "transcendent" sphere that is definitively NOT owned by them.* Against the soporific theologians and Heidegger himself perhaps, for us Heidegger's fourfold as a nomination of a philosophy of difference is most useful when taken as a thought of an aggressive tear in the fabric of the social most readily accessible to us in the thought of the aggressive appropriation—or declaration of ownership—of surpluses and surplus values of all sorts. Humanity does not so much "look up" at the Sky as look for it over one's shoulder, searching for this vampire in every mirror of the fourfold (and realizing it is all the scarier when the mirrors cannot directly register the monster).

After all, as we have already mentioned, these days in order to operate effectively expropriating transcendence just needs to graze us (in order, as it were, to graze on us). Any click will do. Vampiric transcendence falls upon us, falls out on us like von Uexküll's hungry tick. Classic critiques of capital miss just these tiniest of vampires, the tiniest ticks of the multiple modes of expropriating transcendences. Recall Deleuze, who declares of the wonderous little blood sucker: "a world with only three affects, in the midst of all that goes on in the immense forest"! The tick is a probe, a satellite sent out as a form of binding attunement around (in this case) only three affective zones, transcendence as a specialized niche market within the "immense forest" of options. Sky's unconscious economy of rhythms and motions and regularities does not just set the tone of our everyday lives, like when we stay out longer drinking beer by the sea as spring days lengthen into the summer season. It is also the patterning, regularizing, and harmonizing of a chaotic multiple of expropriating spheres which *feed off* mortal life, ticks feeding off the slightest tic or flinch of life "here below." Against the soporific effect of some of the recent formulations of transcendence, excess, or surplus as that which we must now cling to like new readers of Bataille, the new science of the dead and dying Gods veers closer to genealogies of transcendence in order better to illumine those modes in which the economies of satellite skies operate between life and death like a vampire, and all this in order to cook transformations of those tyrannizing regularities of expropriation that define different groups of us in our everyday existence (e.g., our becoming hot-blooded mammals through the tick's drop, our becoming academics through underpaid and overworked early careers, our becoming experts on religion through the contest of niche publishing). No wonder Heidegger could believe in transitive or displaced identities only as he mixed a visual metaphor of "mirror play" with the nonvisual implications of a "fold," as if struggling more and more to be true to what Stoker had already taught us a half century earlier, namely, that vampires cast no reflection.

What is so great about Heidegger as a reader of his traditions of religion and philosophy is the way he, like Freud, situated himself as the revelation of an aspect of the underlying cultural game everyone else was suppressing or acknowledging only at the level of unconscious symptom. In Heidegger's case, the onto-theology machine stamped philosophy and religion with the same binding or unifying operation, implying already that binding only emerges within an experience of separation, of mirroring without ground or *difference*. Onto-theology *already* exhibits wonderfully the game of deferral or autoresponding into the void—but it does not often *acknowledge* that it does so. One labors at e-mailing the lover, securing the lover's affections, expressing in return an enthusiasm one has received in turn. But one doesn't often wonder whether the lover exists apart from the apparatus or machinery of message-and-response in which the larger affair takes its life. Truth be told, and in ways never apparent in his own letters to Hannah Arendt or to Elfride Petri, Heidegger makes a wonderful counselor for lovers in the digital age, unable to shake the imprint of the new media wherein they found, "authenticated" and "undergirded," love.

And with that in mind—this highest of praise: a philosopher for the age of online dating—we find the reception history of his next famous comments generally beside the point:

> God entered philosophy through the issue which we think first of all as
> being the advance point in the essence of the difference between being

and existence. Difference represents the ground plan in the essential structure of metaphysics. The issue yields and cedes being as the pro-ductive ground, which ground in itself requires an appropriate understanding on the part of what it helped found. The appropriate understanding is equivalent to causation by the ultimate and original reality. This is the Cause as *causa sui*, and this is the just and proper name for God in philosophy. Man may neither pray to his God, nor may he sacrifice to him. Confronted by *causa sui* man may neither sink onto his knees nor could he dance and sing.

Accordingly, this thinking-less-God which must abandon the God of philosophy, God as *causa sui*, is perhaps, closer to God the divinity. In our context this means merely that thinking-less-God is less restricted in dealing with him than onto-theo-logic would acknowledge.[24]

Our disappointment stems from the mode in which readers seem to have forgotten the basic ruse of the "step backward" into the history of philosophy as the history of the *emergence* of the very "problematic" or pincered oppositional pairs in question. Forget that we know so many philosophers—or, even worse, theologians—who don't dance worth a damn (though I swear on all that's sacred that many in both camps these days seem to sink to their knees rather easily). The "issue" is that there always was an "issue" that gave rise to the oppositional pair in question, a "game" that both interpellates (or solicits, enables, and challenges) particular types of player. If there is a criticism of onto-theology here, of course it is not simply that it *needs* to learn to dance, but only that it must recognize that it was dancing and sacrificing all along, even as it mistook these unthought vibrancies as the diktats of a "One" who was still, in Sloterdijk's terminology, a "strong sender."

Perhaps Heidegger participates in the unhelpful propping up of the merely formal opposition in the "fourfold" when he immediately begins to worry that "language" will continue to suture our attentions to the onto-theological pairs without allowing other modes of being gamed to percolate to the vibrant, buzzy surfaces. One should be clear about the new science of the dead and dying Gods in relation to such gestures. Our wise advice is that the "step back" of the insurrectionist archivist should allow itself to engage in an opining for an "event" to come only if it is also happy to wait until the theologians and professional philosophers finally discover the club scene. Heidegger was already onto the more excellent way here when he suggests that our writing click over from the received histories or *problēmata* of philosophy and theology to the genealogies of the gyrating hip. Much more important than the institutional and representational games played by most in relation to theology or philosophy is simply to get back to the archives of these and other gestures, like that stunning religio-sexual movement of subservience and the pleasure of submission—all those irresistible paths downward that become our "sinking" to our knees. Tick world, lobster world, dating scenes, never have they been more mysterious, more miraculous, once we realize that we live in a world without adjudicating Other, without closure or final frame—in a word, without "onto-theology."

Time Pressures: New Science of Divine Pincers

To summarize, as a vibrant and always specific practice of insurrection, the insurrectionist archivists link these two moments in Heidegger's perennially significant texts on the fourfold, namely, the aleatory gesture and the vibrant force of the pincers. On the one hand, the archivist of insurrection elaborates genealogies of the *gestures* that onto-theology as metaphysics tended to consider irrelevant (in this case bending knees and quivering hips). But, and here is where things become of essential significance for us, what we find in such genealogies is not simply a baseline of a "material practice" which then functions as a different type of cause or unified ground for the rest of the "onto-theological" story. Such reductive materialisms simply reshuffle the dualistic pack of the idealist hucksters, something I have tried to explore much more fully in *A Materialism for the Masses*. Rather, insurrectionist genealogies hit upon migrant meanderings of a gesture that, at different moments, takes on modes always at least minimally *mysterious*, haunted, possessed, deified. In every case, it is the archive of the pinching of the Lobster *Gods* that we need to amass for further exploration, trying to get at the very vibrancy or pressure of a kind of vibrating investiture without which the gesture will lose its compulsive force of repetition. There is a comedy, and an eroticism, endemic to the everyday work of the insurrectionist archivist's cataloging that can illumine those vampiric skies from which we will not finally escape. In all seriousness, one should forget the discourse of epochal distinctions between "onto-theology" and postmetaphysical thinking. As we have declared, what we need is a new *discipline* for constituting an archive of the gestures bearing those dark vibrancies that come—comedically, impossibly—to regularize and invest repetition itself, giving buoyancy and girth to what becomes the actual, real world (as we tend to say, language that normalizes a state of affairs by repressing the mad dances, laughter, and ecstatic moans which inhere in the gestures that continue to make it so actualized). The real import of Heidegger's reflections is not really in the way that, in this tradition, the articulation of being and the articulation of God mirrored each other from Plato to Nietzsche. That is clear enough. What is more pressing is, rather, the pressure of Heidegger's folds and hyphens themselves, the oddly ubiquitous machinery of an evocation and installation of repetition that carries the performance (and success) of the game in the gamers.

Put differently, the insurrectionist Gospel of a new Sky is just that, a *bookish* Gospel attempting to hook a mobile movement—a faster, oral (and even autonomic) *euangelion,* as it were—into the slower informational flows and more secure informational storage capacities of the archive, the library, or the culture of learning. Indeed, our bookish gospels are not merely a slowing of faster oral gospels but also a tracking of gospel vibrancies operative at faster rates of speed even than the oral, gospels of the moving hip, nondiscursive quivering lip, flick of the finger across the screen. Not a *kerygma* about an epochal break, but a call for a new research *discipline,* our provocatively entitled new science of the unconscious Gods should here also evoke the Gospel of Luke, its effort to situate "gospel" by placing it within a world of (real or imagined, paid-up or prospective) patrons, historical writers about weighty matters: "Oh, Most Excellent Theophilus, having investigated everything more than the rest, my new organization of the material will certify its truth."[25] Conjurers of a new archival discipline (rather than mere proclaimers of the event of the New), the insurrectionist archivist slowly, patiently rewires the history of theology into a genealogy of pincers and their stimuli, attempting to catalog the *vibrancy of the specific gestures of linking* whereby divinities irrupt as shareable, social solidarities—the opening and enforcement of countable multiplicities. Call it a new materialism, call it an object-oriented ontology, call it the capitalization of God or an interdisciplinary disciplining of the postsecular, the only thing we care about is the crystallization of new analyses of those alchemical vibrancies whereby divinities as social solidarities come (as Heidegger liked to say) to a stand.

Read this way, the hyphen of Heidegger's onto-theology, linking not so much two sciences as naming the problem of repetition as such, blurs into Deleuze, the ethologist, that organologist of an unconscious Lobster God, beast and sovereign all at one go. After all, Deleuze suggests in the opening epigraph to this chapter that the name God becomes usefully displaced by a focus on the "overcoding" of an aggregate, as if God were the "worldhood" pinching together multiple affective zones as a regularized form of life. Juxtaposing these comments of Deleuze and Heidegger is useful here to suggest that we consider a form of life, worldhood, as haunted by a kind of excess, an "overcoding" within coding itself, a strange *drive to repetition* of a sameness that both exceeds and retroactively grounds the identities imagined as *same* over time at all. It is in this technical role of God as a "pincers" operation, or as the possibility that a complex ecological happening will regularize itself, set itself up as a form of regularity, that we should give weight to Deleuze's consistent fascination with the topic of the "apparatus," in his own writings and in those of Michel Foucault. In a word, the buzzing apparatus of Deleuze is the real force of Heidegger's hyphen in his discussion of the onto-theological nature of metaphysics.

We need to take seriously that, with a gesture's "clearing" (Heidegger) or the immanent "pincers" movement whereby a Lobster God overcodes an aggregate in an excess of desire (Deleuze), what we are considering is a sort of miracle in the machinery of repetition. We are attempting to name, in an immanent mode, that obscure instantiation of a new modus vivendi. Here is the cut of reality instantiating itself, setting itself up as a form of repetition, a mode of organizing life. Archivists of *this* insurrection have some work of mapping ahead: after all, this is that obscure foreign land where all our Gods, our vampires, our transcendences come from—along with that whole "Fail Army" of organized humanity (and cats and dogs and birds and monkeys), running away with its own success on YouTube.

Thus marks the end of a gospel of vampiric transcendence, a gospel that (as always) seems to leave us only with a lot of work to do. We look up, as ever, to see a promising task slowly receding from the capacities of our vision, as if this task were—before our very eyes—withdrawing itself back into the refuge of the sky as if riding upward on a cloud . . .

Acts of the Immanentizers of Transcendent Authority: From Sacher-Masoch to Paul of Tarsus

Countercultural sages don't boast in any property or propriety—except that dark spiritual exercise which projects them as crucified to the world . . . and the world crucified before them in return. Through this expropriating mirror play appears a new creation without ownership.
Think of yourselves as dead . . . and yet living . . .
—Gloss on Galatians 6:14–15, Romans 6:11

In keeping with the problematic of vampiric transcendence, surplus value, or the "immanent manufacture of transcendence," Brett Buchanan summarizes Deleuze's interest in "problems" as a cut into a situation that is both, we might say, question and answer: "problems and questions are what frame the ontological agenda of modern thought."[26]

"It must be remembered," Deleuze writes, "to what extent modern thought and the renaissance of ontology is based upon the question-problem complex." But it is not just any question problem; it is the question of being. Alain Badiou, in his book on Deleuze, puts it in the following manner: "Our epoch can be said to have been stamped and signed, in philosophy, by the return of the question of Being."[27]

In ways that have hardly begun to be mapped, we should note that this configuration of the problem of being as vampiric transcendence provides the pith for Deleuze's intriguing reflections on the writings of Sacher-Masoch. Indeed, this configuration of the question of being is what, finally, blends the Stoic radical passivity of Deleuze not only with the perversions of constitutional power that one finds in Masoch's *Venus in Furs*, but also—surprisingly—with the perversions of nomological agencies that we find in important moments of the writings of Paul of Tarsus.

In each respect the early Deleuze's fascination with Sacher-Masoch and the perversion of nomological gaming fits almost without seam to the paradoxical structures unearthed in our earlier discussion. Consider Deleuze's Masoch (indeed, his Lacan) as a variation of the dynamics of Heidegger's gift and repression of "clearing." Deleuze writes in his précis to Masoch and his *Venus in Furs*:

In Lacan's words, the law is the same as repressed desire. The law cannot specify its object without self-contradiction, nor can it define itself with reference to a content without removing the repression on which it rests. The object of law and the object of desire are one and the same, and remain equally concealed.

The fact that anarchy can only exist in the interval between two regimes based on laws, abolishing the old to give birth to the new, does not prevent this divine interval, this vanishing instant, from testifying to its fundamental difference from all forms of the law.[28]

The paradoxically redemptive gesture of Deleuze's text on Sacher-Masoch, and indeed of Deleuze's radical Stoicism more generally, is that it does not struggle *against* normalizing *nomos*, representational norms, or the naturalization of powers of judgment. Rather, he *bears witness to an excess within them, an inflation without which they cease to exert any jurisdiction.* Here, too, is a crucial factor for the archive of Gods as instances of solidarity, and we should not miss the way there are important similarities between these earlier moves of Deleuze—reading Masoch and echoing a long history of reflection on "Paul and the law"—and Deleuze's later efforts in *Cinema 2* to philosophize power in an immanent mode. As Clayton Crockett and Paola Marrati have both articulated in important ways, there is a strikingly shrewd contestation of and for "belief" in Deleuze's *Cinema* projects.[29] As Deleuze wrote: "The cinema must film, not the world, but belief in the world, our only link."[30] In order to stay with the immanence of belief in this world (rather than belief as pseudo-knowledge or conviction about "another world" or even a "transformed world" (169), then cinema must follow a "new direction" of Renoir and Welles that is "no longer metaphorically or even metonymically 'figurative' but more demanding, more constraining, in some sense *theorematic*" (168).

It is this immanence of operational *theorēmata*, indistinguishable from cinematic "belief," that calls back Deleuze's frequent vocabulary of the "spiritual automaton." Moreover, in a way that recalls the absurdism of juridical obedience in both Masoch and Paul, Deleuze articulates the faith of this cinematic figure as susceptible to explication by way of the *problem*: "A problem lives in the theorem, and gives it life, even when removing its power. The problematic is distinguished from the theorematic (or constructivism from the axiomatic) in that the theorem develops internal relationships from principle to consequences, while the problem introduces an event from the outside" (169). The new direction of a cinema of depthless immanence—the very figure of a *belief* in *this* world—becomes intertwined with the capacity to "impose this problematic, uncertain and yet non-arbitrary point: grace or chance" (169). Bearing an impossibly *kerygmatic* demand for decision from the "outside," boring into us an "uncertain and yet non-arbitrary point" on which everything depends, Deleuze points to Pasolini's famous and ingenious film, *Theorem,* as the exemplary instance. "Thought finds itself taken over by the exteriority of a "belief," outside any interiority of a mode of knowledge." Such is the introduction of a Deleuzean "event" as a new direction in cinema, this mode of a Deleuzean redemption by a chance occurrence of belief in *this* world that neither laments nor reconstructs the "break in the sensory-motor link (action-image)" of a world in which—in every sense—we no longer believe (167).

Clayton Crockett has developed important comparisons between the event philosophy of Gilles Deleuze and the messianism of Paul of Tarsus, and I would like now to add some additional lines in the development of a kind of Paulinist Deleuzeanism.[31] As I develop in more detail in the introduction to *Paul and the Philosophers* and elsewhere, it is possible to list recent biblical scholarship as another discourse that has, as it were, passed through the break Deleuze identifies in the history of cinema, namely, the break between the hegemony of the movement image to that of the time image. Consider that a very long and still dominant history of Christian reading of Paul orients itself around a supersessionist narrative premised on the idea that Paul represents a break with Judaism, its spatial, temporal limit. In this tried and tested mythology, Paul is presented as the one who pierces Judaism's veils, steps outside it, breaks its shell, starts anew, these and a panoply of other supersessionist images constituting, effectively, a "movement image" of Paulinist drama. Here the drama emerges inasmuch as it is plotted along a given category of measurement, such that newness remains territorialized within identities capable of being in themselves, out of themselves, beyond themselves. Interestingly, however, just as in the cinematic history Deleuze describes, biblical studies has increasingly attempted to find other modes of articulating narrative drama and the process of newness, contestation, and vibrancy than those that submit to these old measurements. More recent biblical scholarship's efforts to imagine a Paulinist partisanship *within* a vibrantly diverse first-century Judaism (rather than as a break from it) coheres nicely with Deleuze's fascination with the time image as a mode of thinking a *singular* process of becoming, which itself precedes its capacity to be mapped (or territorialized) onto preestablished categories of measurable differentiation between stably existing or idealized entities. In keeping with this development in scholarship and this comparison with Deleuze, I would like to highlight a few aspects of Paul's perennially provocative reflection on law in Romans 7, which seem very useful in our archival resistance to the Divinity Managers.

Recall that in the ancient text of Paul the apostle imagines an economy whereby a perverse mode of power operates behind the back of an otherwise docile or submissive imaginary self, this hidden operation functioning to effect the self's agonizing splitting or doubling. While this chapter is not the place fully to explore the implications of such a comparison, recall as well that it is possible Paul played out this splitting of the subject in Romans 7 as a repetition of a theatrical tableau of Medea, whose desire to act violently against other impulses within her became a favored touchstone for Hellenistic philosophical diagnoses of the "problem of passion."[32] It is in this mode that Paul writes: "So I find it to be a law that when I want to do what is good, evil lies close at hand. For I delight in the law of God in my inmost self, but I see in my members another law at war with the law of my mind, making me captive to the law of sin that dwells in my members. Abject person that I am! Who will rescue me from this body of death?" (Romans 7:21–24). For our purposes it is useful to allow Romans 7 to operate as a machine with which to think the idea of an economy of a consumer society whereby the producer/consumer is *simultaneously* victim and victimizer, and this because of a capacity—as the ancient Paul put it— "to seize a chance opportunity" (7:8, cf. *aphormēn de labousa*) to create a surplus desire or excess of relation within the otherwise fixed poles of the juridical scene. As we will see, this comparative constellation articulates an impish mode whereby an open economy of power relations can be formulated as the possibility for any of its moments to be subtracted from the dominant form of structured power, a potential which ends up meaning that the form of power itself *only* emerges retroactively, therefore, in relation to this (open) operation of exceptionality or surplus. Put differently, Paul's quirky articulation of what is often traditionally named as the theologico-political "problem of the law" in Romans 7 emerges hand in hand with an epoch in which capitalist power as vampiric production of surplus operates at once expansionistically but also eventually, as an event or an emergent production of surplus relationalities, an eventalism that deforms alternative models of linear cause and effect.

In the text of Romans, notice the way in which the dialectical stand-still or suspension of the originally imagined hierarchical agency within juridical economy does not simply operate in the splitting or doubling of the inner man/wretched man of this scene, fissuring his agency into antagonistic strategists (cf. 7:21–24). Much more striking than this ostensibly Platonic splitting of agencies, I think, is the way there is here clearly a matching split or duplication of *nomos* (law) as well, as if the agency of *nomos* (itself) appears as *both* prohibition *and* transgression of the same. Paul is explicit about the matter, as if his rumination has hit upon a "law" (his term) of law itself, as if having "discovered" a law within law or a code inside of code. Paul's text articulates a little shadow of law that becomes, in a retroactive effect of duplication, law's opposite, its resistance, indeed, an active rebellion and criminality against it rather than docile acquiescence to law as appropriate delimitation of proprietorial spheres. "So I find this law: when I want to do the good, evil lies ready to hand . . . [That is] I see in my members another law (*heteron nomon*) at war with the law of my mind (*nous*)" (cf. 7:21f.). We should resist a schoolbook Platonic reading of the section. Rather, here the very impasse or obstruction within the otherwise smooth functioning of power in a system of juridical compliance itself comes to name *another nomos*, namely, the *nomos* of the way the arrival of the commandment is always a repetition of the immanent "springing to life again of sin" (cf. 7:9), a return of the repressed that displaces the "I" from itself, effectively "killing" it (cf. 7:10). Most important for the immanentizers of transcendence against the textbook two-tiered reception of this passage among the Platonizing Christians, we must never forget that this displacement and splitting of the I emerges from a "chance" that is itself susceptible of being grasped as a "production" (cf. *kateirgasato* 7:8) of a surplus. Surplus, as produced by this tableau, is capable of inverting the value of the intentions of the actor in question. No wonder that most of the recent philosophical readings of Paul have taken Romans 7 as a primary touchstone. In a world of vampiric transcendence turned against the immanence of the I, Paul's "problem of law" returns forcefully at a moment when new types of production of surplus value seem, precisely, susceptible to a value-inverting seizure in an economy that grows by transgressing its own limits.

But this is just the beginning. It is this little shadow of law, this excessive surplus within law, that effects in this intriguing Pauline passage a doubling and self-suspension of juridical authority as an imagined form of emancipation and the basis of a life one might call good.[33] What Paul does in Romans 7 is very intriguing inasmuch as elsewhere in his writings he seems much more comfortable than he does in Romans 7 with presenting the juridical economy of *nomos* solely as an agency of enslavement or as an apparatus for the production of transgressors. One could certainly wonder on reading his letter to the Galatians, for example, whether Paul imagined the juridical economy to found itself *only* by way of the manufacture of criminality as the exception to juridical norms (see, e.g., Galatians 3:10–13, 19, 22f., 4:3, 9). In the later letter to the Romans, however, Paul seems more intent on supplementing the otherwise short-circuited, suspended, or exhausted polarities of agency into which the juridical economy seems to have fallen for Paul. Indeed, note just how in the Romans text "sin" is relied upon as a crucial supplementary agent, this "third" agency being imagined as the localizing *cause* of the displacements of activity and passivity within the otherwise short-circuited functioning of juridical economy. In what many commentators over the centuries have even imagined as a kind of response to possible views of Paulinism emerging from the more trenchant earlier letter to the Galatians, Paul presents a virtual conversation with an interlocutor who asks: "So what are we saying, that the law is sin?," to which he responds: No! Rather, it is *sin* which "seizes an opportunity" within *nomos*, this extralegal act of partisanal warfare itself yielding the perversely split (and perhaps Medean) scenario described in the seventh chapter of Romans.

We should hesitate before we repeat Paul's language at face value or without considering what it is that makes possible precisely the agents on the Pauline scene. Note, for example, that despite Paul's efforts to stabilize the otherwise destabilized juridical economy by way of the naming of "sin" as a supplemental agency or the nameable *cause* of disturbance, the *function* of the agency of sin within this Pauline tableau is very simply the operationalized function of the power of exception making that is yielded by a potentially productive surplus and its appropriation. It is this production of an excess, capable of being seized, that displaces the status of otherwise perceived laboring roles or, we might say, makes "sin" possible as that retroactive agent which comes to stand in opposition to the will of the "inner person."

In this sense, one must read Paul's "sin" here as the retroactive appendage of the "chance opportunity" itself, that agent always already the effect of a more primordial zone from which arises the potential for partisan co-optations, rogue attacks, and potentially revolutionary emancipations alike. Consider that it is no accident that Paul appropriates in this passage the favored lingo of "seizing a chance" from a panoply of Greek texts about military history. Random occurrences, chance encounters, enable the polemically inclined to "seize" or "take" the opportunity afforded by chance, transforming the nature of sovereignty in a kairological moment of opportunity that effects new orders of power. The seizure of chance in these texts constitutes a kind of Schmittian act of appropriation, though one not at all merely at the disposal of regnant powers. On the contrary, regnant power maintains itself by immunizing itself against the arrival of these unformed moments of chance. As the first-century Jewish historian puts it, much more effective than defeating one's political enemies is to immure the current situation of power against the "chance" (*aphormē*) of viable contest in the first place.[34] Paul's exposition of works and the weaponization of surplus against would-be workers here fits such descriptions exactly. Note, for example, that Paul's scene here emerges against the backdrop of a *lack* of power in law—he designates its status as *adunaton*—opening the way to understanding the productive economy of commandment as one constituted through an originary "weakness" or inoperativity within the (active, sovereign) law—(passive, docile) flesh pairing (cf. 8:3, *to gar adunaton tou nomou en hō ēsthenei dia tēs sarkos*).

It is only at first glance, therefore, that Paul's tale seems like it sides with traditional sovereignty, as if bemoaning the weakness of effective order and longing for a moment when the role of *nomos* in a representational economy of commandment could be stabilized. Many commentators, docile sorts themselves perhaps, assume that Paul *merely* laments the deformation of the sovereign command of *nomos* at the hands of the radical partisanship and interventionism of "sin." But this is to miss the implications of the way Paul has here made sin a partisan properly speaking, postrepresentational and insurrectionist, what Paul himself calls (in a line of great interest to Lacan and Bataille alike) sin's manifestation through the (inoperativity or surplus activity of the) commandment, the revelation of "sin beyond measure" (*hina genētai kath' huperbolēn hamartōlos hē hamartia dia tēs diathēkēs*).[35] Here, too, we should pay attention to the specific modes in which Paul maps his discussions of sin's partisanship onto the seizure of chance motif, a motif that was never in the ancient Mediterranean contexts *simply* about the anxiety of the powerful to immunize their situation against it. Seizing the *aphormēn* or chance was also, we should never forget, about the capacity for transformative insurrections, a discourse of partisans without acceptable political representation, none of which was far from the advocate of a brutally murdered messianic figure.

Genealogically, philosophically, there is chance to be grasped, the act itself as an allowance or fund by which one insinuates one's own stance into the stream, say, of philosophical ideas. As he trots out one after another philosophical argument in order to seize them all by an indifferent middle wherein his skepticism finds an uneasy resting place, Sextus Empiricus articulates Zeno of Citium in the same way that Paul articulates "sin" as a subversion of nomological hierarchy: "And Zeno of Citium, taking Xenophon as a point of insertion (*apo Zenophōntos tēn aphormēn labōn*), says that . . . " (*Against the Physicists*, 101).[36] Zeno here grasps Xenophon as his opportunity, his mode of self-insinuation, his starting point, and he does so with the same language as sin in Paul's text about a doubled and subverted legal order. Xenophon, in providing the capitalizing fund of a chance opportunity or openness to intervention, appears here citationally. Zeno starts with a quotation from another, this move of the other opening a way for someone else to take up residence therein, indeed, to steer the whole conversation differently. After all, in this passage, the chance *aphormē* of a citational "starting point" of another, the other as a "base of operations" for some other project to take root. It is unfortunate that, in our genealogical lineages and family trees of ideas and political traditions, we tend not to see the immediate associations of a figure like Paul with the radical skeptical *époche* or, in a latter-day instance, the everyday subversions of sovereignties in Deleuze's Lacan or in Sacher-Masoch.

Jacob Taubes earlier intervened in the political history of Pauline reception in order to develop a genealogical subversion of the dictatorial exceptionalism of Carl Schmitt, Taubes looking to Paulinism for a mode of attending to transformative contingency or the (as if *ex nihilo*) *surprise* and openness of transformative sovereignty, just as Schmitt did. But Paulinism, Taubes argued, enables a way of attending to the same rogue potentials, except that one could think them, he stated famously, "from below" rather than from the position of Schmittian institutions or dictators. In this project Taubes never picked up on some of the things we are describing here, including the rather astonishingly inverted Schmittianism we might find in Paul's use of Schmitt's beloved theological term of the *katechon* or "suppressive" capacity of power.[37] At Romans

7:6, for example, it is through the community's adamant identification with the criminalized and effectively suppressed messianic figure that they "have died" to the effective grasp of *nomos* generally. The Paulinist insurgency of the crucified is described as excepting itself from the juridical economy, *their having subtracted themselves from the effective force that, he writes, "suppressed them"* (*nuni de katērgēthēmen apo tou nomou apothanontes en hō kateichometha . . .*). A long history of imperial Christianity's interpreters fashioned the *katechon* myth into a naturalization of empire's use of suppressive power against the emergence of "chaos"—but before these divinity managers were the radical Paulinists, inverting emancipatory juridical boasts through perverse forms of immanent identification. And in doing so the Paulinists claimed to be undoing law's *katechon* myth, rendering it inoperative in its capacity to suppress *us*.

Far from being a "Christian" break from Judaism, moreover, here Paul's rhetoric is in keeping with a rich and diverse tradition of early Jewish partisanship and contestation of inherited norms of all sorts. Note, for example, that the first-century commentator and philosopher Philo of Alexandria could also imagine that a divine law installs within itself the *aphormē*, as if Philo, too, were reflecting on the possibility of a divinely sanctioned chance (chance as divine sanction) for the deformation of identity, causality, and the economy of commandment. Thus, Philo writes, in legal traditions of scripture, strangers are given a "chance" or opportunity to appropriate legally those goods and rights that were not officially or originally afforded them because of their identity as outsiders (cf. *Special Laws* 2.118.2).[38] Philo also narrates key moments in the surprising scriptural deformation or revolutionary transformation of the identity of the people by way of the terminology of chance, as when a non-Israelite prostitute becomes the crucial bearer of the people's legacy, indeed the very "origin" of their justly constituted *polis* (cf. *On Virtues* 222.6).[39] Similarly, identifying with the partisan against repressive power structures, Josephus, too, understands that what was the eventual *destiny* of Moses (to be the cause of both the downfall of the Egyptians and an exodus of the Israelites) nevertheless had to occur in a moment of chance openness to transformation (namely, the unexpected and destabilizing invasion of Egypt by the Ethiopians). Josephus's Moses, just like Paul's sin, effects the transformation of agencies, territories, and sovereignties by "seizing the opportunity," both writers appropriating the same Greek terminology of sovereignty and partisanship (cf. *Antiquities of the Jews* 2.239.1).

In other words, the "seizure of chance" is itself the unformed, deforming moment in the economy of identity, sovereignty, and commandment whereby radical transformation may be effected. Or, as I have already intimated, one might even say that the drama of divinity in these ancient texts is *nothing but an attentiveness to this open space of transformation*, almost a monotheistic variation of the question of causality and openness, which the polytheistic traditions deified as *tuchē* or chance. After all, the potential seizure of chance is at once imagined as both the origin and possible revolution of modes of life, the singular aura or surplus value of which has always been the stuff of religion. To add one further genealogical twist, we might even say that, in keeping with another of the ancient meanings of seizable *aphormē*, in Paul's confounding of the efficacy of *nomos* by way of the "chance opportunity" of this economy's inversion, we have a witness to that "*capital*" *which funded* both the promise and the debts of ancient religiosity, the surplus value or excessive forcefulness of its stability *and* its openness to radical transformation.[40]

To put the matter differently, was not the secret of Paulinism that his own *kairos* or now time of a surprising event (cf. Romans 5:6, 9:9, 13:11), the moment that for him constituted the transformative power of a new age, was already precisely in keeping with (or formally the same as) *the operation* of sin's "seizing an opportunity"? This is the case despite the way that Paul *likewise* attributes to the aleatory or supplemental forcefulness of a chance perversion of efficacy within "the commandment" a structure of agency or causality by invoking the name "sin." Stated more starkly, we should not be misled by the ostensibly gut-wrenching, soul-searching rhetoric of a split subject: "Who will rescue me from my split subjectivity?" (cf. 7:14–25). After all, it was only because Paul's catastrophically criminalized Christ was taken by the apostle as the messiah's having "been made sin for us" that Paul was to have anything creatively emancipatory to say about his Christ at all (cf. 2 Corinthians 5:16–19, 21). It was this suppressed messiah which was for him the exemplary clue that the merely believing may "become" outside the economy of the manufacture of representative transgressors. It was, in other words, not only sin that seemed to have learned the affinity between partisanship, transformation, and seizing on a subversive chance. If the *nomos* of the current order makes transgressors of you, you might consider how transgression itself speaks doubly as the end of transgression, even as a kind of redemption to be seized upon.

Like Lacan's Joyce, Paul the partisan repeats tradition while deforming it, deforms it while repeating it, following the singular declinations and inflections of the seizure of chance (and, as we have pointed out, in keeping with his Jewish hermeneutical contemporaries).[41] For the Paulinist, the messianic age as much as "sin" was capable of "seizing an opportunity," and this to turn agency and agencies against themselves, splitting their operations into conflictual multiplicities of identity and radically altering their capacity to maintain themselves as hegemonic forms of power in the process. Playing the role of a kind of "sin without measure" in relation to the effective economies of "commandment" constituting Roman imperial domination over the intractably rebellious Jews, for example, Paul declares that the Roman transformation of a would-be messiah into a form of stupidity and failure should itself be grasped as a moment of divine wisdom and triumph of the undying divinity of the partisan (cf. 1 Corinthians 1), indeed a divinity that has given rise to an alternative "city council" (*ekklēsia*) of the undead, a council consisting of those who act as if *already* dead so that they might live beyond the "suppressive" or katechontic economy of *nomos*. Carried away by the life of this very gesture, Paul even boasts that if the "rulers" knew what they were doing when they put down this messianic figure, they wouldn't have done it (1 Corinthians 2:8). His point here is not simply that the rulers were "mistaken" in their crucifixion of another rebel from Palestine. Much more in keeping with his argument, the issue is rather that in their very enactment of imperial control and legal condemnation of a messianic figure from a dissident state, the "rulers" became susceptible to the doubling, splitting, undying power of the divinity of emancipatory partisanship. Roman imperial power, too, knows not what it does, living as it does off of a surplus or excess that is only imagined to be owned. Here, too, we return to the expropriating "mirror play" of the Heideggerian fourfold.

On Laughing with Vampires (and Adding More Agreeable Endings to a Gospel)

All three had brilliant white teeth that shone like pearls against the ruby of their voluptuous lips. There was something about them that made me uneasy, some longing and at the same time some deadly fear. I felt in my

*heart a wicked, burning desire that they should kiss me with those red
lips. It is not good to note this down, lest someday it should meet Mina's
eyes and cause her pain; but it is the truth. They whispered together, and
then they all three laughed—such a silvery, musical laugh, but as hard as
though the sound never could have come through the softness of human
lips. It was like the intolerable, tingling sweetness of water-glasses when
played on by a cunning hand.*

—Bram Stoker, *Dracula*

On finding no body in the tomb, a "young man dressed in white" assures
some of Jesus's followers that Jesus has been raised ("look, he is not here,
here is where they laid him!"). The shiny youth then asks these women
to tell the rest of the disciples about a resurrection, instructions that set
up the infamous final line of the original ending of Mark's Gospel: "So
they went out and fled from the tomb because terror and amazement
had seized them; and they said nothing to anyone—because they were
terrified" (Mark 16:8). In the "Hollywood" versions that soon began to
circulate in Christian communities, the shock of the ending was soon
transformed into what we now politely call "longer endings," endings
replete with heavenly ascensions, convincing resurrection appearances
to the otherwise absent mortal menfolk, not to mention the all-impor-
tant dissemination of superpowers: power to exorcise demons, power
to speak in new languages, immunity to snake venom (cf. 16:8b–19). In
keeping with such a tendency, I want to add here some indications of a
"longer ending" to my Gospel and Acts of vampiric transcendence.

"A world with only three affects, in the midst of all that goes on in
the immense forest!" Tics and ticks of transcendence, sometimes you,
Jonathan Harkers, should "let it be" and learn to let your hair down with
some of your vampiric admirers. To this end, we believe that insurrectionist archivism may also be read as a kind of collective therapy of the
soul, a form of understanding, reworking, and rewiring the recursivi-
ties and feedbacks of desire. As we have tried to indicate, insurrection
today must take upon itself a discipline that imagines primarily neither
return nor great leap forward. Insurrection, we believe, is a more austere practice than those oriented around these two idealist and imaginary categories that love to masquerade as emancipation. Let insurrection rather be freed to constitute a series of exercises that need not waste
time and energy parading as a breakthrough, a piercing of the collective
or epochal veil, the revelatory bearer of ungovernable newness, or the

pushing of words, things, or their economies to an exterior or otherwise fantasized "limit." With insurrectionist practice we are free to cast about, even just to shuffle around, for instances of solidarities that these other stratagems, these other visions, tend to have missed, occluded, mocked, or accidentally sold down the river. (And, for a start, we've all been overlooked, overladen, laughed at, and sold down the river.) The insurrectionist drama incited, conjured, or—why not—prayed for is not so much coming, on the way, breaking through as it is yawning and yelling within the practice itself. Our practice, our life's discipline? Primarily we like to harness our attention to the patiently inventive practice of archiving—recategorizing, realigning, and differently accessing—that category "religion," and this in search of solidarities we might enhance, encourage, develop.

We need to be clear. This attention to religion is, ironically, not generally because religion names the most general or the most useful modes of access to grand questions of humanity, life, and politics, but rather because it is, often enough, completely useless, the detritus of hegemonic immediacies or the detour of the direct. It is in these detours, deferrals, and aleatory events, however, that we find ourselves true believers and faithful messengers, precisely, of unremarked instances or gestures of solidarity, collectives announcing themselves in their very failure to appear, their falling out of repetitive vibrancy, their active suppression or their sheer impossibility, all these failures to show up on the historical or conceptual radar. Endemic to our practice thus far is the archival shuffling of religion in its ancient Mediterranean, European, and North American modes. If the instances of unremarked and provocative solidarities we find therein sometimes seem to flutter as if floating free of space and time, then our sense is that the archival work is precisely there, beginning to tinker together a creative form of the instance in question. At any rate, archivists of this sort, we should say clearly that we have no anxiety about the fact that this very creativity may appear only against the backdrop of a hesitation, uncertainty, or hilarity, all our solidarities without ready-made functions and endgames.

Buried in Bergson's analysis of laughter is an important rationale for remaining activist archivists of the genealogy of "religion," and our practice is as faithful to laughter as to relevance. We repeat, in all seriousness, one of those jokes of Bergson to which he appends an important maxim:

A man who was once asked why he did not weep at a sermon when every-one else was shedding tears replied: "I don't belong to the parish."

What that man thought of tears would be still more true of laughter. However spontaneous it seems, laughter always implies a kind of secret freemasonry, or even complicity, with other laughers, real or imaginary.[42]

Insurrectionist archivism is neither more nor less the register of such secret freemasonries, registered as much in laughter and tears as in blue-prints and the justifications of historical success and failure. "We played the flute, but you wouldn't dance! We sang those sad, sad songs but you wouldn't cry!" In keeping with the comedic messianic traditions of Jesus and John the Baptist, we're getting really good at tracking, developing, inventing new modes of breakdown between flute-machines, jiggy-feet machines, sad-sad-song machines, tear-jerk machines. For the messianic archivist, those who laugh should do so as if it were not because they have succeeded, and those who weep as if it were not because they had failed (cf. 1 Corinthians 7). Rather, it's time for laughter and tears to come into their own against what our Paul of Tarsus—that huckster and yuck-ster of the living dead and the still-kicking sacrifice—named the *para-deigmata tou kosmou*, the schemata of a world order (cf. Romans 12).

As a close philosophical repetition of this messianic, Paulinist point, I suspect it is this fidelity to instances of solidarity that emerge from a reshuffling of the pack constituting a predominantly European and North American archive of religion or theology that inclines us toward a consistent fascination, despite his many recent detractors, with the philosophy of Gilles Deleuze. With that latter day Stoic, who found in weird constellations of philosophy and other forms of life precisely "machines with which to think," we work and unwork this archive of religion, and this, very specifically, from two wrong sides of the Atlantic.

Insurrection is for us, therefore, indistinguishable from conjuration as an incitement of practices, exercises, and communities that operate at a distance from many of the typical fantasies on offer these days of emancipatory or redemptive alterity, inasmuch as this category func-tions as the supreme lure of a duty of "breakthrough" or promise of an approaching "limit," not to mention most of those discursive panoplies of the radically new and transformed. Just count on it; taste and see if its true: fetishized alterities, now more than ever on offer and in triumphal parade, almost always crystallize into categories that—despite them-selves—tend to become quaintly, safely, and securely otherworldly and enslaving. Once invested with the (divine) sheen of the totally different, the grand breakthrough, the new world, or the self-absolvent and self-secured, the gaming of structured alterity becomes, very quickly and predictably, co-opted by the very worlds and systems these alterities are meant to resist, threaten, or transform.

It is in this specific sense—though only this—that we archivist theologians of dead and dying Gods as instances of solidarity read with admiration recent philosophical provocations to be *more* austere in relation to, more subversive of, the philosophical and political afterlife of inherited theologies of redemption.[43] Amen and so be it! It is just that insurrectionist archivists have no interest in a would-be secularist austerity proving itself by a *lack* of sophistication about that massive and monumentally wonderful archive that are these strands of "religion." It's always those who do not see the seething restlessness and unease of this archive who seem always to convince themselves—and others—that it is finished, over, come to nothing. Wanting to unearth, invent, and extend emancipatory instances of solidarity without the tumultuous and shifting archive of religion seems to us like cutting down the rainforest in order to see if useful plant and animal species are lying there beneath it. Such programs are the least interesting of our tradition's secularist fantasies, these premised on notions of ground and justification that will always deteriorate into boring assertions of territory, ownership, and control. Laughing with Bergson and practicing with Deleuze, we prefer rather to give ourselves over to the secrets and freemasonries of the thicket that resists encapsulation or control. Indeed, we give ourselves over to the thicket without ready-made inroad, efficient extraction plans, or markets ready for distribution.

"Plato defined the human as a two-footed animal without wings, and was applauded for it; so Diogenes the Cynic plucked a cock and took it into the lecture hall, held it up and declared: 'I've got Plato's "man" right here'" (cf. Diogenes Laertius, *Lives of the Philosophers* 6.40).

"Diogenes the Cynic used to reason: 'The All belongs to the gods. The wise person is the friend of the gods. Friends hold everything in common. Therefore, everything belongs to the wise person'" (Diogenes Laertius, *Lives of the Philosophers* 6.37).

Archivists therefore of a revolution no longer of a simple name (especially the name *religion*), insurrection is the patient, disciplined development of peculiar philosophical commons and communities. Archivist solidarities, still instances and therefore ungroundedly available for use, are sometimes as strange as the ancient Epicureans (who sought to practice vibrant philosophical living through the cultivation of a form of unknowing as a being-unknown). Experience of our solidarity has always shown us, quite clearly, that our invested instances of solidarity are also intensely comical as the practice of our Cynic forbears (as when they preferred as much to become mice or dogs or plucked chickens as beasts imagining their reason to exist in order to be turned against themselves). With the Cynics (and perhaps with Jesus, that best-known Cynic of all, that missed, suppressed, and mocked inventor of a messianic Cynicism, as it were, "for the masses"), we consider the birds of the air, the wildflowers of the field, and prefer not to let even our revolutionary fantasies make slaves of us any more than our aspirations to reason: "Take no thought for your life . . . " Insurrectionist practice is something rather more comical and unknown than all such slave-making machines as are capable of reason, revolution, reformism. Without these centralized institutions, we have no greater advice for a radical archivism than that from this same rogue Cynic messianist: pick up your walking stick, strap on your cloak, take your empty purse, and strike out in pursuit of an economy sustainable only through trust as the concrete gesture of friendship. Tomorrow is already worrying about itself: go look for economies sustained only by instances of solidarity.

Our allegiances may be peculiar—strange practices of solidarity implied by odd philosophical and religious genealogies. But these allegiances are also, we believe, peculiarly tailored to our specific political moment. A few dog bites and home remedies for a physician's diagnosis of our thinking of this moment: is there not altogether too much melancholia at present, too much loss, too much lamentation over the fallen state of the world? Just for an archival start, poststructuralist melancholy always sounded to us—untimely born (and, let's face it, perhaps just a decade too late)—like the eighties trader on Wall Street waking up the morning after and feeling that, somehow, the affluence flowing from the union busting and deregulation of Reagan or Thatcher leaves him, nevertheless, with a "kind of emptiness." Ah, poor bastard, sounds like only another potential recruit ready to aspire finally to become with us that mouse or that dog of our good news—except, let's face it, it's more likely he'll sign himself up for that daily pharmacological dosing that will keep him hard at work even after his vibrant, buzzy, and believing soul has clearly fled the scene. Consider the lilies of the field: if it weren't for all the Prozac currently being pissed back into our drinking water, even they would have long since dropped the pretense by now. (Stupid flowers, doing everything without the indirection of reason and its deferral to causality and telos: you'd think they were actually enjoying this shit.)

Even more awkward for us these days—given our genealogies, influences, and ongoing reading practices—is our experience of those beloved mass meetings of Marxists or those conferences driven by denunciatory intensities of the critical theory bunch, all those deplorably exiled academics (poor employed souls). We commiserate, fulminate with gusto, being from the same parish. But, damn the secret freemasonries and their subterranean solidarities, we soon smile, too, as if at a Puritan revival meeting with tales of the Fall and hopes of salvation that leave us flat and move us very little. Nevertheless, we try to nod with conviction at depictions of our place in the Evil Scheme. I positively light right up at those hushed or slightly veiled references to that coming Final Battle between the all-knowing and sovereign good (puppet master 1) and Satan himself (puppet master 2). Happy scene of solidarity, except—archivists of real laughter and deferred tears— we clearly can't shake the homophonies and echoes on the scene with us. At any rate, touch it—you really must go there to know—and see if tales of Capital dangling potential new recruits over an abyss covered in cobwebs is only the tiniest bit more emancipatory than imagining God were doing so. Homework for readers of this insurrectionist *protrepsis*: if you haven't read it since high school, do yourself a favor and checkout that classic sermon of Jonathan Edwards, all those sinners in the hands of a pissed off Sovereign.

Indeed, we could start with that sermon to trace some crucial affiliations and differences not only with Puritanism but also with Marxism and post-Marxist critical theory. Edwards is great—what a Yalie— but he never had enough of the dog, mouse, or comic about him to be much use to us for the long haul. Nevertheless, his sermon is not simply wrong or stupid either, particularly in its underlying sense of being dropped, like a pebble, straight through the cobwebs into an abyss. Insurrectionist archivism and the reshuffling of the pack of religion to tinker new instances of solidarity does indeed start here as well, with an Edwardsesque tarrying with a few of the cobwebs that we're already falling through. Everywhere, the sinews of emancipatory solidarities snap without sound, and we plunge downward. God hasn't dropped us as Edwards needs to think, but we are all nevertheless falling, as if so many atoms in a void. Epicurus here had it much better than Edwards.

Unlike the Puritans, and against many of the Leftists, we won't be saved from this particular tumble in which we currently find ourselves, and no amount of projecting backward or forward the promise of safety or security (lost or to-be-found) is going to change that. We will therefore need to follow the thread of commitment, solidarity, and hope much differently from old Edwards in order to reconfigure how we might begin to imagine the formation of a new covenant, a dream of Edwards to which we, too, are faithful. Our closer ally Epicurus looked for "strange federations" founded only on the chance of the faintest swerves of atoms falling in the void. Our favorite "materialist" Paul the apostle did something similar (and contrary to inherited opinion), gambling everything on a swerved "covenant" marked by "unnatural" graftings of identity.[44] But, with the Epicurean Paulinists, was this not likewise—despite himself—Edwards's strategy also, a revamped gamble on *conversio* as an aleatory possibility of hitting upon a form of "covenant" with a universal or global sovereignty whose economy is otherwise brutally opaque and undetermined? Siding with Epicurean swerve over Democritean reductivism, Marx would call this opaque and undetermined tyranny the empty universalism of capital. Itching for the solidarity of a "covenant," which would determine and pacify the emptiness of this alienating universal sovereignty (that which renders us, in Edwards words, "always liable to destruction"), Edwards (quite rightly) hit his favorite media channels. From the pulpit and in the pamphlet shop he fulminates.

> So that, thus it is that natural men are held in the hand of God, over the pit of hell; they have deserved the fiery pit, and are already sentenced to it; and God is dreadfully provoked, his anger is as great towards them as to those that are actually suffering the executions of the fierceness of his wrath in hell, and they have done nothing in the least to appease or abate that anger, neither is God in the least bound by any promise to hold them up one moment; the devil is waiting for them, hell is gaping for them, the flames gather and flash about them, and would fain lay hold on them, and swallow them up; *the fire pent up in their own hearts is struggling to break out: and they have no interest in any Mediator, there are no means within reach that can be any security to them. In short, they have no refuge, nothing to take hold of; all that preserves them every moment is the mere arbitrary will, and uncovenanted, unobliged forbearance of an incensed God* [my emphasis].[45]

Always passively registering the secret freemasonries of the archival thicket—all those assertions and limits of concrete solidarity—we cannot help but to approach the trappings and mise-en-scène of Edwards's tale through the *epoché* of comedy or the ironic gleam in the eye. And yet, against the obvious, we are not in such a different situation from the old fulminator, with the ineluctable threat of real catastrophe approaching through agencies that seem always capable of stripping us of all rights of resistance. Ever liable to destruction, everywhere today are globalized forms of difficulty with conjuring types of "covenant" whereby one might hit upon a fulsome "interest" (Deleuze spoke of "belief") in forms of "mediation" and buffer between ourselves and the dispossession to which we are liable. Here we elect an affinity with old Edwards, and anyone who has not yet worked in a situation whereby further labor—indeed endless "works" (as Edwards liked to say)—yields no buffer against dispossession or global catastrophe has perhaps not yet hit upon the strangely relevant solidarities percolating through Edwards's fearmongering manifesto. We, too, quest for movements that imagine themselves to constitute solidarities capable of binding the horror of a world whose commons, whose universals, appear only in the form of refusal, dispossession, and threat. Edwards's revivalism was a Promethean, even Epicurean, venture that did not know how to declare itself as such, something we don't really hold against him. As Edwards's incarnated God is remembered to have said: "Tomorrow will worry about itself." That wasn't Edwards's job. And now, as if faithful to his master, he comes to the insurrectionist archivists in the naïveté or trust that marks the full comedy of friendship. Secret freemasonries, parishes, solidarities, all those swerved "federations" and "unnatural" renewals of the need for "covenant" against catastrophe.

Conclusion: Archivist Radicalism Against the Divinity Managers

> *Globalization is basically a force that pushes people together. And if religion is a force that pulls people apart, it becomes actually a threat to the way the twenty-first century works.*[46]
>
> —Tony Blair, "A Fireside Chat at Yale University"

We could greatly expand the archival references from Epicurus, Paul, Edwards. And you must, if you want to wake up to the peculiar possibilities affording themselves to you today. Our dream, a small army of archivists practicing remarkably creative modes of approaching the constitution, crystallization, and transformation of collective solidarities. Here we diagnose rather cruelly the frequency of the notable fact that, in academic disciplines, disciplinary conferences, governmental funding schemes, international funding bodies, there is currently a near obsession with a form of parliamentary democracy neatly filled out as an easily recognizable form of hierarchical representationalism. Go to any panel from the lowest to highest spheres of the well-endowed academy, church, or state and see if it does not consist of a selection of tokens for a simple representational game, token Christians meeting token Muslims, token Jews, token Buddhists, and so on. If there are anxieties or criticisms marking the event, these anxieties or criticisms almost always express themselves by remaining docile before the *form* of this parliamentary or representational model: not enough of category X or Y, and what about the missing (but equally obvious and readymade) category Z? As a practice, insurrectionist archivism enacts a brutal diagnosis of the ubiquity of such events at the moment, events that—we believe—participate in a broader and more sweeping event, which is, above all, the effort to manage the name *religion* and the *sensus communis* that this name projects for social, political, and economic life. To return to Edwards and our Epicurean Paul, it is apparent in these evental radiations of a larger social event that the emerging system of power relations needs to maintain the hegemony of a sense that "covenants"—as forms of intensive social solidarity that mediate or concretize the category of the universal or global—are already given, set in stone, written in the past or a manageable future, in any case fundamentally prefabricated and ready-made by and for our current hierarchies and hegemonies.

Radiating from event to Event (or, as that messianist Paul would have it, "from trust to Trust"), here as always there is emerging a form-of-life in which the micro- and macro-cosms are taught how to mirror each other. Tried and true funding from wealthy industrialist benefactors, new investment in humanities and technology from (as it were) nouveaux riches tech-stock holders, reconfigured and "modernized funding streams" from the United Kingdom or the European Union all collude to repeat—through the object "religion"—a Tao of international managerialism. All these levels of investment, all these acts of *pistis* or trust, enact in other modes the same patronizing inflation of the question of "constitution" in ongoing revolutionary moments in Syria, Egypt,

China. The unification of these diffuse cultural strata, their synthesis, is a great fear of free solidarities that do not map onto the functional demands of a singly developing "economy," that most zealous, jealous, and providential monotheism of our currently dominant political/theological rhetoric. No doubt because it accomplishes so much "good work" at home and abroad, the strangeness has gone relatively under-remarked that—under the twinned auspices of "religion" and Tony Blair—Yale Divinity School has "partnered" with the Yale School of Management in order to develop new models of education about "faith and globalization."

The epigraph to this concluding section, from one of Blair's first public self-presentations at Yale, summarizes what Blair described as an underlying "theory" of the new venture with the would-be divinity managers. Described early in the partnership, Blair was here present-ing publicly a trial balloon of his classroom "theory" whereby econom-ic "globalization is basically a force that pushes people together. And if [he continues] religion is a force that pulls people apart, it becomes actually a threat to the way the twenty-first century works." The over-tones of the theological in the description of economic managerialism intrigue us here, with new definitions of sinful recalcitrance, resistance, and lack of fraternal feeling coming alongside in a new invention of one god to supplement the faltering mechanisms of another. If it was once important to point out the Calvinism of the Scottish economics of Adam Smith's "hidden hand," it is perhaps the moment to note rath-er the way a visible "religion" is being called upon by governments to prop up the faltering providences of the hidden god in whom they had placed their trust.[47]

On the other hand, Blair goes on to suggest, religion *could* function to make the force of togetherness "work for all people" rather than just "elites."

The partnering of Blair and Yale in the guise of a fairly massive proj-ect of divinity management (divinity as management) first caught our eye. This was so not only for Blair's early enunciations of a theory of a kind of faith-based economic development. It was also because of the way the foundation then began—as Blair suggested it might in his inau-gural conversation with the then president of Yale University, Richard Levin—to host training sessions for other academics at the American Academy of Religion meeting in how to teach "Faith and Globalization" courses back at their home institutions.

But perhaps not much here needs to be parsed: the Sovereign Good of economic development is either helped or hindered by the capacities of "religion." This help or hindrance does more than set in motion the ubiquitous nomination of "religion" into those competitive twins of "good" religion (as that which fosters the good development of a global economy) and "bad" religion (as that which resists incorporation in new economic developments). Rather, this capacity to help or hinder the "demands" of emerging universalities through economic development calls for the development of new partnerships in order to predispose "religion" toward the "good." Forget the usual tokenistic game of religious representationalism, the real issue here is the function of such institutional partnerships to foster the development of an affective sphere of solidarity that will itself mirror at the level of tendencies, trusts, and temptations the given "demands" of a global economy. In this respect, Blair and his Yalies are a fascinating repetition of the gamble of Jonathan Edwards's sermon. For our latter-day missionaries, however, the catastrophe looming in the form of an unmanaged and potentially rogue universal sovereign—that "liability to destruction" which affects us all—is designated as "global economy," a slight modernization of Edwards's God-over-all, though a modernization that leaves the basic functions of the sovereign intact (e.g., origin of moral imperative, providential holder of blessing and curse, rationale for redemptive conversion). Moreover, just as Edwards famously developed extensive "measures" or exercises of a conversion that must be real in relation to the sovereign, so Blair's partnership with Yale may be read as the development of a panoply of measurables, "deliverables" (as the British funding bodies like to say), concrete "exercises" of an expanding global economy finding its will, as it were, enacted on local earth as in global heaven. It is in this sense that it seems particularly obvious, and particularly useful, that the "faith and globalization" movement at Yale would call for the partnership of Yale's Divinity School and its School of Management.

The insurrectionist allegiances and its fidelity to thinking and reworking the archive of "religion" are here perhaps not quite what is expected. On the one hand, we say, forget the new mercantilism of all these paid-up representatives of this or that community, faith, tradition, academic discipline. This is an expanding game whose spontaneity or naturalness never, ever should be taken for granted. At stake is whether there remains structurally recognizable space for the essential political affirmation of contingent, tinkered, and emerging solidarities, solidarities that traverse and elude strict limits of the regularities and rhythms of the current identitarian regimes, solidarities which we earlier referred to as those worthy of the name. (Or, perhaps more important, at stake here is whether the gatekeepers and institutions "representing" the hegemonic identity markers on offer today will be in a position always to take credit for, and therefore to reterritorialize in their own interests, the breakout of new instances of solidarity.) Even if all you ever do is to "live unknown" or like a mouse, flower, or dog—better to be committed to the instantiation of a new internationalism founded, grounded solely in the risk and wonder of our own gambles on togetherness.

On the other hand, though related, the radical archivist of all people should not be outdone by the important thinking implicit within the "faith and globalization" movement or, indeed, implicit in Tony Blair's shrewd enactment of a partnership between the Schools of Management and Divinity. Universalities, as enforced and enforceable demands of the "global," are—just as Edwards warned—precisely the opening onto new forms of solidarity that we cannot fill beforehand, that we cannot predict, and, therefore, that we cannot manage. They are that liability to destruction in the face of which we attempt to concretize new instances of solidarity in the form of new "covenant" structures to mediate, buffer, and protect us from the open threat of the global.

Tony Blair and the Yalies may be everything we want to condemn, the enemy that gives body to the concrete orientations which—flowers in the field—give shape and pattern to our solidarities. Nevertheless, we do not disagree with the gist of Blair's "theory" of economy and "religion" in the sense that we, too, are aware that the universal, the "economy" of the "global," is a generic sovereignty filled by the affective dispositions inherent within our everyday practices, all of which "intend" a global solidarity—a global sovereignty—that operates with or without our "intention." If we may say it this odd way, this is the great insight of the Tony Blair Faith Foundation: global sovereignty and the enforceable demands of a global *oikoumenē* are conjured, enacted, solicited by our trusts, our faiths, our dispositions, and the localisms in which they participate. For good and ill, we're all conjuring into existence the Gods who will be both rogue sovereigns alienating us and placated providences giving buzzy repeatability and actualizing effect of our implied "covenants." It is with this shareability, indeed, this common, universal ground at work between us, that, more than ever, we want to take radical issue with projects such as these.

And so, most excellent reader, having investigated everything more than the rest, we conclude this longer ending to the Gospel and Acts of the vampirisms of transcendence with an old, old gauntlet constituting a tradition to which we remain faithful. Choose today whom you will serve, becoming through your choice—the options are stark, demanding— either a Divinity Manager or an archivist of insurrectionist solidarities.

3

A THEORY OF INSURRECTION
Beyond the Way of the Mortals

Jeffrey W. Robbins

> *When I switch on my radio and hear that black men are being lynched in America, I say that they have lied to us: Hitler isn't dead. When I switch on my radio and hear that Jews are being insulted, persecuted, and massacred, I say that they have lied to us: Hitler isn't dead. And finally when I switch on my radio and hear that in Africa forced labor has been introduced and legalized, I say that truly they have lied to us: Hitler isn't dead.*
> —Aimé Césaire, *Political Speeches*

I.

The link is made at the very end. A secret so plain that it lies hidden over the course of six interlinking lives, times, and even worlds: *those who resist the natural order of things will be crucified or lynched.* And so too, it is thought, will they be forgotten, without hope for change or significance. This is the way of the mortals, a brutal savagery of consumption: to eat or to be eaten.

Giorgio Agamben's *Remnants of Auschwitz* tells us this tale all too well: what hope is there for redemption when there are no remains, no archive?[1] In this way, redemption is dependent upon memory. But the moral imperative to never forget rings hollow when there is no memory with which to begin. So it is that, after Auschwitz, any suggestion of redemptive suffering—of God making instrumental use of death and destruction—rightly strikes us as a perversion.[2] Think also here of Walter Benjamin's haunting image of a messianic force so weak as to go unnoticed, a messiah who might just as well have come and gone without so much as a second glance or a moment's thought. The instant gone. Humanity's best chance or only hope dead and buried. The one who would redeem history, the one who would proclaim that nothing is lost, nothing forgotten, is the one who slips through the straight gate of time only to be plotted in the ever expanding sequence of events that is in fact the single and continuous catastrophe of history.

There is no resurrection in this tale. No new exalted life born from the ash heap of history. No recovering what has been destroyed. Instead, make no mistake, what is dead is dead, and the lost will not be found.

This natural order of things would render life utterly absurd were it not so terribly bleak. We might rebel against it with all the existentialist might we can muster. We might wish it otherwise by imagining the sweet hereafter where justice is restored and love is everlasting. In some ways, this is the temptation that Heidegger resisted when he famously repudiated the existential humanism of Sartre. For Heidegger, there is the distinction between a good humanism and a bad humanism that rests on the difference between being and beings—or, more precisely, on the difference between metaphysics and the task of overcoming metaphysics. Sartre's humanism was a bad form of humanism in that it was "determined with regard to an already established interpretation of nature, history, world, and the ground of the world, that is, of beings as a whole." Sartre's formula of existence preceding essence did not rise to the task of overcoming metaphysics. Instead, it was merely a reversal and, as such, remained a metaphysical statement.[3]

"But in what does the humanity of the human being consist?" Heidegger asks. The way of the mortal, so conceived, is to be thrown into existence—to be thrown without reason, without recourse, and without any sense of finality or comprehension. The way of the mortal is always to be incomplete as a being toward death wherein the essence of our being is destined to be factually unknown and structurally unknowable. To invoke the term from Antonio Negri that will be discussed during the course of this chapter, there is a certain "ontological immeasurability" at work, a ruination in the law of measure that requires a radical rethinking of the very idea of justice and the very essence of humanity.

It is no wonder that in our hour of agony over life's uncertainty and loss we have the will to believe that there is more to this life, another world—a better world. Freud understood this more than most by locating the enduring power of religion in the power of our wishes arising out of the depths of our disappointment and despair.

So to return to this secret: the cross and the lynching tree are not only the threats voiced at the conclusion to David Mitchell's s novel *Cloud Atlas*, but it is of course also the title of the book by the black liberationist theologian James Cone. The central motivation of Cone's career has been "to reconcile the gospel message of liberation with the reality of black oppression" and "to develop a liberation theology that could be both *black* and *Christian*—at the same time, and in one voice."[4] The imperative and indictment are clear: any theology that does not directly engage with the religious struggle for justice is morally and spiritually bankrupt—more specifically, any theology in the United States that does not directly challenge the reality of white supremacy is bankrupt.

After all, Cone asks, why has it taken so long, with so few, to notice the resonances between the cross and the lynching tree when both are "symbols of terror, instruments of torture and execution, reserved primarily for slaves, criminals and insurrectionists?"[5] During the lynching era in American history (1880–1940), there were nearly five thousand African American victims. Following on the heels of Reconstruction and the removal of federal troops from the South in 1877, lynching emerged as a form of mob rule and vigilante justice—"slavery by another name"—wherein the American South was able to garner a cultural victory after their military and political defeat. Look no further than D. W. Griffith's gross cinematic masterpiece *The Birth of a Nation* (1915): the United States was born as a nation only *after* the Civil War and as a result of the collective realization of white supremacy. The movie depicts Northerners and Southerners relinquishing their past grievances to join together in common cause against the specter of mongrelization. As Cone writes: "Although white southerners lost the Civil war, they did not lose the cultural war—the struggle to define America as a white nation and blacks as a subordinate race unfit for governing and therefore incapable of political and social equality. In the white imagination, the image of black men was transformed from docile slaves and harmless 'Sambos,' to menacing 'black beast rapists,' the most serious threat to the virtue of white women and the sanctity of the white home."[6] During this time the killing of African Americans was so commonplace that the law was rendered utterly ineffectual, providing sanction for violence rather than justice. Or, as Ida B. Wells rightly put it, lynching was the "unwritten law" of the land. Entire families were known to enjoy the spectacle of lynching as they sat down to picnic, collecting and sending out postcards as memorabilia. As historian George Fredrickson recounts, this was the time when the United States was established as an "overtly racist regime," with a systemic, violent and virulent form of racism even worse than the worst form of colonialism, a "hate-filled brutality" fellow international segregationists found appalling.[7] It is for this reason that Cone identifies lynching as "the ritual celebration of white supremacy" and the "metaphor for white America's crucifixion of black people."[8]

Cone is indignant that the lynching tree *should* have a prominent place in American Christians' reflections on the meaning of Jesus's crucifixion. But it has not. This theological silence is "profoundly revealing," reflecting a "defect in the conscience of white Christians" (32). But where for some there was silence, not so among African American poets, novelists, and artists who have served as society's best ritual priests and prophets. It is they who have repeatedly made the linkage between the cross and the lynching tree. With each ritual execution, lynching was seen as a recrucifixion. In the effort to make sense out of this tragic history, attempts were made to relate the message of the cross to African Americans' own lived social reality. Jesus was lifted up as the "first lynchee," and the theology of the cross was restored beyond one of merely personal suffering and redemption to that of social suffering and redemption. It was realized that Jesus's death was not an isolated incident. On the contrary, *what both the cross and the lynching tree reveal is not a single, exclusive point in human history wherein an innocent victim was made to die, but that this is a terrible truth that societies repeat, almost ineluctably.* This is the perversity of the natural order, that justice is twisted to kill the victim as criminal.

This is an obvious, but still neglected, truth that remains a challenge to contemporary theology. As Cone makes clear, by reading the cross and the lynching tree together, not only might we know "at the deepest level . . . what it means to be crucified," but this also reveals the dialectic of despair and hope in African American religious life. That is to say, crucifixion rightly understood is not the story of a bloodthirsty God demanding the ritual sacrifice of his son to atone for the sins of humankind, but instead, it is "God's critique of power" (2). "It is one thing," Cone tells us, "to think about the cross as a theological concept or as a magical talisman of salvation and quite another to connect Calvary with the lynching tree in the American experience" (108). As Rene Girard has so powerfully argued in his analysis of the mimetic structure of violence, *Jesus's death may very well have been inevitable, but that should not be theologically misconstrued to mean that it was necessary.* To do so would make the mistake of providing divine legitimacy to violence. On the contrary, what Jesus's death signifies is how God's "powerless love [snatches] victory out of defeat" (2). It is a radical reversal of the natural order of things whereby the lynching tree is not the final word. And to hold fast to this belief is what Cone calls an "essentially religious stance" born from the double consciousness unique to the African American experience (106).

II.

Where Cone speaks of the religious imagination, *Cloud Atlas* creates what Deleuze has called the time-image.[9] According to Deleuze, the creation of a time-image as a pure image of time itself is a directly political and revolutionary event. Time not in a linear sense, but in terms of "the series of time, which brings together the before and after in a becoming, instead of separating them; its paradox is to introduce an enduring interval in the moment itself."[10] This is an opening up, an interstice if you will, in time creating the interval that gives time its dynamism as thought.

While Deleuze spoke of the time-image exclusively in reference to cinema, by the plot structure of Mitchell's novel, which contains within it two distinct series of time—forward and backward—that open up an enduring interval spanning six centuries, it is the novel, perhaps even more than its film adaptation, that is positively cinematic. So much so, in fact, that when it was eventually released as a film by the visionary and daring team of Tom Tykwer and Lana and Andy Wachowski, there was widespread skepticism that such a book ever belonged on screen. As one film reviewer wrote, "It took three directors . . . to capture the breathtaking reach of David Mitchell's 2004 novel." Others remarked on the novel's supposedly "unfilmable" nature. Mitchell himself speaks of the "ontological wow" and "primal kick" he got from seeing his words made flesh on the screen. He even ascribes a theological graph onto the adaptation by identifying himself as the once monotheistic creator who in a gesture of kenotic self-sacrifice released his creation into the hands of others, inviting their faithlessness, knowing that it is often too much faithfulness that leads to the failure of many film adaptations of well-known and beloved novels.[11]

In the words of Andrew O'Hehir, both the novel and the film are oversized and "potentially ridiculous . . . arguably too much of a good

thing, with too many characters, too many stories, too many directors." But this oversaturation is by design, and thus also potentially "the
source of its power."[12] More specifically, by the compounding of stories,
characters, epochs, and even creators, *Cloud Atlas* helps to visualize and
incarnate the revolutionary impact of the time-image.

Mitchell's reflections on the differences between a novel and a film are
instructive: "Perhaps a novel contains as many versions of itself as it has
readers," Mitchell writes, "whereas a film's final cut vaporizes every other
way it might have been made." As Mitchell sees it, a film "vaporizes" a text's
strive toward ambiguity by the film's inclination toward specificity.[13]

But there is more than this. Much has been made, for instance, of the
filmmakers' decision to replace the Russian doll structure of the novel's successive stories with that of a mosaic of transmigrating souls. The
novel depicts six self-contained stories that take place over the course
of six centuries, both from the past and the future. These six stories
are first introduced in chronological order and then each is returned
to in reverse chronological order. The film, on the other hand, presents them all as one continuous intertwined narrative. To accomplish
some semblance of continuity with all the splicing of the narrative necessary to fit the six into one, the filmmakers' made a further decision
to have the same actors play multiple roles. No sooner do you get used
to Tom Hanks playing a contemporary petty gangster and pulp author
than you see him as a goatherd from the year 2321 or a thief posing as
a ship doctor patiently and deliberately poisoning his friend to death
from the year 1849. Likewise, the film's other veritable Hollywood star
Halle Berry plays a slave from an aboriginal tribe, an investigative jour-
nalist from 1973, a male Korean doctor in 2144, and a representative of
the last vestiges of advanced civilization in the postapocalyptic world
of 2321. Doona Bae is at once a white wife, a Hispanic factory manager
and a genetically engineered Korean "fabricant" who gets worshipped
as a goddess over a century after her death. With the same actors playing different roles and even different genders, races, and ethnicities
from different epochs, many took this obvious homage to the fluidity
of personal identity and gender and racial construction as the sole work
of Lana (formerly Larry) Wachowski, who famously underwent gender reassignment surgery after her success with *The Matrix* trilogy. Too
many also got hung up on the actors' relative fit to the different types,
wanting and expecting a seamless transition from one character, story,
and time to the next.

What if, instead, this deliberate mixing of genres, gender-bending, and racial reversals was meant to be disruptive? It is a shock to our system to see a single actor becoming-man-woman, becoming-white-black. The Hollywood dream factory can stand only so much transgression written in a standardized visual script. So what in the novel was an epic that spanned six centuries, which builds to a climactic future of destruction and beyond, only to return back into the past one age, one story, one character, and one act at a time, becomes in the film a more specialized emphasis, or at least suggestion, of the artificiality—better, the partiality—of personal identity. We are not who we think ourselves to be—at least not entirely. No doubt, this was partly the cinematic vaporization Mitchell had in mind, a drive toward specificity that lifted out one of the novel's motifs for special attention. By thematizing inter-connectivity, the film also provides striking visualizations of the fissures in time and the moral fabric that make up the cosmos. Single acts of meanness or kindness, cowardice and heroism are exalted to world-historical significance.

The clearest case of this is with Somni-451, the genetic "fabricant" waitress that eventually wakes up to her oppression and first becomes an agent of revolution before becoming deified as the lone voice of historical memory after the hyperlogic of consumer capitalism ends up devouring the world in a state of near total destruction. Somni-451 can be compared simultaneously to the prisoner in Plato's allegory of the cave, who finds courage in her curiosity to discover the source of the truth of her own reality, to Neo, from the Wachowski's *Matrix* franchise, as the One chosen from the preexistent resistance as the cipher for their emancipation, and to the Wizard of Oz as the subject of confused worship. Her enlightenment was born from a friendship that develops and awakens her curiosity. The important thing about this is that she was thought to be incapable of both friendship and curiosity because such capacities had been engineered out of her specimen type. Her enlightenment, thus, was the genetic anomaly that put the truth to the lie of the biopolitical regime's forced oppression of a permanent servile class. Once discovered, her curiosity was fed and set free by the armed resistance with the aim of fomenting a revolutionary consciousness. As she later recalls when confessing to her crimes to an archivist, she was fully cognizant that her path to enlightenment, liberation, and insurrection was one that had been elaborately orchestrated by others. She was a willing pawn, wherein a seemingly infinite series of small acts and small discoveries had been lined up in advance like dominoes set to fall and trigger Armageddon.

Likewise with Adam Ewing, an American notary from the mid nineteenth century whom we meet in the story as he is seeking passage back to San Francisco from the Chatham Islands, an archipelago off the coast of New Zealand. He proves to be less a pawn and more a reluctant and unwitting hero. He is treated as a friend by a runaway slave who entrusts Ewing with his life, while at the same time he is being methodically poisoned to death by his lone confidant who is masquerading as the ship's doctor. It is Autua, the runaway slave, who discerns the supposed doctor's cure as poison and thus saves Ewing's life. But as Ewing tells the strange twist of fate, "Autua insists that had I not prevented him from being tossed overboard as a stowaway he would not have saved me + so, in a sense, it is not Autua who has preserved my life but myself." Even still, Autua's moral courage and fidelity impressed and indicted Ewing. He had already seen enough to know the cruelty and degradation of slavery. Indeed, before meeting Autua on the ship as a stowaway who was ready to entrust his life to Ewing's care, Ewing had previously witnessed Autua being brutally beaten on the shores of Chatham Islands. He was struck, if not awakened, by the sight and by Autua looking at him from afar square in the eye as if the two had some mutual understanding. He could not have known then how their fates were intertwined.

Nor could he have known how his eventual common cause with Autua would splinter his own life. From the brink of death and having been restored back to life, there was no going back: "Upon my return to San Francisco," Ewing announced, "I shall pledge myself to the Abolitionist cause, because I owe my life to a self-freed slave + because I must begin somewhere." The splinter would be his father-in-law, the voice of respectability, of reason, and, above all, of measure. It is he who knew the natural order of things, and of the price that would be paid for those who defy it. Just as assuredly, at the precise moment that Ewing was awakened to his own moral courage, he knew in advance the condemnation, if not ridicule, he would receive from his father-in-law.

The novel ends with what is only an imagined conversation between Ewing and his father-in-law, an internal dialogue in Ewing's head by which he fortifies himself against his own built-up resistances, which had long prevented him from seeing what was in plain sight. "I hear my father-in-law's response," Ewing tells us. "Oh, you'll grow hoarse, poor and gray in caucuses. You'll be spat on, shot at, lynched, pacified with medals, spurned by backwoodsmen! Crucified! Naïve, dreaming Adam." Thereby the decisive link is made between the cross and the lynching tree, a moral empathy that surpasses the defect pointed out by Cone with regard to the successive generations of white Christians turning a blind eye to what is plainly there to see. The imagined response from Ewing's father-in-law does not stop there though. "He who would do battle with the many-headed hydra of human nature must pay a world of pain + his family must pay along with him! + only as you gasp your dying breath shall you understand, your life amounted to no more than one drop in a limitless ocean!"

Ewing had been brought low. This is his hour of temptation: an internal warning of life's futility and insignificance coming at the very point when he is awakened morally and politically. The wisdom of the world bespeaks his own political impotence and existential irrelevance. This is the way of the mortals with the common fate of mortality. But his deprivation goes deeper. He is alive only because of the discernment and fidelity of a runaway slave. His only friend and confidant on his journey home from the ends of the earth turned out to be his would-be assassin. The words of his father-in-law were the words of the wisdom of the world—a brute, inarguable, tormenting truth that he must somehow find the means to resist. From a living death to a death outwitted or at least deferred, Ewing received a new lease on life. Only now he realized his life was not his own. Merely a mortal man, he now was being required to *defy the natural order*. Not by sacrifice, per se, but by a life of exchange. Once recognizing he owed his life to another whose survival had already been bound to his, the exchange was now a life for a life. Born into a new life, not by the way of death but by a most intimate exchange: a life held in, and restored by, another's hands and thereby awakened to a new moral and political consciousness. The creative becoming of a cause for emancipation and justice begins in a life shared, suffering witnessed, and death forestalled.

By staging the encounter between Ewing and his father-in-law as a purely imagined one, in point of fact we do not know what Ewing decides, the ultimate strength of his resolve, or the staying power of his newfound empathy and courage. Here is another instance of how the film vaporizes the essential ambiguity of this psychological drama when it renders this internal, purely imagined, dialogue into an actual face-to-face exchange. With the novel, the psychological is shown to be simultaneously moral and political: where the brinkmanship with death for some would lead to a psychological breakdown, for Ewing, it was the moment of his moral and political awakening. Could it be that Mitchell is suggesting some linkage between suffering, strength, and courage? Put otherwise, is it possible to conceive of Ewing's moral and political awakening apart from his physical torment? Was torment the condition of possibility for awakening?

Or, in a formulation from Antonio Negri that will be explored shortly, *is insurrection necessarily linked to pain?* Further, might we achieve life *before* death? To repeat, the thing to note from the chronicle of Adam Ewing is that his is a life achieved by a death forestalled. Before and beyond any well-meaning on Ewing's part, a bond had been forged between him and Autua. Two lives hanging in the balance. Both indebted to the other. Each the other's source of salvation. This bond is a life-giving power, a creative force. *Solidarity beyond sacrifice. Life before death.*

Where the novel leaves us with Ewing facing within himself the inner conflict of his sudden resolve to resist the natural order of things, the film cuts from one life, epoch, and world to the next, giving Ewing's defiance in the face of his father-in-law's voice of reason and measure a moral force that echoes through the centuries. The suggestion is clear: it is Ewing's moment of resolve that makes possible Somni-451's liberation and subsequent insurrection three centuries later. Time, which is traditionally conceived as a gulf of separation, is reordered by the overlapping of the past, present, and future. Time as a permanent passing and point of fissure becomes thereby a point of connection—or, better, infinite points of connection that do not run in a single line or follow the flight of an arrow but cross back and jump forward. Time as a folding wherein each and every moment contains within itself an explosive potential.

Put otherwise, what *Cloud Atlas* has achieved is a deconstruction of time—so long as we understand deconstruction as Jacques Derrida once defined it as the speaking of multiple languages all at once, simultaneously.[14] Understood in this way, deconstruction can be seen as the differentiation and thus temporalization of time—not only language's, but time's own surplus, which gives time its own permanent and immanent possibility. Time without exteriority, but, nevertheless, time and its other. In the words of Catherine Malabou, this would be "the excess of time over time."[15] Not time out of joint, but as a joint or a hinge that simultaneously joins and separates with a spacing that gives play, allows for movement, and opens and closes back and forth, time and again.

Cone and Mitchell's *Cloud Atlas* have brought us to this turning point or hinge as they have both managed to think the cross and the lynching tree together. Such a linkage is a violation of time and history as traditionally conceived. To assert a common dynamic that inevitably leads to the torture and death of those who violate the natural order of things is to open up an enduring interval of time that cuts across centuries and cultures. Once linked, we might know the reality of senseless suffering, meanness, and loss while still holding out the faith in change. A faith that holds out hope that the lynching tree is not the final word, that the seeming intractable cycle of racism, discrimination, and degradation might be overcome, and that the perversion of rendering death sacrificial might be replaced with a theology that cries out with righteous, prophetic indignation over the tragedy and loss of each and every death. It is not God that wills murder and destruction. On the contrary, it is God whose power is revealed by standing in solidarity with the suffering as testimony to the natural order as a violation against God's good design for creation. It is not God who singles out the death of only certain choice individuals as meaningful and leaves the rest dead, buried, and forgotten.

From an insurrectionist theological perspective, then, whether the cross or the lynching tree, they are no more the single point of time and history than are the infinite other points of connection. Further, they are not willed by God, but demonstrate just how far we as a human species have fallen. And just how often.

III.

What follows aims to be an extended meditation in that same spirit. As such, it will attempt to theorize insurrection—the insurrection that lives from life to life and thus does not have to pass through death.[16] It is in this way that insurrection will be contrasted with resurrection. I want to remember and insist that some wrongs can never be made right, some sufferings so painful, so inhumane, so destructive, catastrophic, and traumatic that they can never be forgotten, precisely because our very capacity to remember them in the first place has been compromised. Consider, for instance, the truism that the only genocides that we can "never forget" are precisely those that ultimately failed or, together with Voltaire, the Panglossian proof that this is the best of all possible worlds because "pigs are made for eating" only works if yourself are not the creature being devoured. So this insurrection may not be redemptive so long as the calculus for redemption still relies on the logic of atonement or, more fundamental even, the logic of measure. A legal code, let alone a morality, of an eye for an eye is not fit for humanity, let alone an adequate measure of divine justice. Likewise, to attribute ultimate meaning to death rather than life may be a standard theological gesture, but it is no less a perverse one.

You would be right to pose the question here of what precisely the point is then of an insurrectionist—in contrast to a resurrectionist—theology if and when its promises are ever so slight: no redemption, no guarantees. Even still, there is and remains the possibility of joy, albeit fleeting. And goodness and kindness. Freedom as well. In other words, an insurrectionist theology, at least in this author's iteration, intends itself as a liberationist theology. It is with this that my two primary questions announce themselves: 1) If not us, then who will decide our fate, and 2) is change possible, or is history just a repetition of the past and a perpetuation of the same? It will be my argument that it is through an ontology of change that insurrection offers itself up as a new species of liberationist theology.

IV.

Thus far I have repeated a mantra for the sake of simplicity when I have written of the natural order of things. Evidence mounts, especially within the burgeoning field of evolutionary psychology, that humans are a tribal species, that the laws of sexual attraction are productive of certain hierarchies, and that violence is endemic to civilization. From a different angle, Michel Foucault's critical history of modernity has taught us that what appears as the advance of reason, scientific and technological progress, and more open and inclusive communities is in point of fact more elaborate systems of social control and that there is a madness to rationality and biopolitical control masking as civilization. As he observes in *Society Must Be Defended*, "if we look beneath peace, order, wealth, and authority, beneath the calm order of subordinations, beneath the State and State apparatuses, beneath the laws and so on, [we will] hear and discover a sort of primitive and permanent war," a war being waged "just beneath the surface of peace."[17]

With this in mind, what follows is not meant somehow as a retraction from the opening paragraph wherein the fate for those who resist the natural order was first announced—namely, the way of mortals is governed by the brutal savagery of consumption. But I do mean to qualify what is presumed as the order of nature and thereby to rethink the conditions of possibility for meaningful and viable forms of resistance. In short, must insurrection be conceived as a force or movement pitted *against* nature and/or the natural order? If so, would this not mean that insurrection itself is unnatural—and thus fundamentally quixotic and doomed to fail? And, more broadly, if insurrection is conceived as a resistance against nature, would this not also doom any hope for real, lasting change? After all, if nature abides by a certain order, who are we mortals to dare defy it? Would insurrection in this case be the ultimate hubris, if not heresy, by its defiance of God's good creation?

Thus it is in the effort to theorize insurrection we may first turn to God—and, from God, only then back to nature. The Bible tells us that in the beginning there was divine violence. More specifically, as John Dominic Crossan has argued, the first eleven chapters of the book of Genesis provide us with four parables on the meaning of creation, the ambiguity of divine power, and the *failure of divine violence.* The first of the four parables is the first story of creation, which Crossan identifies as establishing the primacy of distributive (as opposed to retributive) justice. This is shown when considering what is looked to as the climax of God's creation—namely, the Sabbath, a day of rest from labor where, in the words of Crossan, God models "the justice of equality as the crown and climax of creation." The fruits of creation are freely available to all. In this way, at least from this first story of creation, nonviolence can be seen as the original feature of creation—not an aberration from nature, but written into the very fabric of nature by God's express will.

The second of the four parables is what is often referred to as the second story of creation in the Garden of Eden. And if the first story of creation testifies again and again to the *goodness* of creation, the second is where notions of the fall of humanity and the theological concept of original sin derive. The question Crossan asks is whether this story is rightly interpreted as a story of divine punishment. His answer is that the story is less about punishment than it is about human choice—specifically, the choice between moral knowledge and eternal life. "We could have had *eternal life,*" Crossan extrapolates, "but we chose *moral knowledge* instead." The important thing to note from this is that it is here where the first rift between nature and culture expresses itself. For by the consequences of human choice, the first humans were not so much punished as there was a change in the state of being. Again, in Crossan's words, a "fall (or rise?) from nature to culture." Exiled from the garden paradise, Adam and Eve were told that they would now have to toil for their food in a permanent struggle with nature. Nature's harmony and God's ideal of Sabbath justice give way to never ending human labor. Note here that *what we take as the natural order is not entirely natural, and, least of all, it is not original. Our nature is derived from human choice. Nature, as we know it, is a human product.* The supposed rift between nature and culture is more properly understood to be a mutual entanglement: *nature is always already culture.*

Parable 3 is the story of Cain and Abel and the tragedy of the first act of murderous violence. Cain the farmer kills his brother Abel, who was a shepherd. The farmer displaces the herder, the human population grows sedentary, and civilization is born in an act of violence God does not punish. From that point, there is a process of escalating violence and disorder leading to the extreme wherein the "sons of God" took the "daughters of humans" as their wives, who bore them the children later remembered as the "heroes of old," "warriors of renown" (Genesis 6:4). If humans were first producers of nature by virtue of the choices made and the consequences derived, then this is human nature in the extreme, a mixing of humanity and the gods, the mortal verging on the immortal. No longer a natural order, but now the height of disorder whereby not only is nature the product of human culture but the natural is actually becoming supernatural, the mortal becoming immortal. To those who insist that nature speaks of fixed limits or an atomistic universe that abides by a rigid deterministic logic or, more specifically, that nature is set and thus the natural order can abide no change—that biology is destiny—this third parable speaks otherwise. Not only do humans have the capacity to change, but this extends all the way to our capacity to change nature, to change our very being from that of mere mortals. The human who was first created in the image and likeness of God, together with nature in a constant state of becoming, is not just *like* the Gods but is *becoming* God.

The fourth parable is where God learns from his mistake and where the ambiguity of divine power is laid bare. With human violence escalating exponentially and the growing disorder of God's once good creation, God was presented a choice: how ought God confront the problem of evil on earth? Or alternatively, what is the nature of justice—distributive or retributive? In the story of Noah and the flood,

God opts for retributive justice by his decision to kill everyone and to destroy all living things on earth in order to start over from scratch with the lone righteous one and his family. Crossan calls this the "Noachic solution," one so dire, so extreme, and so destructive, that God immediately follows it up with a promise of "never again." Not only was God seemingly bound by moral scruples after the near total destruction of the earth, but, as we quickly learn from the stories that follow, the solution itself does not even work. From the very (re)start, humanity (again) spirals out of control. *God's violence proved ultimately impotent in taming human rebellion.* And so, with the Noachic solution foreclosed, what Crossan calls the "Abrahamic solution" commences whereby God chooses blessing over slaughter.

The lingering problem, however, is that just as there is now introduced a rift between nature and culture, with the realization that the very being of nature could become otherwise, so too are we introduced to a rift within God's own character—the *irresolvable ambiguity of divine power.* To be sure, with the Abrahamic solution, God vows to keep God's violent tendencies in check. But the *question is whether God is always as good as God's word?* For Crossan, an understanding of that *ambiguity between a violent and a nonviolent God* is necessary in order not only to understand the Genesis narrative, but the entirety of the Bible. By Crossan's reading, while the Bible might tip the balance it does not break the scales. Contemporary readers of the Bible, therefore, are presented with a choice between God's radical vision for nonviolent, distributive justice and the normalcy of an unjust and violent civilization.

More radical still, this is not a struggle that is resolved by the Bible, but rather depicted *within* the Bible itself. That is to say, there are times where God falls short of God's own promises and, correlatively, when the Bible fails to live up to its own liberative standard. Womanist theologian Delores Williams identifies this as the "nonliberative thread running through the Bible," wherein there are certain instances "where the texts supports oppression, exclusion, and even the death of innocent people."[18] This leads Williams to question the assumption of liberation theologians such as Cone who make the exodus story paradigmatic to their biblical hermeneutic. In other words, the Bible's silence with regard to the suffering and oppression to non-Hebrew victims is a problem that should not be ignored. After all, by identifying so completely with the exodus story, one runs the risk of being blind to the genocidal "reality of victims making victims in the Bible." And, for Williams at least, such blindness suggests the question: "Does this kind of blindness with regard to non-Hebrew victims in the scripture also make it easy for black male theologians and biblical scholars to ignore the figures of the Bible whose experience is analogous to that of black women?"[19]

And to think this is merely the triumphalist Christian trope that contrasts the New Testament God of grace with the angry, vengeful, and jealous God of the Old Testament would be a mistake. The ambiguity of divine violence—or, in Williams's terms, this nonliberative thread of the Bible—does not end with the Hebrew Scriptures. On the contrary, Crossan insists that the New Testament also presents us with this choice, as contemporary readers must ask themselves the question of which Jesus is to be normative for Christians.

Consider, for instance, what the New Testament has to say of Jesus's first and second comings. With Jesus's first coming we are told of his triumphant entrance into Jerusalem riding on a donkey. Such a gesture could only be an act of irony, a processional rendered farcical and thus staging the confrontation of Roman imperial rule and the violent repression upon which its order rests with Jesus's talk of the kingdom of God. But what must not be missed, Crossan insists, is that there was no mistaking this ironic gesture as a nonviolent demonstration. Contrasts this with what we are told of the second coming from the book of Revelation. Written during a period when followers of Jesus were facing their first bout of systematic persecution and when they were coming to understand the brutal repression under which Jesus himself suffered and died, here, instead of the nonviolent Jesus on a donkey in an ironic mimicking of a triumphant processional, we are presented with the image of Jesus descending from the heavens on a war horse leading a violent attack. Crossan sees this second biblical story of Jesus's triumphal procession as the "double negation" of the first, one that "libel[s] the body of Christ" and "blaspheme[s] the soul of Christ." Libelous and blasphemous, perhaps, but no less biblical, and thus from start to finish the Bible remains ambiguous regarding divine power through and through.

Unresolved and perhaps irresolvable, we are left with one version of the natural order of things wherein there is the presumption of the normalcy of violence. By Crossan's formulation, this is "peace through victory," an ideology exemplified by Roman imperial rule. It has a compelling, if world-weary logic to it, which is a temptation that even God godself is not exempt—let alone self-proclaimed followers whose faith under assault would naturally lead to the prayers and tears that cried out to God to vanquish their foes so that they once and for all could live out their faith in peace, a *prayer for peace that in truth is a bloodlust masquerading as faith.* In contrast to this logic of the world is the alternative formulation of "peace through justice," the Abrahamic solution also exemplified by Christ. The fact that the Bible gives credence to both formulations within its pages is what gives it its integrity and authority. "If the Bible were only about peace through victory," Crossan suggests, "we would not need it. If it were only about peace through justice, we would not believe it."

Unresolved and perhaps irresolvable, but at least clarified. So long as we are posed with this choice, we are sharers in the good news of the gospel—namely, in the words of Crossan, "the violent normalcy of human civilization is not the inevitable destiny of human nature." *The natural order of things can be resisted.* And so long as we accept that nature is a product of human culture—or, put otherwise, that the rift between nature and culture is better understood as a point of mutual entanglement—this resistance need not be conceived as a defiance against nature as such. That is to say, *resistance against the natural order is not unnatural.* Nature itself is in a constant state of change such that even if the natural order of the cross and the lynching tree seems positively ineluctable and irresistible, it is this very logic that stands as the fundamental temptation that *we—like God—must resist.*

Resistance is divine.

V.

If by the term *nature* we mean things as they are and should be from time immemorial, then what the preceding discussion of the four parables on the meaning of creation was meant to convey is that this conception of nature is a faulty one, at least from a biblically informed theological perspective. Nature, as we know it, is always already cultural. Further, what God wills is not always what God intends. In the pages of the Bible not only does God sometimes fall short of what God promises, but the Bible itself leaves unresolved the issue of the proper path to peace (via victory or justice?). And so we must conclude that, when it comes to theorizing insurrection, the Bible is not the answer, though it certainly helps in clarifying the question. The theo-logic that sanctions the presumed natural order as God's good creation misses the point. As God learned, *violence, death, and destruction are a permanent temptation, not the solution* to the problem of exponentially escalating violence. *God's violent interjections into human history are an expression of divine failure, not triumph.*

Make no mistake, for Crossan at least, the Bible remains a gospel story in the sense that it is an expression of hope and the bearer of good news. The point is that the violent normalcy of human civilization could be otherwise. Our destiny is not written in stone. By reading the Bible attentively, we can discern how this counterintuitive, if not contranature, vision of peace through justice not only gets domesticated but negated, libeled, and blasphemed. So understood, the Bible is a staged confrontation that presents the reader with a choice.

This confrontation is also what lies at heart of the existential struggle in the book of Job, which Antonio Negri has read as a staged ontological break with direct ethical and political implications. As Crossan does with the first eleven chapters of Genesis, Negri reads the book of Job as a parable—in this case, a parable of what Negri terms the "ruination of the law of measure."[20] Unlike Crossan, however, it is questionable whether Negri's reading of Job can be classified as a gospel story. Negri explicitly rejects any notion of redemptive suffering. While there may be no redemption, there certainly is freedom in Job's story. Indeed, for Negri, the political project of liberation necessarily excludes repentance altogether. That is because whereas repentance operates according to the law of measure, Negri insists on an "ontological immeasurability."[21] In other words, when a righteous man is made to suffer, there is no restoring the scales of justice, no making right the wrong, no moral law of cause and effect, and, perhaps most important of all, no undoing the pain endured. When faith in God's justice has been destroyed, the world, as such, is unjustifiable. Job's pain and suffering force him to reckon with the reality of *being* terribly out of whack. Put otherwise, Job's pain and suffering present an ontological problem.

Another way to speak of the ruination or crisis in the law of measure is to speak in terms of equivalence and the inadequacy of the logic of retribution. For Negri, as he states in the preface to the 2002 edition of his book *The Labor of Job*, the book of Job poses a "practical problem, not a theodicy."[22] Negri turned to Job in the midst of his own political ordeal as a prisoner and exile because he was seeking after "a means to resist through the analysis of suffering."[23] And, as Michael Hardt points out in his foreword to the book, Negri proposes an analogy between the injustice Job suffers and the injustices faced by labor in contemporary capitalism.

Consider here Karl Marx's familiar labor theory of value—namely, that an item's economic value, which is distinct from its use value, is determined by the total labor hours put into its production. Beyond the alienation suffered by the worker whose productivity is externalized by the commodity produced, there is the additional issue of exploitation. The capitalist is driven by the incentive for surplus value, to find efficiencies or cost-saving measures such that profits might be shaved off the value generated by labor. In this way, labor time is devalued and the profit motive endemic to capitalism is built on the logic of exploitation.

This theory of value assumes an industrial workforce whose labor time can be calculated, whose workday can be measured with the punching of a time clock. It is for this reason that Negri announces that Marx's theory of value is no longer adequate for the culture of late capitalism and with the shift toward a postindustrial information economy in which the immaterial production of ideas, images, and affects—"intangible assets"—have redefined the working day and blurred the divisions between labor and leisure. As the site for today's workforce for many has transformed from the factory floor to a form of biopower wherein there is an extension of state and corporate power over the totality of life—whether as work or leisure—then it becomes impossible to quantify production.

The analysis here is akin to that offered by Antonio Gramsci in that the regime of control functions not by way of overt force or coercion but by the power of cultural hegemony. Also useful to understand here is an analysis of contemporary forms of alienation, as detailed by the Italian theorist of postindustrial capitalism Franco Berardi, wherein "privacy and its possibilities are abolished. Attention is under siege everywhere. Not silence, but uninterrupted noise, not the red desert, but a cognitive space overcharged with nervous incentives to act: this is the alienation of our times."[24] This alienation creates a crisis in political subjectivity. The exploitation of physical labor has been superseded in some senses by the captivity of mental labor. Returning to Negri, this is what he means when he reflects on the ruination of the law of measure: *Value has become immeasurable at the same time that all measure fails.* And further, "Once measure is removed, *labor works without an end.*"[25]

Further, if Marx's theory of value is no longer adequate for the culture of late capitalism, then neither can the solution to capitalist exploitation be a socialist rebalancing of the law of measure. When the nature of work has been so radically transformed, the labor theory of value finds itself in crisis. In this case, Negri tells us, labor "does not reveal value—it exhausts it."[26] *Notions of fairness and justice must be rethought in nonquantitative terms.* This conviction places Negri in direct contrast with the traditional Marxist heritage, which, even in its resistance to capitalist exploitation, is still bound by the same notion of value predicated on the allure of equivalence. "Where old measures had fallen," Negri announces, "it was necessary to create new ones. . . . Only from this perspective was it possible to imagine communism anew."[27]

It is this contemporary economic and political reality that provides Negri with the analogue to Job's suffering. No better image of the ruination of the law of measure can be provided than the absurdity of the conclusion to the book of Job wherein God restores to Job his family and fortune. "The Lord blessed the latter part of Job's life more than the former part" (Job 42:12). If all things were equal, then Job would have come out of this ordeal ahead: more sheep, camels, oxen and donkey, more sons and daughters and descendants, and more time to live out the days of his blessing. But this would require a callous indifference to the actual loss of life and the enduring reality of pain. No amount of wealth or new sons or daughters can fill the hole in the heart of a parent who has lost a child. Anyone who suggests otherwise would rightly be perceived as a moral monster. There is *no rebalancing or equalizing* the imbalances created by the ordeal of pain, suffering, or death. Yet we persist in the dogma of retributive justice, the notion of an ethical measure by which God can somehow make good, of life as a zero-sum game.

While there may be no undoing the ordeal of pain, there is no shortage of explanations and justifications for it. For Job's friends the calculation was a straightforward one borrowed directly from Israel's covenantal-sapiential tradition, which was, in the words of one biblical scholar, the belief that "the world governed by God is morally reliable, wherein obedience yields prosperity while disobedience yields adversity."[28] The series of disputes in the long middle section of the book of Job testify to this "unbearable mismatch between [Job's] lived reality and [Israel's] traditional explanations." Job's friends repeat the dogma of retributive justice, whereas for Job there is no ethical measure that can account for his suffering and pain. In this way, Job moves beyond retribution and thus also beyond both capitalism and socialism in one fell swoop: "Job's protest to the *retributive model*, in which he recognizes *pure and simple charlatanry*, is merely intelligent—not yet revolutionary. Despite this, the great historical time of the Occident has been dominated by empty retributive conceptions—from Aristotle, through Christianity's reactionary accounts of it, to the more advanced capitalist ones. Socialism is the apologia for a retributive theory of justice, human action, and social rewards."[29] This dogma of retribution turns Job's friends into accusers who perceive him as a threat to the established order. Their consolation turns to accusation when Job testifies to his pain and refuses to repent. As Negri shows, it is precisely this path from a supposed clear-eyed, calculating objectivity of measure to retribution that so often "turns religion into an instrument of Power" (40).

There also is the mismatch of the contrasting images of biblical faithfulness. The sapential formula from the book of Proverbs, for instance, identifies wisdom as an instrumental value that makes possible a life of virtue. A virtuous life is then presumed as the guarantor of success. In this way, the wisdom traditional and literature sought to understand and live in harmony with the moral laws that govern human existence. God was seen as the fount of justice who sought to regulate human behavior so as to ensure human happiness and success. The book of Job, on the other hand, exposes the simplicity of this formulation, if not condemning it altogether as wrongly posed. In the book of Job, *God is no more bound by the exercise of retributive justice than human suffering is explained by it.* It is we the reader, better than Job himself, who know the backstory of God's moral indifference as he enters into a deal with the devil to treat Job as a pawn.

If by its implied critique of the coventantal-sapential tradition's moral law of measure the book of Job is not a proper theodicy, then how are we to read this ancient text? Beginning with the fact of what he calls "unreflecting violence" and "unbearable ontological pain," Negri reads it as an insurrectionist text par excellence. Job stubbornly insists on his pain and refuses all justifications for it. Job resists the counsel of his wife and the wisdom of his friends and eventually achieves a vision of God: "If Job's desert ends with a vision of God," Negri proclaims, "defeat and every prison of the multitude will end in a new insurrection" (xxiii). There are three things that we must garner from this proclamation.

First, as has already been noted, Negri's reading of Job is important to the present effort at theorizing insurrection because he makes the *link between insurrection and pain.* It is in his ordeal of suffering that Job cries out to God for a hearing. When God finally appears, God's sovereign power is revealed in all its omnipotence, if not capriciousness.

Where most would cower in fear, Job showed the strength of his vulnerability by remaining totally exposed by his pain. Hardt explains:

> Job's primary affect with regard to God's power is not fear but pain. Fear is the primary weapon of transcendent sovereign power, as Thomas Hobbes and numerous other authors throughout the history of political theory have taught us. A subject that fears is willing to give up freedom for security. The fact that Job does not react with fear even to God's display of absolute power is itself an act of insubordination. Instead of fear, Job expresses only his pain.
>
> (xiv)

The formulation offered by Negri is the following: "*Pain is a key that opens the door to the community.*" Even further, "*Pain is the democratic foundation* of political society, whereas fear is its dictatorial, authoritarian foundation." Just as pain is to democracy what fear is to authoritarianism, so too the revolutionary power of *potenza*, which Negri distinguishes from the congealed, state-form power of *potestas*, "is established in pain." This is the power of nonbeing appropriate to a measureless ontology—"an inconclusive essence within an indefinitely creative process" (90).

Return here to the previous discussion of Cone, specifically with regard to the meaning of the crucifixion. What exactly do the cross and the lynching tree reveal—a divine sanction for violence or God's critique of power? For Cone, the cross and the lynching tree are not written into God's plan for history as the bloodletting necessary for salvation or social cohesion. On the contrary, they are the positively revelatory expressions of pain and suffering, the very sign of human sinfulness, and the markings of how far, and how often, we have fallen from God's goodwill for creation. Further, for Cone, it is those who have made the critical link between the cross and the lynching tree—by and large, African American poets, preachers, artists, and musicians—who have been the agents for social change. In short, just as Negri links insurrection with pain, so Cone deftly articulates the productive and creative value of suffering without legitimizing it whatsoever. For them both, *pain is a constitutive process*. By the experience of pain, we might become fearful and cruel or identify together with the suffering of others. If it is the latter, then this becomes the bases for a new and different community. As Negri puts it, a reconstruction of the world from pain: "The ontology of the community is uncovered through suffering together" (94). In this way, suffering is not a mere passivity, but has the potential to become constructive, if not necessarily redemptive.

It is with this question of redemptive suffering where Negri and Cone disagree. Negri can be aligned with Delores Williams in her theological critique of the idea of redemptive suffering. For them both, it would be a perversion to persist in the notion that Jesus died in humanity's place as an atoning sacrifice, an ultimate expression of the law of measure whereby the end justifies the means. On the contrary, it is not Jesus's death that is redemptive, but his life. In the words of Williams, Jesus "came to show redemption through a perfect *ministerial* vision of righting relationships." While Cone is unwilling to let go of the redemptive theological power of the story of the cross, he nevertheless makes it clear when he writes, "I find nothing redemptive about suffering in itself. . . . What is redemptive is the faith that God snatches victory out of defeat, life out of death, and hope out of despair."

Likewise, the source of Negri's caution with any language of redemption should be clear: redemption still abides by the law of measure. What is decisive in the experience of suffering is not that it achieves a rebalancing, as in theories of atonement, nor does it restore what was lost before the onset of the ordeal of pain, but that in suffering and pain we are forced to encounter the ontological break. Job's rebellion is seen as a constitutive act because it is a generative, creative act, not restorative or retributive. It admits the failure and inadequacy of old standards of justice. Life does not balance out to a zero sum.

Earlier it was pointed out how Job's ordeal of pain countered by the "restoration" of his family and fortune exposes the ruination of the law of measure. Here the point is a similar one: *Job's unbearable ontological pain bespeaks a measureless ontology.* It is nonquantifiable. His loss is irreplaceable. His ordeal of suffering is an everlasting torment. But the mistake is to read this experience in relation to a supposed standard of equivalent measure, the false belief that if only God heaped enough blessings on Job this might make up for his suffering, rebalance the scales for his previous loss, that death is the necessary price for everlasting life. Negri's proposition is a much different one: suffering happens, but we must not justify that suffering by some abstract notion of fairness as equivalence, nor should we misconstrue the inevitability of suffering with its necessity. Even while linking pain with insurrection and recognizing suffering as one condition of possibility for the generation of a new community and a different world, this is still no sanction. The pain and suffering must still be resisted. And what Negri shows is that resistance is not a reactionary force but a creative and constitutive one. This is where liberation *begins*.

Second, *Job's resistance is not to be thought of as a Promethean subjective revolt. It is, instead, ontological*, "a refusal as profound as the pain that one has endured: an ontological refusal that follows an ontological pain" (12). It must also be distinguished from stoicism. For Job, there is no resignation and, most significantly, there is no separation of the ethical from the ontological. There is no indifference to good and evil, no manly charge to soldier on despite the vicissitudes of being. On the contrary, as Negri announces, "*for Job ethics is being*" (25). The pain and suffering endured by Job was a wrong inflicted in the heart of an ontology of measure. There is no steady state to being by which the scales of justice might be rebalanced. It is in this way that Job's antagonism with God is a form of ontological resistance.

As an ontological resistance it goes beyond justice to outright war with God. He addresses God not as a judge but as adversary: "a challenge of power against power" (44). Correcting the cliché, Negri insists that *Job's virtue was not his patience, but his power*. After all, Job is the one protesting against the unlawfulness of divine command, the amoral nature of God's omnipotence, and the perverse logic of retribution in the face of suffering. Job is the aggrieved prosecutor. God stands as the accused. And the theodicy that would defend the justice of God in spite of the brute fact of the unreflecting violence, suffering, and pain in the world is exposed as morally bankrupt.

God's response to Job's ontological rebellion is no less ontological. It is why God invokes the behemoth and the leviathan. These primordial beasts do not represent a future threat, but the rift in being at its very origins. They represent the "primordial chaos," a world "without measure or law" that was thought—even by God godself—to have been subjugated by God. By their subjugation God was thought to have gained the monopoly on violence. God's sovereignty was thought to be established as sacrosanct. Which is why Job's charges cut so deep: "The destruction of the ancient order has offered us not a well-ordered world but precisely the opposite: a great chaos, a great immeasurableness" (52).

Third, *liberation is not the end, but the beginning of an insurrectionist theology*. Negri places liberation theologies at the center of his evaluation of the book of Job. With the analogy of contemporary conditions of labor and the inadequacy of the labor theory of value with Job's story of suffering and his ontological revolt, we are placed squarely in the ruination of the law of measure and value. This present crisis of meaning also helps us to understand the emergence of liberation theology. Negri charts the impetus for liberation theology as follows: beginning with early patristic theology, the story of Job was reduced to order by appealing to a theology of redemptive suffering. It was only after Auschwitz and Hiroshima that God's silence in the face of human suffering because a genuine theological problem. Liberation theologies arrive at this point in history as part of the larger decolonial political project. This broadens the evaluation of the book of Job as redemption or atonement gets transvalued as liberation. Negri also expresses his own preferential option for the poor when he shows how the drama contained within the book of Job "does not unify, it separates—masters from slaves, the powerful from rebels—and redemption is on the side of the latter, of those who through suffering have understood the lightness of matter and the ingenuity of labor" (73).

Job's rebellion constitutes his freedom. By his rebellion, he is neither raised to the level of God nor is he atoned to God. Instead, God is lowered to the level of Job, forced from his role as sovereign judge to that of the defendant. The old model of justice in which God served as its backstop, wherein God's monopoly on violence was still thought an improvement to the primordial chaos of the behemoth and the leviathan, has been decimated. "When power opposes Power, it has become divine. It is the *source of life*. It is the *suberabundance of charity*. The world can be reconstructed on this basis and only what is reconstructed in this way will have value" (75).

Liberation is the beginning. Creation is the end. "The book of Job exhibits a sarcastic existentialism that, through pain, denies all dialectics and understands being only as creation. After Auschwitz and Hiroshima God is no longer—but there is the ever more human necessity to create" (59).

Insurrection is the creative force proper to us mere mortals.

VI.

Building on this argument, we must return to the question of whether insurrection must be conceived as a force pitted *against* nature and/or the natural order. When asking this question previously, my aims were clear: the purpose of this analysis is to qualify what is presumed to be the order of nature and, thereby, to rethink the conditions of possibility for meaningful and viable forms of resistance. Let me put matters here in schematic form, which will be developed with reference to the work of Catherine Malabou in the pages that follow: (1) Insurrection may adopt a defiant pose, but it is not a defiance against nature per se. (2) Insurrection may reject talk of a natural essence when it implies, is associated with, and is employed toward the end of a fixed essence, a naturalization of social norms, an ideological construction that then provides the rationalization of, and script for, continuing prejudice and oppression, but it does not reject essentialism per se. (3) Insurrection may reject a theology of liberation predicated on a politics of difference and identity, but it aspires to provide its own basis for liberationist thought.

(1) Earlier it was established, at least by reference to a biblically informed theological perspective, that nature is not purely natural if by natural it is meant original or exempt from cultural influences. Henceforth, we will appeal to, and make use of, the concept of plasticity to make this point. It is Malabou more than anyone else who has developed this concept, proclaiming it as the new motor engine of thought that has effectively drawn the limits of deconstruction and the epoch of writing deconstruction has come to signify. In this way, Malabou belongs together with figures such as Alain Badiou, the speculative realists, and the new materialists by her suggestion of an alternative to a purely linguistic philosophy. But, whereas Badiou and the speculative realists directly repudiate the paradigm of philosophies of language, Malabou reads textuality as a materiality, thereby retaining the flux and indeterminacy associated with Derridean deconstruction, but not by way of an indifference to the natural sciences and/or a repudiation of essence. Instead, Malabou demonstrates, for instance, how neurobiology, properly understood, teaches us that the brain has a history—that it is in part constituted by its experience but also is in the permanent, never ending state of constituting itself. The brain, and not just the mind, is adaptable. This is a nonreductive materialism that has profound implications for the nature of human freedom, moral responsibility, and the individual's relationship to society.

In perhaps what has been her most noteworthy claim—or the analogy that first brought her widespread critical attention—in *What Should We Do With Our Brain?* Malabou analogizes from the neurobiological to the biopolitical. That is to say, how we think of our brain both reflects and partly determines our social and political world. Neuro-biological reality is just as much a biopolitical reality. She claims a neu-ronal ideology that blinds us to the actual nature of brain plasticity, an ideology that, throughout the early part of the twentieth century when industrial capitalism in the West was at its peak, stubbornly mistook the brain for a machine or a control center. This faulty understand-ing of the brain pairs up with an industrial mindset and managerial regime wherein the worker is the subject of control and domination. With shifts to a postindustrial economy in the West, however, this neu-ronal ideology has undergone a shift—the brain as command center or machine gives way to a faulty understanding of plasticity wherein plasticity is reduced to pure flexibility. In Malabou's words, "flexibility is plasticity minus its genius."[30]

The genius here refers to the dual aspect of plasticity—that is, the concept of plasticity means not just the capacity to receive form or to be acted upon but also the capacity to give form or to resist. So the cur-rent neuronal ideology gets it only half right. Yes, the brain is not a fixed entity. It retains the permanent capacity to open up new neuronal path-ways, to adjust to certain traumas, and to actualize almost an infinitude of possibilities. The brain demonstrates a remarkable resiliency and flexibility, adjusting and responding to almost any environment. Like-wise the worker in a postindustrial economy—the worker is nomadic. To thrive in today's global economy, the worker must be willing and able to adjust to new market demands, adjust to the rapid pace of change, learn and relearn new skills and capacities. As such, it is a biopolitics of extreme flexibility that renders the subject almost entirely pliant, a blob of clay that can be molded and remolded at the market's whims.

But, this is only one half of plasticity. Malabou draws a hard line between flexibility and adaptability. What differentiates them is the latter retains its resistance. Our current neuronal ideology blinds us to the possibility of resistance because such agency runs counter to the demands of a global workforce. We see in the brain only what we want to see. Or, more precisely, the brain lacks self-awareness because of the biopolitical restraints imposed upon it by virtue of certain economic realities. This is the biopolitical culture of late capitalism as described by Fredric Jameson. If the plasticity of the brain is misconstrued only as a flexibility, then this naturalizes and thus justifies all forms of the dislocation and exploitation of labor. Recall here the previous refer-ence to the work of Gramsci and Berardi wherein it was suggested that contemporary exploitation takes the form of the captivity of mental labor. Malabou goes one step further: this captivity must be understood not only as ideological, but as material—because, after all, the mind is nothing other than the brain.

This is the contemporary crisis of political subjectivity, and what is desperately needed is *a reschematized philosophy of freedom founded on a thoroughly materialized notion of resistance.* Put otherwise, a materialized notion of resistance demonstrates resistance as a necessary part of nature, not as a form of defiance against it. The adaptability of the brain is the material means by which the self achieves its autoconstitution. But adaptability is not flexibility, and so this autoconstitution, in the words of Malabou "cannot be conceived as a simple adaptation to a form, to a mold, or to the received schemata of a culture." Thus, when she describes the plasticity of the self in terms of "a necessary split and the search for an equilibrium between the preservation of constancy . . . and the exposure of this constancy to accidents, to the outside, to otherness in general," it is not unlike Negri's critique of the law of equivalent measure. Being does not operate by a steady-state principle. Instead, in the words of Malabou, "What results is a tension born of the resistance that constancy and creation mutually oppose to each other. It is thus that every form carries within itself its own contradiction. And precisely this resistance makes transformation possible" (71). *Resistance is not reactionary, but generative, not restorative of an equilibrium, but constitutive of form.* As such, it is integral, not opposed, to nature.

Further, not only are there built-in resistances within the neuronal itself, but so too must we speak of the resistance between the neuronal and the mental. Malabou writes, "The transition from the neuronal to the mental supposes negation and resistance. There is no simple and limpid continuity from the one to the other, but rather transformation of the one into the other out of their mutual conflict" (72). To describe this transition, Malabu speaks of "energetic discharges . . . that progressively transform nature into freedom." And then she concludes with a paradox: "Paradoxically, if we were flexible, in other words, if we didn't explode at each transition, if we didn't destroy ourselves a bit, we could not live. Identity resists its own occurrence to the very extent that it forms it" (74). Resistance, then, so conceived from Malabou's nonreductive materialism, is the continual process of creative destruction—a natural passage from life to life, from one form of life to another. And if we accept the analogy between the neurobiological and the biopolitical, then this thoroughly natural brain process might also hold the key to a politics of insurrection. That is because not only does the plasticity of the brain reveal resistance as integral to the self-formation of the natural and biological themselves but it also shows how we are blinded by a certain neuronal ideology that naturalizes flexibility and thereby gives credence to and reinforces a purely pliant subject who is entirely victim to a supposed natural, though no less savage, order of consumption. Such an ideology would make us into mere pawns of capital, confining us to a fate of endless and nomadic laboring in which our only tangible asset is our pliancy, and hence, our docility. But, as Malabou shows us, just at the brain *needs* resistance, so too does society. Resistance to this supposed natural order is no more unnatural than it is unwanted: "*Creating resistance to neuronal ideology is what our brain wants, and what we want for it*" (77).

(2) What is it about essence to which we rightly object? When employed in discussions of sexuality and gender or with race, the problem with talk of essence is that it implies a fixed essence that then provides the rationalization of continuing prejudice and oppression. Indeed, when examining identifying the essence of racism, George Fredrickson insists that it "is not biological determinism per se but the positing, on whatever basis, of *unbridgeable differences* between ethnic or descent groups—distinctions that are then used to justify their differential treatment." For Fredrickson, this is a much more helpful understanding of forms of discrimination than his previously held view of the mere combination of prejudice with power. As he explains, "I would now put more stress than I did then on the presence and articulation of a belief that the defining traits are *innate or unchangeable*."[31]

But what if, in contrast to this fixed view, essence is thought of in plastic terms? The differences would be no less real—even no less material or biological—while being recognized as a product of our own making. In this sense, Malabou's intervention into gender theory can be likened to W. E. B. Du Bois's early study of urban black life where he sought to prove the value of social scientific studies in combating the pseudoscience of racial bigotry. As Du Bois put things in his autobiography from 1940: "The Negro problem was in my mind a matter of systematic investigation and intelligent understanding. The world was thinking wrong about race, because it did not know. The ultimate evil was stupidity."[32]

Perhaps the essence of the theory of insurrection I am advancing here is this present point with regard to rethinking essence. This builds on the deconstruction of nature already accomplished. Whether from a biblically informed theological perspective or a new materialist perspective, the binary between nature and culture is overcome—the world of nature is at least partially the world of our making. The being of nature bespeaks an open, measureless ontology constituted by explosive discharges. The being of nature bespeaks a world of *change*—in the words of Malabou, "a metabolic ontology." Resistance goes all the way down. *Insurrection is not only what we want, but it is nature's ownmost possibility.*

But the question that must be asked is *how* we make the change that we want. Malabou's most direct engagement with this question is from her book *Changing Difference: The Feminine and the Question of Philosophy*. It is here that Malabou takes up the deconstructionist critique of essentialism and, in so doing, formally declares her independence from Derrida by her attempt to "alter the trajectory of deconstruction, to plasticize *difference* and *différance*."[33] Not only Derrida: the book is also haunted by the specter of queer theory and the work of Judith Butler—or, more fairly, as Malabou announces in the introduction, the "two types of feminism today." The one is what Malabou identifies as traditional feminism that is based on the biological differences between the sexes. Traditional feminism is most concerned with rectifying the power imbalances between the sexes, but makes the mistake of reifying identity and difference by assuming a fixed essence to biological differences.

The second is "post-feminism. It bases its critique of misogyny and patriarchy not in the biological differences between the sexes but in the ways by which gender identities get socially and culturally constructed. By differentiating between gender and sex, it accepts the deconstruction of nature we have advanced thus far—namely, biology is not destiny. The binary division of the genders is an artificial construction that grossly simplifies the whole spectrum of sexual identities. As such, it goes beyond feminism as traditionally conceived by exposing not only phallogocentrism that underwrites patriarchy but also the heterosexual matrix of man-woman.

Put in different terms, what queer theory accomplishes is a pluralization of the ontological difference. Beyond the man-woman binary, wherein each is attracted to and constituted by its opposite, there is a full spectrum of identity—not just one difference, but many differences. If gender can be seen in terms of a spectrum, this suggests ontological difference must be conceived as more than a simple duality. Even more, identities may be freely chosen, a self-fashioning liberated from presumed metaphysical restraints, bringing with it a sexual ethos of transvestitism. "So long as we think ontological difference outside the transvestitism to which it necessarily gives rise," Malabou writes, "no theory of the pluralization of difference will be able to shake the rigidity of the dyad."[34]

Despite their important differences, the two types of feminism share much in common. Most significantly, they share a systematic critique of patriarchy and a commitment to full gender equality. Queer theory goes beyond traditional feminism by its critique of how traditional feminism naturalizes sexual essence and thus unwittingly reifies traditional conceptions of identity and difference. But this too exacts a price. Queer theory's pluralization of difference operates on the cultural plane exclusively, severing all ties and claims to the biological and the natural. By its social constructivism, it is antiessentialist through and through. As such, it is bereft of any ontology whatsoever.

Malabou, on the other hand, argues that the proper means by achieving these shared feminist aims must come by thinking being otherwise. This is where her reading of ontology as change comes in. Her claim is that before and beyond both the ontological difference and its pluralization with the full spectrum of possible differences, there is being as change. It is the mutability of being that gives rise to difference(s). *Differences are derived and produced by the change of being.* It is by this fundamental insight that Malabou then seeks her rehabilitation of essence. Differences are real. Differences matter. But, returning to the point about the essence of racism from Fredrickson, this need not translate into the belief that differences are innate or unchangeable. The affirmation of difference(s) need not come at the expense of a scientific and material discussion of the natural and the biological. *Once change is understood to be more fundamental than difference, then this displaces the ontological question and suggests a plasticity to identity.*

Returning to the script of antiessentialism, Malabou links the deconstructive with queer theory and thus has both Derrida and Butler in her sights. Whereas the former opposes the essential because of its ontological meaning, the latter expresses its opposition in terms of the natural, biological, and anatomical meanings ascribed to essence. "If . . . we must clarify the intersection of gender theory and deconstruction," Malabou writes, "it is in so far as whatever the difference of their approaches, there nonetheless appears to be a consensus regarding a definition of essence as stability, self-presence, and nature, in both the ontological and biological meaning of the term."[35] So, while sympathetic to their caution with regard to how the natural has traditionally been conceived in terms of a stable equilibrium, she nevertheless insists that there is a different and better way to think about essence. "Because woman historically has been denied her essence—characterized by her deficiency or deviance from the (male) norm—the assumption of an antiessentialist position has struck many, if not most, gender theorists as the necessary position to take. To the extent that this liberation is theorized in terms of a pure social constructivism, though, the freedom is purchased at the price of materiality—by which I mean in this case a materiality embedded in nature and informed by biology."[36] Malabou begins from the point of the historical legacy of the damage done to woman by man, giving special attention to the very "impossibility" of there being a genuine woman philosopher. On this point, you can read Malabou's struggle here along the same lines as Cone's animating concern—namely, the pursuit of the possibility to be "both *black* and *Christian*—at the same time, and in one voice." As Malabou shows, the possibility of philosophy is predicated on the impossibility of woman. So there is no specifically feminine philosophical tradition: "It's certainly not a matter of inability; it's the lack of theoretical possibilities. All the 'philosophical' topics are and always will be borrowed topics for women. The questions are and always will be given to them."[37]

If at best women can only possess a borrowed tradition, then it is a legitimate question to ask about what is the value of philosophy at all—for women in particular and, more generally for our purpose in theorizing insurrection, for making change. Malabou answers by turning the problem on its head: women may not invent philosophical questions, but, in so being, they create philosophical problems: "The impossibility of being a woman thus becomes the impossibility of philosophy."[38] Women "act without": "This is where she feels hope—perhaps delusional—beyond essentialism and anti-essentialism, a new idea of the feminine that starts from her own philosophical impossibility."[39]

Malabou has shown by her ontology of change that the essence of being is its own transformation. Essence is always becoming different because to be is always to be changing. This is what she means when she speaks of woman as acting without an essence. But to say that woman acts without essence is not to deny the real, biological differences between man and woman. Rather, it is to insist that this nature is not a fixed essence, that our differences are not innate and unbridgeable.

In the end, Malabou makes a definitive philosophical claim about woman, a claim that I am invoking as potentially insurrectionary by *its simultaneous affirmation of biology and the capacity for change, the natural and the cultural*. If woman is emptied of her essence by the violence done to her, by the philosophical negation of her own possibility, then the "new era in the 'feminist' fight," according to Malabou, may come by imagining woman as "an empty but resistant essence."[40] To be is to resist. This aligns with what was previously said about the energetic discharge that transforms nature into freedom. Though marked by the "stamp of impossibility," and thus always at least a tacit acknowledgment of a violence done and a suffering endured, this empty but resistant essence is generative, not reactive. By harnessing the resistant power of ontological mutability, the essence of woman reveals the conditions of (im)possibility for the production of life itself.

(3) It is by this understanding that our theory of insurrection may provide the basis for a new and different liberationist thinking. That is to say, instead of predicating liberationist thought on concepts of difference and identity that follow the larger script of a politics of identity, liberation may be seen as ontological. To think being as change is fundamentally an insurrectionist gesture. It is aimed toward the end of making change.

As mortal beings, we are earth creatures, rooted in the materiality of nature. There is both great danger and hope in this realization. Danger because we run the risk of naturalizing the presumed natural order, which operates by the law of competition for finite resources. This is a mortal danger to our being because, by its logic of consumption, we steel ourselves to the seemingly inevitable fate of eating or being eaten. Hope because *this presumed natural order contains only the most superficial understanding of nature*: nature void of culture, stripped of choice, opposed to freedom and creativity; nature void of life insofar as it precludes resistance, and resistance void of nature insofar as it poses insurrection as an unnatural violation of the natural order.

Whether gods or mortals, to be is to change—which means not only to have the capacity to change but to have the capacity to make change. Insurrection is the divine capacity written into the very heart of mortal being.

4

THE GOSPEL OF THE WORD MADE FLESH

Insurrection from Within the Heart of Divinity

Noëlle Vahanian

A theology of insurrection cannot think the sky in opposition to the earth. This much is a given.

What was once called by the name God can no longer be cordoned off and separated from the world. Likewise, any treatment of divinity in insurrectionary terms cannot be isolated from the rest of the world. That is, for a theology of insurrection, Heidegger's famous declaration in his posthumous interview with *Der Spiegel* that "only a god can save us" signifies doom and fatalism. If only a god can save us, then no god should bother. It is hopeless. We, human mortals, are hopeless. Thus what is at least as evident as this hopeless claim is that God cannot and will not save us. This acknowledgment is one of the constitutive elements of this insurrection.

What is more, if we take Heidegger at his word in this same interview when he said that "it is no longer an earth on which human beings live today," then we have all the more reason not to think the sky in opposition to the earth—all the more reason to rethink the ethereal sky and the solid earth. The two concepts are joined at the hip, as it were. The passing of the god that Heidegger discusses in his *Beiträge zur Philosophie* signifies the end of metaphysics, but for such a theology of insurrection this must mean that any thought of the world cannot be born of or grounded in an earth that could alienate us for losing touch with the sky above.[1] The otherworldly cannot simply be denied or forgotten; it must be folded in. That is, we cannot deny our propensity to reach for the heavens or the stars, even in the face of the refusal of being to show itself. Similarly, our technological condition cannot be thought in opposition to our natural condition, whatever that condition may be. If the world must be thought in relation to the earth rather than the heavens, then the earth must be rethought. Estrangement as the ground of being—the estrangement that results from the passing of the god and subsequent loss of determinate being—estrangement that marks a new beginning in the refusal of being to show itself is, as a leap into Dasein, both *theological* and *technological*—that is, it is a leap in and of language.

Thus, and to repeat what was postulated at the outset, a theology of insurrection cannot think the sky in opposition to the earth. At the same time, there is a dangerous logic lurking behind the desideratum to be part a fourfold, earth, sky, mortals, and divinities. The ghost of metaphysics beckons us even from within the fourfold. This ancient metaphysical logic creeps in (as) the foundations, as the very ideal notions, of what it might mean to dwell within the fullness of the fourfold. To dwell, Heideggerian-style (as in the Heidegger of Derrida or Irigaray), must be exposed as metaphysical trickery. The radical materialism of a secular theology of language cannot abide by the solid earth-crusted plane of Heidegger's idealized Black Forest farm.[2] Such a dwelling, in its appeal for its naive and phantasmagoric intimations of caring and nurturing of the earth, falls prey to a facile, all-too-metaphysical conception of preservation—a preservation of an ossified Being. This is why, here, we must conceive of insurrection from within—within the fourfold, within phallogocentric language, within the history of colonial oppression and white supremacy, within capitalism, within the sin of Christianity—without exoticisms.[3]

I.

Paleonymy, this Derridean neologism, refers to the subversive use of an old word to transform the symbolic order. The old word now means something new, but, paradoxically, it does so by referring to what it previously erased as the condition of its marking. For instance, Derrida's own use of the word *writing* is paleonymic. After Derrida, *writing* is, as Malabou will write, the new "motor scheme" of an epoch.[4] In a sense, then, paleonymic writing is a writing that makes immanence instead of transcending it. Or writing is no longer a transcending act even though it is a transforming act. The immanent is no longer a passive, inert, or solidly static remaining within. It is not that "writing" transcends speech, but that there is no speech that is not always already a "writing."

Keeping paleonymic writing in mind, the question of insurrection from within can be seen as, in the words of Naomi Schor, who so lucidly articulates the logic and the aim of Luce Irigaray's theorizing of feminine specificity, "the question of the difference *within* the difference."[5] From this feminist perspective, woman's liberation from the phallogocentric world she inhabits is doomed if it calls for her rejection of the specificity that has spelled her oppression as well as her exclusion from dominant discourses. The point of liberation is not to reject the status of the feminine; it is, instead, to transform and take back the concept by cultivating—breathing air into the nostrils of the crusted earth—and loosening the packed ground within which the fluid feminine has been emptied out. In the work of Irigaray, mimesis is the way to do just that: a deconstructive discursive practice that repeats the myths of the dominant discourse while changing the moral of their stories. In so doing, mimesis instantiates the positivity of the feminine, in other words, "the difference within mimesis *is* the difference within difference."[6] It is not that "woman" finally realizes her essence through her projects, in action, outside of herself, but that woman's immanence does not condemn her to the destiny of the parasitical, flightless gypsy moth.[7] If Schor suggests that Irigaray's use of mimesis is paleonymic, there is yet another example of paleonymic writing, the power of which is to reclaim Being, without repudiating "writing," and this is done through the new motor scheme of "plasticity."[8] This, of course, is Malabou's use of the concept. She rescues *différance* from itself, from the linguistic monism to which epistemological undecidability otherwise condemns it. The plasticity of Being is what makes "writing" and "difference" possible, but it is also what makes real change possible. This, then, is one way to begin to think about the meaning and the possibility of an insurrection from within.

Taking this possibility at face value, a theology of insurrection, too, can aspire to reclaim ontology while dispensing with the bad metaphysics. Or, put more bluntly, insurrection from within might very well look like "an effort to hold onto the baby while draining out the bathwater."[9] But put this way indeed, what is the alternative? Dispensing with ontology altogether might condemn us to what has been termed linguistic solipsism, and that in this way becomes hopelessly ineffective in instantiating any real change. The way of a radical theology as a theopoetics or theology of language, in evacuating the traditional language of ontotheology, may appear to leave ontology behind. But the antiessentialism of a theology of language serves its iconoclastic (antimetaphysical) verve, and, for that reason, it could not be held fast onto without contradiction—without essentializing its antiessentialism and thereby mourning a pure being of its own making: original ground or full presence to come. This is where Paul Tillich's formulation of God as the ground of being, as being itself, is paramount to radical, secular theologies.[10] Another one of Tillich's formulations of God as the only nonsymbolic symbol can be interpreted as a sort of apologetics for ontotheology in that while the classical metaphysical formulations concerning God as being are avoided (Highest Being and so forth), the oneness or purity of God as being is nevertheless intimated in the fact that God, as now unspeakable or unrepresentable, maintains for that reason a pure identity without difference.[11] But such an interpretation aligns with a postmodern reading and critique of Heidegger and his reduction of ontotheology to metaphysics—which is that his project of overcoming metaphysics still betrays a desire for purity.[12] Or, as Irigaray avers, Heidegger never leaves the earth, and, in this, he never leaves metaphysics.[13] The Tillich of a theology of insurrection does not simply appropriate or apologetically recuperate the language of ontotheology: he transforms the meaning of ontotheology by opening being to change in the same way that Malabou opens Heidegger's being to change.[14] It is Jeffrey W. Robbins who combines Malabou's ontology with Tillich's ontotheology such that, in his words, "The identification of God with being means that God is seen as the very being and source of change. This claim does not rest on the hope for the impossible, but instead is grounded in the very nature of our being."[15]

Thus the question of the difference *within* the difference goes beyond the straightjacket of the binary from which it stems: the difference within the difference that stands opposed to the same is a change of difference. Femininity no longer stands opposed to masculinity as the latter's other or as confined and defined by heterosexual patriarchy. It does owe something to women, as Malabou would say, its "empty but resistant essence, essence that is resistant precisely because it is emptied, *a stamp of impossibility*."[16] This is the positivity that transvalues the difference because it can transform the symbolic order—by resisting it. Likewise, being no longer stands outside the machine, a dead ghost of metaphysics that haunts the most secularist discourses or opposed to becoming and constitutionally warding off differences. Instead, being is change, transformability, hope in living—in expenditure.

Hence, insurrection from within—within language—is not to be confused with linguistic monism. To the contrary, *within*, here, refutes this monism. Insurrection from within does this, first, in acknowledging that the constitutive outside of any discourse refers back to its inside. Thus insurrection from within always eludes the abject—the neither subject nor object; neither self nor other. If we stopped here, we would need to concede that insurrection from within is no real insurrection; it moves the furniture around, and maybe in doing this the bottom-feeders get bigger and the big fish sink to the bottom of the ocean. Nothing has really changed.

But, in acknowledging that its constitutive outside refers back to its inside, what is then posited as always elusive—some abject (noumenal) realm—appears precisely as an object, as nothing but the effect of our grammatical condition. Here, too, though, if we stopped, we would be forced to admit that besides nominal change, nothing could ever really change without divine intervention, some salvific event from God knows where.

If insurrection from within means anything besides its opposite, if it actually subverts the norm that it adopts, this is because *a word is not made flesh by being stamped on a body.* A word is made flesh only insofar as flesh can differ with itself. In this way, what must be conceded is that writing belongs to materiality—a radical materiality. But what this means is that the abject, even as a grammatical surface effect, does not wholly belong to writing as one of its personal effects. The abject is also, and always, a material effect. When being differs with itself, writing remains within being. And the way out is a better way in.

Insurrection from within can now be seen as a discipline, a religion, a practice—a wording—of the flesh that works the plasticity of the materiality of being and that, in doing so, resists the otherwise thoughtless mimicry of everyday living, which mimicry reinforces normative identification at the expense of any Other. Like the performativity of gender as expounded in Judith Butler's now seminal *Bodies That Matter,* which materializes sexuality as the condition of identity through iterative citationality, but also, and more important, through what Karen Barad names iterative intra-activity, insurrection from within understands that the discursive limits of bodies are also material limits of discursivity.[17] In this sense, discourse and materiality interact. It is not simply that discourse impacts matter and shapes it through mere repetition, but that discourse is always already material and matter is always already discursive, or, in the Malabou sense, it is plastic, not some extrahistorical and extratemporal referent. Agency does not belong to a subject, but is instead "a matter of intra-acting; it is an enactment" and a "matter of making iterative changes to particular practices."[18] Insurrection from within is possible because subjectivity or subjective identity is a production that is never established firmly but needs constant confirmation. Such confirmation is aided through the forgetting of what Nietzsche called a fundamental human drive, namely, the creation of metaphors. That is, language functions through the forgetfulness of its arbitrariness, a forgetfulness facilitated or an arbitrariness erased by the materiality of speech, voice, and sound, the smell of ink, the touch of paper, or the tapping and clicking of keystrokes—an arbitrariness that is crossed by history, a story that captivates, transports, and interpellates. This intra-activity becomes habitual, until one experiences a crisis of meaning and one's flesh grows apart from one's words. It is at this point that confirmation is like a second baptism, the recognition of the act of faith at the basis of every (in)decision to enact a subjectivity. For such a theology of insurrection, this can be said to be the Christian insight into God, the Word made flesh. Such is the gospel of insurrection from within. It should not be confused with historical and imperial Christianity, which denies this very insight through its Christologocentrism.

The radical materialism of this theology of insurrection conceives of the ground of being as a materialization in the sense just unveiled: no pure being, no pure ground, but always a materializing nevertheless, which therefore spells a future, one for which we are responsible in this present for the limits we set on it through the dreams and machinations we have for it. One such dream is found in the Black Forest, as it were; it is Heidegger's idea of the dwelling that is a building that is a thinking grounded in the fourfold earth, sky, mortals, and divinities. This idea of a dwelling that is a building (that is, therefore, a thinking) is *in* the Black Forest, which is, this must be avowed, also the forest of werewolves, Little Red Riding Hood, Hansel and Gretel's edible house, and Black Forest cake. Countless legendary witches and factual witch trials mark the fourfold ground of this idea of a dwelling that is a building in the Black Forest. The ground of this dwelling is a ground spun of sorcery, a word whose Latin etymology means fate. Thus, the fourfold ground weaving earth, sky, mortals, and divinities is fate. Take it as you wish: chance, luck, opportunity, or destiny. A theology of insurrection operates within fate, which can turn on a dime or simply slowly spend a life span. Insurrection does not rebel against fate, but against fatalism, the warped dystopian distortion of fate that leads to various exoticisms, spurious transcendentalisms, and academic turf wars. For instance, a theology of insurrection is neither a repudiation of Christianity and an indictment of its universalism, nor is it a Christian apologetic clamoring the triumph of post-Christian, yet Christian, secular universalism.

II.

The Black Forest farm, as a dwelling that is a building that is a thinking, expresses a notion of caring, a thinking that is a caring. It is what the notion cares for that is misplaced and betrays a metaphysical dream of simplicity and purity, a longing to preserve autochthonous, earth-sprung folk spiritedness. There are other *buildings* that betray a different kind of thinking, even if such thinking could be said to be born of a caring just the same. Doubtless, Heidegger would not count these buildings as authentic dwellings. But, just as Heidegger's Black Forest farm fails to be the dwelling that it cares to be—nonmetaphysical—so too, these other *buildings* are also claimed as dwellings. They, too, are the product of a thinking that is a (kind of) caring. Let us explore just a few of these, to get a sharper sense of both, the exoticism of the Black Forest farm as dwelling and, in general, the exoticisms, metaphysical or not, that come to define *the way we live now*—the way of global capitalism.

It is men who wage war, so that to wage a war on terror sounds patently absurd. At the same time, precisely like an idea *in* the Black Forest, so-called terror turns forest dwelling into global drone-surveillance-and-remote-control-precision-weapon-building. The war on terror knows no bounds; it is a license to eavesdrop on allies and to institutionalize racial profiling; it is to the imagination like water to the seed as it beguiles and bewitches. It is fairy dust in the service of the transcendental vampirism of global capitalism as it blurs the boundary between national security and corporate interests, confusing and confounding them. The little people may wish to own a house, but the players dwell in a marketplace of pies in the sky. And this kind of global dwelling is all the more a thinking that is grounded in the fourfold earth, sky, mortals, and divinities. It is no less a ground spun of sorcery than the ground of the dwelling that is a building that is a thinking *in* the Black Forest.

It is *The Way We Live Now*, as in the 2001 TV miniseries based on 1875 satirical novel by Anthony Trollope, in which Augustus Melmotte, a European-born, mysteriously rich financier of uncertain European origins, swindles the whole city of London. Or again, it is a ground spun of sorcery, as in the actual Bernard Madoff 2008 investment scandal, which revealed that Madoff's grand Ponzi scheme targeted a wide array of investors, from individuals and nonprofits to hedge funds and big banks. Or, in between fact and fiction, there is, and by his own admission, the James Bond–like villain, and real-life Kim Dotcom (aka Kim Schmitz), the Internet entrepreneur and hacker, whose persona and lifestyle are derived straight from an Ian Fleming playbook. As he put it in an interview with CBS *60 Minutes* correspondent Bob Simon, "I was inspired by the James Bond movies, you know? Where, you know, some characters had private islands and super tankers converted into yachts and space stations and underwater homes."[19] A Dr. No in the flesh, Dotcom, the founder of the cloud file-sharing service Megaupload, was indicted in January 2012 for, among other charges, criminal copyright infringement "with estimated harm to copyright holders well in excess of $500,000,000."[20] He currently lives—dwells—on sixty acres of rolling hillside in New Zealand.

It is mortals who think, build, and dwell in a Christian, secular, or postsecular universe. It is mortals who aspire to transcend the mortal universe and make-believe or simply and squarely believe that God bleeds into his, sometimes her, creation or that Jesus Christ dies for their sins. And, again, it is still mortals who condemn Christianity or capitalism or colonialism in another, more subtle and self-exculpatory, gesture of transcendence, that of self-righteous indignation. Forgetting that, once more, and as always, it is human mortals who preach, pillage, rape, and annihilate the wretched of the earth. Because it is mortals who, born of the earth, reaching for the sky, believe or make-believe in or mourn or long for the majestic, the extraordinary, the august, the divine.

III.

The way we live now can be seen as the product of an experiment in thinking that is a (type of) caring aspiring to a modern humanist idea of a dwelling that many, including that bastion of liberalism, John Locke, have sought to legitimate in a Christian, biblical mandate derived from the Noachic covenant. Even if subjectivity is a constant process of iterative intra-activity, a performative production—in short, a habit, because this production is plastic and malleable—and a materialization that could not be without a fundamental resistance at the core of being, human beings are responsible for the ideas that they hatch and the beliefs that they fasten on to. At the same time, and for the same reason, human beings cannot really change the plasticity of their being. They can learn to be flexible, to adapt to an environment, or to resist. Each of these terms—*flexibility, adaptation,* and *resistance*—inherits an ideological and semantic tag within a historical conceptual scheme (for instance, the capitalist prizes a flexible workforce). All these terms seem to hinge on materiality and materialization. With this in mind, we can think of colonization as a form of deterritorialization of the colonized, of reterritorialization by the colonizer, where, in this *exchange,* flexibility, adaptation, and resistance come into play. The settler must reckon with *primitive* accommodations, the *native* must be plied into a worker bee. The concept of assimilation suggests a different story of *exchange,* one closer to the idea of identity as a social, cultural construction. Accordingly, the *savage* will be *civilized,* will be Christianized, will learn proper manners, will abandon her native tongue for one deemed more intelligent and befitting of human beings—even of *lesser* races. But is her assimilation necessarily a mark of her flexibility and adaptation? Or can one be flexible enough to adapt without assimilating the violent logic of the colonizer? What would this form of resistance look like?

Take the poet Aimé Césaire, who wrote in French against assimilationism. He was fighting colonialism from within colonial language and culture. What choice did he have? Which African dialect should the Martinican have adopted instead, or would any do just as well, and as though one could trade language in like a used car, as though one could undo one's past and start over? Language encircles us. If it is important to recognize that languages shape us, if our horizons broaden when we think and speak in more than one language, we must not therefore assume that in learning a foreign language we are freed from the prevailing group think of academic circles, from ethnocentric bias, or from the objectifying lens of the anthropologist measuring, cataloging, and classifying differences. Just as Thoreau's *Walden,* where the experiment of the simple life in a natural environment is nevertheless a social construct—a construct born of life in a social environment, in the same way, learning Arabic to think Islam in a non-Western way is an experiment born of, let us say, a native English-speaking being. It is a form of consumerism bridled by entitlement, which is to say, unbridled.

It was Ataturk, that great twentieth-century father of modern Turkey, who imposed the adoption of the Latin alphabet, to *modernize* Turkey by Westernizing its language. Here is yet another experiment in deterritorialization aimed toward a form of identity colonization: Turkey for the Turks, away with the Kurds or the Armenians. The novel component—not so novel in light of the French Republican calendar experiment a good century prior, which was intended to expunge religious and royalist sentiments from the French citizen—of the Ataturk experiment was its indiscriminate imposition on all citizens. It was a form of ethnocide meant to solidify a positive, homogeneous national identity. But the idea of fashioning identity by way of a *civilizing* education, the idea of saving souls by forcing the acquisition of a new language and forbidding the oppressed from speaking their native tongues is an old one, or, to be sure, it is of course one of the instruments in the arsenal of colonialism.

It was Captain Richard Pratt who could pretend to belong to the circle of more humane-minded reformers when, challenged by the persisting "Indian problem" and bothered by the bloodshed of the Indian Wars, he proposed (forced) assimilation of the natives to Americanize them. This founder of the Carlisle Indian Industrial School openly agreed "in a sense" "with the sentiment" of the saying attributed to General Phil Sheridan that "the only good Indian is a dead Indian." [21] He agreed "only in this: that all the Indian there is in the race should be dead. Kill the Indian, and save the man."[22] Pratt's evidence for his position on the "advantages of mingling Indians with Whites" rested on his certainty that the American way is superior for its allegiance, in principle, but that remains to be made actual in every "locality," to the "Bible principle of the brotherhood of men and the fatherhood of God," to the doctrine of the Declaration regarding self-evident truths, and to the Fifteenth Amendment to the Constitution concerning the rights to vote of all citizens regardless of race or creed.[23] He found spurious proof of this superiority in his assumption that blacks were benefited from their oppression, as it is what forced them into proximity with white American culture. That is, to the contrary of the policies of Indian removal from American territory that physically and legally alienated Native Americans and in effect condemned them to remain "savages," slavery exposed blacks to civilization even as it denied them the right to benefit from civilization's promises of freedom and enlightenment. Pratt's point is triumphant: "Left in Africa, surrounded by their fellow-savages, our seven millions of industrious black fellow-citizens would still be savages. Transferred into these new surroundings and experiences, behold the result. They became English-speaking and civilized, because forced into association with English-speaking and civilized people; became healthy and multiplied, because they were property; and industrious, because industry, which brings contentment and health, was a necessary quality to increase their value."[24] And thus "the greatest blessing that ever came to the Negro race" was "concealed" in the "ways of Providence" and of "slavery."[25] In light of this successful capitalist experiment, the boarding schools for young Native Americans forcibly removed from their parents, stripped from their tribal culture, forbidden to speak anything but English, and their long hair cut short, seem *civilized*. And yet the sentiment is genocidal through and through; the "savage," wherever she is from, is "life unworthy of life."[26] The only difference is that Jews or the mentally disabled under the Third Reich cannot be *converted* and saved. They are essentially and fundamentally inferior and corrupt. The irony is not lost that the racialization of the Jew ontologizes the dictum "once a Jew, always a Jew" and neither is the apparent contradiction that the one who is a convert to Judaism is no less a Jew than Abraham, the first Jew, is a convert.[27] If we continue this unpalatable chain of reasoning, we can perhaps expose the kind of logic at work in the ontological racialization of religion. Those who are assumed to be without religion, the "savages," may be assimilated, and converted, because they have, as it were, to the European settler, no religion. Jews, however, have the *wrong* religion: the one from which there is no coming back, the one that should be barred from conversion . . . because, Jews are too white to be mingled with whites without risk of corruption.[28]

IV.

Assimilation, forced conversion, modernization, and Westernization all collude ontologically in forgetting the other prong in the production of subjectivity, in only envisaging the "thingification," the objectification of subjects. The other prong is the essential resistance at the core of any being. Matter, racialized, dehumanized matter—a blank slate with its own limitations—is what this essential resistance is substituted for in the grand scheme toward *the way we live now*. A theology of insurrection refuses this poor substitution. But the question now becomes, why do so many allow it? The obvious answer is that they believe it; they believe in their dwelling, that it is a building that is a (caring) thinking. Kim Dotcom believes in his persona, Ataturk in his modern vision, Richard Pratt in his humaneness. All believe in a great coming of some sort, a new world order. Strangely enough, if some are still waiting for the parousia, Dotcom, Ataturk, and Pratt's visions have all come *true*—they have all come to pass. And if you see the lies in these truths, insurrection is at work.

In "Immanent Refusal of Conversion," Daniel Barber, reading Jacob Taubes, suggests that the ground of Christian identity is denial.[29] Specifically, it is a denial of the failure of messianic hope, the denial through which failure converts to survival, such that "Christian identity *is* conversion . . . the conversion that makes failure unthinkable."[30] This emphasis on messianic hope as a denial of messianic failure (as a failed historical prediction) would suggest that the folly and the scandal of the cross—that is, on the one hand, the scandal of the incarnation of a God made flesh in the son whom God forsakes for love of his people and allows to die on the cross the death reserved for slaves and, on the other hand, the folly of the resurrection, of one god who renders all others inconsequential and who, in faith, is the promise of eternal life after death—this folly and scandal of the cross, which in themselves sound *too good to be true*, must be transcended in (the) denial (of history) for Christianity to endure.[31] Or, otherwise put, faith is now more than a passion that belies reason or certainty, because faith is rooted in the misidentification of a failure (a historical failure) with a(n illusory) success (with an illusory future)—in denial. This denial is the condition for the Christian identity in Jesus Christ as Lord and savior. Denial would therefore be the condition for the "survival," in Barber's term, of an interior dialogue effecting a (hopeful) personal relationship with the divine in the flying face of messianic failure. This then is how Christian identity is "conversion that makes failure unthinkable." Or simply put: avoid disappointment and convert to hope deferred.

For Barber, the Freudian psychoanalytic critique of religion, as it emphasizes the illusory nature of eschatological hope or redemptive futurity (mired as these are in wish fulfillment writ large through mass delusion), helps make clear that Christianity is the culprit underwriting the racialization of capitalism from precolonial times to postcoloniality. In other words, the secularization thesis is reinterpreted here as a process of conversion bent on repeating the same dualistic logic (pagan/ Christian; savage/human being; etc. . . .) under a new name. Christian identity, predicated on denial as it is, cannot endure but through forced conversion, forcing the others to find God in Christ, to identify with Christ's message of unity, to rally under the banner of humanist ideals. Denial of the failure of the messianic gives hope deferred to the masses—that there is life after death for the true believer or that tomorrow's humanity will bring all peoples together as one. Tomorrow is another day. Christian identity is why, Barber appears to say, we can forget and deny genocides and pretend that the future holds promise for all of humanity, even its victims. In this sense, conversion, as a survival mode of Christian identity, seems to depend on the transformation of the psychic violence required for the maintenance of denial into a racial and colonial violence toward the others.

While Barber's critique stems from an immanent view of history (as in history is the now), it is a Christocentric view of history, where "now" starts with Christianity. If it is, as Barber writes, "not about getting back to how things used to be," but "about making present that which has disappeared," and if this, too, I would suggest, is a form of insurrection from within, so that "the past is not past," but "it is now," then I would like to suggest that the problem is not Christian identity as original cause, Platonic idea in which all divisive universalizing tactics of oppression participate.[32] Just as when the Holocaust is held as the exemplar of genocide, this leads many to infer that genocides are the exception to the rule—that there's only the one studied in all school textbooks, so, too, let us not make the same mistake when it comes to the problem of identity. Christian identity, or its *survival*, may indeed be grounded in the denial of messianic failure, but the logic of conversion at work in this identity is eerily similar to the logic of language: a name calls forth, makes present, what it names—the name negates the fact that it is nothing but a name. Insofar as a denial of (a historic) messianic failure is a denial that a future did not become present with an affirmation that it has, that it is present, this denial operates the same way that negation does in language. I can name my mother only when I can negate (deny) that in naming her I have lost her.

It is Julia Kristeva who, in *Black Sun*, theorizes that the move to the Symbolic and into language necessitates the "negation" of the infantile stage of primary narcissism—of oneness with the mother. For her, denial of the negation spells depression as a mourning for some unattainable Primal Thing. Negation finds no loss in the substitution of primary oneness with the maternal body for the name with which that mother body is recognized. But the depressed person is, like the unbeliever, the one for whom the word is a trickster that hides its failure to be what it represents. This is why we can venture to say that it is from the depressed person's perspective that Christianity is "a denial of the failure of the messianic." Otherwise put, Christianity is negation in language. You believe in Jesus Christ, son of God and savior because the words are meaningful, so meaningful that they might as well *be* that to which they refer. The promise of salvation is enough because it *is* the salvation, as though in naming my mother I could forget myself in oneness with her, as though the promise of the word performed itself in its utterance. It happens that the word is made flesh. But, if Christianity recognizes this logic, then it also recognizes that the limit of its universality is language: not that we all speak the same language, but that when we speak we believe, we trust, we want to trust that our words are true. We know, though, that such is not always the case.

Thus there are bastards, Dotcoms, and Madoffs, for whom conversion is a duplicitous act. It is too good to be true: you're James Bond; you're going to be so rich. And there are Christians, and Young Turks, for whom conversion is the solution to that moment when the recognition of the self can't abide in itself, can't believe itself, unless the others do as well. The story is too good to be true, so that to maintain the fiction of a new world requires the destruction of the others who would not convert to its story. A story too good to be true, but "he who will not be baptized shall die." A savior? What does that mean? And of course I am usurping Kristeva's own logic of sense, because for her negation is not a denial of the failure of words to be what they name. Only the depressed, or the unbeliever, sees it this way. We extrapolate: only the savages and the uncivilized see it this way. Conversion either already is—you believe, negation is at work, there is no loss in language; or it won't happen, it can't happen: you can't believe what you can't believe. Who is in bad faith? Who is in denial? The one who believes her words and their story or the one for whom the words cover up the Real?

V.

Between "One God, one people," and "Follow me, I am the way, in me there is neither Greek nor Jew," between the Islamic perfection of monotheism and Christian universalism in discipleship, who has the better story? Whose story is less violent and bloody? Apples and oranges? Immanence or transcendence? Or is it the other way around? For Mohammed was a peacemaker amidst warring tribes, suggesting that the first pillar of Islam, of submission to Allah, marks a moment of conversion, that it is in the conversion that one comes to grasp what already is: which is that the oneness of God dictates the oneness of God's people. You don't need to believe that Jesus, the forsaken son of God, saves all humanity when he dies on the cross a death reserved to the lowest of the lowliest kind. Humanity is already saved; it is already one. But you do need to believe in one humanity. This means that whether humanity already is one or its oneness is to come amounts to the same thing. The result is the same, and the mechanism of belief is the same.

How so? In the first case, you dispense with the holy water, this much is true: the earth, its mortals all reaching for the sky with their little gods, all really already is One and with God. But if you are not a believer, then you are, indeed, an infidel, an enemy of humanity's immanent oneness. In the second case, God intervenes, something happens, and in Christ we are all united. But if you are not a believer you are also an infidel, an enemy of humanity's transcended oneness. So it is true, in the second case, there are ontological shenanigans; whereas in the first there are none. But the belief is the premise for both ontologies—the immanent or the transcendent—and the belief is in language, in the language we fall for. The belief transforms—it transcends—what you see: and now, either you see it for what you believe it always already was, by the grace of God, or, now again, you see it for what you believe it has become by the grace of God. Belief, in effect, and paradoxically, implies that it does not matter which ontology you favor because, precisely, it is all a matter of belief.

Still, is not the point of contention a seriously problematic one? Namely, that Christian identity demands a violent rejection of ontic differences in order to make place for ontological universality; it stamps out difference; it is exclusive, by definition. Whereas, on the contrary, Islamic identity, in principle, demands no such rejection of ontic differences? Opposites, one and many, are not contraries. Perhaps they are more properly understood as binaries. But slippage is easy, as for instance even the de facto motto of the United States, *e pluribus unum*, can attest. It is surmised that the motto was directly reproduced from an English publication widely distributed in prerevolutionary America.

The *Gentleman's Magazine* featured the motto on its title page together with the same illustration of a bunch of flowers handheld into a bouquet, from the magazine's inception in 1731 into the nineteenth century.[33] Yet it is the metaphor of the melting pot that most would likely associate with the motto today. Out of many, one: but how? The flowers bunched into a single bouquet retain all their differences. The melting pot clearly does away with differences. Slippage of the ideal is easy, but, worse, the ideal itself might be a subterfuge. And, as alluded to a moment ago, this is the common critique of the Enlightenment that issues forth into a downright indictment of Christocentric Western civilization and global capitalism. A theology of insurrection agrees with this critique. But it is suspicious of ideals, even when they clamor their immanence. Perhaps especially for that reason. Let us see why.

Social contract theory would have us believe that human beings stand to benefit equally from relinquishing some of their liberties, and yet, historically, some human beings, to wit, women, slaves, colonized peoples, African Americans, gays, lesbians, bisexuals, queers and trans-gendered, and proletarians have been and remain subjugated by the structural inequities underwritten by the purported egalitarian and libertarian nature of our polity. Like a verbal dispute, the one evoked by William James in his lecture "What Pragmatism Means," for instance: the ones, let us say, the hard-core idealists, will tell you that the man chasing the squirrel around the trunk of a tree does go around the squirrel in going opposite him from all four cardinal directions. Whereas, the others, in this case, the hardened materialists, will say that the man and the squirrel both go round the tree, but not each other. But, says James, it all depends on what you mean by "going round." Likewise, it all depends on what you mean by Oneness. Do the many become one? Or are they always already one in spite of being many? In accepting God, are they now joined as one? Or, in submitting to one God, do they now accept that the many are really one? Or, again, it also depends what you mean by out of many, one: the bouquet of flowers or the melting pot. And finally, thus, when it comes to the principle themselves, the ideals, and the creeds: One God, one people; follow me, in me there is neither Greek nor Jew; *e pluribus unum;* all men are created equal, etc.—when it comes to these ideals spun out of earthbound mortals shooting for the sky with their hidden aspirations to become little gods, it is simply too hard to believe that some ideals are better than others because they presumably interpellate the subject without forcing an impossible conversion on her, without implicating her in a deep web of denial the return of which is violence to the others.

VI.

What would such an interpellation look like? Would it be more *natural*? Or would it require instead a certain *cultivation*? Where would it come from? Would it be *autochthonous*, the earthling of chthonic gods? Or *allochthonous*, the Other buried deep within the earth, haunting voice of unconscious dark chthonic spirits and demons? Whose thinking would be building the dwelling in which this being would be interpellated? Would such interpellation be refractory to insights? That is, would it be safe from, well insulated against the shock and fright of the new and foreign idea? I ask, again, in whose language would it speak? Would the interpellated subject be any less interpellated if he were to speak the language of the one whom he, in his interpellated being, perceives as the other? But if you say yes, then you are guilty of the same colonial logic, that the civilized one would become a savage for speaking a savage tongue or that the savages could be civilized: it is just a matter of beating the savage out of her. Or that Aimé Césaire could never write in French against French assimilationism. Yet, if that were the case, untranslatability would explain double lives: Nazi executioner by day, and loving father by night. All in one and without contradiction. But, again, this would also mean that one could be both savage and civilized, that in becoming savage, or in becoming civilized, one simply added another mask to wear, like a change of clothes, so that both the violence against the other and the love for one's kin become symptoms of the denial that one's identity is nothing but a costume. How can there be no cognitive dissonance, might ask the psychologist. Only if there is no necessary impetus toward an integrated personality; only if the many selves are better served by their disunion, their heterogeneity. Oil and vinegar. Finite and infinite. Secret lives = different selves = changing person. Savage and civilized. Civilized and savage. Both, savage or civilized. And, yet, this is not the case, unless we count Batman's Harvey Dent, the hero district attorney, who is also Two Face, the disfigured, unpredictable, and schizoid criminal whose coin toss determines whether he will kill you or spare you. Only in this madness can we reconcile this two in one without contradiction.

In his *Surviving Auschwitz,* Primo Levi defines the grey zone of morality in which the saved, those who will not drown, those who will not give up on survival, dwell. Thanking God for escaping from oven selection next to one's condemned bunkmate; owing one's survival to theft and connivance . . . how, indeed, does one survive the survivor's guilt? Here, again, it is not madness, but it might as well be madness. It is an infernal no-man's-land, out of which there is no way precisely because one cannot be reconciled with oneself. Yet countless ordinary citizens, those who gave up their neighbors and benefited from it and so forth, go on living as if the fault was never theirs. If their inaction makes them complicit, why are they not burning in hell? They live matter-of-factly, falling in place wherever the wind blows. But is this a Taoist *wu wei,* is the ordinary bystander really living her life in a mode of non-interference with the Tao of the universe? Or is this entropy at work? Is interpellation in the service of entropy? Is this ordered structuring of subjectivity in the service of equilibrium by way of survival? Is dif-férance not in the service of life beyond the immediacy-craving human? And how does interpellation trump this différance if not by hiding the latter's temporalizing mark, by timing cognition to trigger immediate recognition through the habit of mimesis: smiling back at a smiling baby until she knows, without even having to think about it, to smile in return for your smile. This trumping might also be how interpellation *changes* the difference of différance. I recognize myself in the behavior that I mimic; I recognize myself in *any* behavior that I mimic. The mim-icry *is* my reflection. This chameleon complex, if you will, might be how one can be Two Face or bystander. The chameleon complex could be a different way of interpreting the Stanford Prison Experiment in which college students were randomly assigned inmate or prison guard status, and where, as prison guards, with the expectations and powers the sta-tus calls forth and without orders from above, these perfectly nonpsy-chopathic young men became abusive toward other perfectly nonpsy-chopathic young men.[34]

If the experiment has been used to show behavior's situational attri-bution and the role cognitive dissonance plays in this attribution, what are the conditions that make these behavioral responses possible, but, one hopes, not necessary? The interpellation of subjectivity happens before the subject responds to meet the expectations set by his situation. Likewise, negation (the negation of the loss of the Real in accession to the Symbolic) precedes the experience of dissonance (dissonance between one's beliefs and one's actions, for instance) so that the greater the dissonance the better one resolves it—as in the denial of the failure of the messianic: the prophesy cannot be wrong, even if it is, because there is always tomorrow. Because you cannot make me do something to which I can't agree, I will agree, says the bystander. Because the more I hurt you, the more I love you, says the sadist. Because the more extreme the oscillation between personalities, the more anchored and unreachable is the being at their center, says Two Face. And différance makes both interpellation and negation possible, but not necessary, as evidenced, for instance, in autistic, anxiety-laden, repetitive behavior and in the world of words without meanings of depression. So again, to resume this bifurcated point, the issue is that of the formation of subjectivity through this operation of transversal negativity that sunders and sutures the consciousness of a nascent subject learning not only to recognize herself in her image, but learning also the habit of reflecting and internalizing the outside—learning behavior in-itself, how to act outside of oneself. Little R.-M. recently learned that showing one's middle finger is an insult. She does not pause to question the nature of the insult or the absurdity of interdicting a movement that, in its absence of signification, is not really a behavior. She wonders what is so bad about her middle fingers and how much she can move them or lift them without being in the wrong. The situation does not matter to her, a fact that reveals how interpellation is always already at work. She is a convert. But is that not why she could write in French against assimilationism (why she could give a *bras d'honneur* in the first place)?

Swapping languages is not what makes the Real changing difference, and especially not if humanity is one in being many. The change cannot just be a matter of transplantation and expatriation. Soon enough, the new language inhabits you, not unlike the old one did. We cannot simply leave earth behind for the ether of spirits. Behavior modification may change a person, but it does not undo or erase a person's past, even if she does forget her native tongue. And, more to the point, it is not a safeguard against the violence of the thought oblivious to its own belief in its building of a dwelling that it can believe in. Let us not confuse the infinite possibilities of immanence with the trompe l'oeil illusion of belief's immediacy. That is the habit that needs our attention.

If there is a theology of insurrection, it must be conceived in the thickness, the opacity, and the recalcitrance of subjectivity. One can envisage interpellation as a Whiteheadian concrescence of feelings and concepts incessantly swirling into actual entities coming to a head into a nexus; a subject/superject open to the breadth and depth of her interpellated being and who, for that reason, cannot have faith in any gods or in any one god, though she cannot help but to have faith or to desist. To have faith or to capitulate. To have faith or to lose face. But to have faith in what?

VII.

George Yancy, in his introduction to his edited volume *Christology and Whiteness: What Would Jesus Do?*, reveals to the Christian reader that white supremacy underpins his faith and his Christian identity. If Jesus were alive today, he would be black and poor and he would be fighting against white power, so that to ask the question "what would Jesus do?" requires you to recognize not only how far you are from the Christian ideal, but that it is you who is the problem. You are, in an echo of Friedrich Schleiermacher, the cultured despiser of Christianity for assuming the identity of Jesus, namely, that Jesus would do what you would do. But the feeling of absolute dependence is far from romantic, it is the despair Kierkegaard relates in his *Sickness Unto Death* and, in Christian terms, it is sin defined as a misrelation of the self to itself. But the interpellated subject is racist and does not even know it; he is in despair, but does not even know it. This epistemology of ignorance, to borrow the concept from Charles Mills, gives the bystander her lifelong buoyancy and is perhaps the virtue of the chameleon complex in which a self comes to recognize itself as it reflects its outside and folds it right in, without even knowing it.

Césaire, in his "Discourse on Colonialism," captured the downside of Enlightenment liberal ideals best when he argued that colonization decivilizes the colonizer and that Hitlerism is nothing but the boomerang effect of colonization. This theology of insurrection agrees. Let us see why.

Perhaps it is easy enough to see the lies, the "dishonest equations Christianity = civilization, paganism = savagery."[35] Perhaps one can come to realize the double standard of humanism, that its concept of the universal rights of man "has been—and still is—narrow and fragmentary, incomplete and biased and, all thing considered, sordidly racist."[36] But we might venture that corruption is at work, that the humanist ideals are true and good. Yet Césaire exposes the lie as inextricably linked to the ideal. As though the ideal were never more than a cover to hide brutishness from plain sight, a grand form of irony substituting a beautiful and inspiring idea of humankind for barbarity, an ideal of humanity effecting the denial of its depravity. A form of self-deception and wish fulfillment, a form of mass delusion that is so powerful that it denies the alienation and the dissonance that it ought to foment. Like one of those powerful deflections: sublimation. Men eventually prefer the life of the mind over that of the appetites. Except that sublimation, here, is a lie. By all appearances, one passes for a humanist: if you really try, you too can believe that slavery is a blessing in disguise, that feeding the labor force into the market and commodifying beings readies them for the day that, free, they will become productive consumers. Great! Today we say "people did not know any better." They believed these asinine positions. And, in Socratic fashion, we maintain that people should not be blamed for what they did not know then. But this ignorance, if it is not altogether feigned, demonstrates the Nietzschean point that all knowledge is a form of deception. Men are in desperate need of the ideal—humanists especially, it would seem. To wit, the great humanist Ernest Renan, who declares, in his *La réforme intellectuelle et morale*, that "we aspire not to equality but to domination. The country of a foreign race must become once again a country of serfs, of agricultural laborers, or industrial workers. It is not a question of eliminating the inequalities among men but of widening them and making them into a law."[37] The lie is at work in the very deployment of the "humanist" thinking that informs the building of the modern, bourgeois dwelling.

John Locke's views on property, as expounded in his *Second Treatise of Civil Government*, have been and still are compelling to many. While Locke's social contract theory is generally recognized as the inspiration behind the Jeffersonian Declaration of Independence in which it is written that "all men are created equal, that they are endowed by their Creator with certain unalienable Rights, that among these are Life, Liberty, and the pursuit of Happiness," the substitution of the right to property with the right to pursue happiness is worth puzzling over.

All this is well known, but as property is precisely the kind of idea that births a dwelling (that is a building that is a thinking), it is worth exploring whether the biblical universalism of the Noachic covenant with which Locke justifies his liberal economy, and which is precisely what compels so many, is not really the product of the wish that robber barons be made captains of industry. Again, here is the question of the virtue or innocence of the ideal. God's covenant is unconditional. God promises never again to destroy His creation and tells Noah that every moving thing shall be food for man (Genesis 9, NKJV). Otherwise put, and also according to Locke, God gives the earth and its creatures to all men in common. But, as Locke develops this notion, even in this (biblical) state of nature, every man has a right to property in his own person and in that of the fruit of his labor, although in such a state of nature no one can take more than his fair share without it going all to waste. Still, as God chased Adam and Eve from the Garden of Eden, he thus condemned them to a life of labor. This is why, in a civil society, the industrious have a right to the land that they develop and to the resources that they exploit. And this is also why the "savages," like all inferior creatures over which God gives man dominion, only have a right to "occupy" the land on which they live but have no right to own it, as it was stipulated in the nineteenth-century "Doctrine of Discovery," which justified land expropriation of non-Christian territories and peoples since the 1455 Papal Bull *Romanus Pontifex* that gave Portugal a right to the "savage" lands and peoples of West Africa.[38] Thus civil society aims to protect, more than anyone's *natural* property, all *expropriated* property, and this *in perpetuity*. The right to the pursuit of happiness is the right of the wealthy to pursue more wealth and the right of the poor to chase after a dream of equality. The secular version of unalienable universal rights would extend to all of humanity, but this humanity's origin, sex, and race would matter—it would be the example as ideal form that excludes all others, far from being what it ought to be: far from the exception that justifies the rule, as, when God chooses Abraham, He chooses all his descendants, Greek, Jew, or Muslim, no exceptions.

A theology of insurrection agrees. But turn to Russian Stalinism, Chinese Maoism, or Khmer Rouge communism. These revolutionary regimes are driven by some form of the agrarian ideal as counter to capitalism or to Christian civilization and to its violent logic of conversion, to be sure. Yet, they, too, have called for conversion, even while maintaining the opposite, namely, that all peoples are one, as, for instance, in the Soviet utopia of a classless, egalitarian, and inclusive society. Here the utopian promise of a harmonious, uniform, and classless society, hinged, as it was, on a belief in the "malleability of individuals" and their ability to "become good Soviet citizens," cannot be reconciled without contradiction to the bleak reality of population purges.[39] While the Soviet Union outlawed work on eugenics and never officially endorsed a genocidal racial ideology, because such "'zoological' thinking" was associated with the "Nazi system in particular" and "bourgeois society in general," the institution of the Soviet project nevertheless called for the extermination of millions for not belonging to the right class, for holding on to bourgeois aspirations to nationalism or national identity, or for not projecting the right image of internationalism.[40] That is, social class, behavior, or nationality, while not defined as inherent biological marks to which inferior or subhuman status might be ascribed, as was the case with race in Nazi Germany, were nevertheless treated as if they were.[41] Revolution and logic of conversion collude.

Just as it is too easy to blame the Holocaust on one man who would be a monster, so is it too easy to blame the lesser-known genocides as the result of one paranoid man or one handful of génocidaires. The ideal might appeal, but to verify it is to refute it. The would-be cure (communism) is worse—in these instances—than the poison (capitalism). But each, as an ideal, can appeal. Cause-and-effect rationalization has to stop somewhere. The sin of capitalism does not exculpate, nor does it give license to, genocidal violence, even if it does explain, as the linchpin cause, such revolutionary brutality. Christian whiteness does not exculpate, nor does it give license to, the state of Israel's mistreatment of Palestinians, even if we posit the proto-Christian sin of whiteness as the alpha and the omega of a "decivilized" global market. And, finally, it is a tunnel vision view of history again, a Christocentric view, that, precisely in attacking this view, would be unable to read history but through its focus. One could take the case of the Armenian genocide as a counter to the equation of Christian identity *alone* (as denial of the failure of the messianic) with forced conversion and genocidal homogenization in the name of a present to come if you burry the past and make it, and its beautiful manifold, disappear into the oneness of the white universal.

Christian Armenians under the Ottoman Empire were a subclass of citizens, with fewer rights. At the eve of the start of the First World War, power over the weakened and shrunken Ottoman Empire was seized by a triumvirate of Young Turks who, when they entered the war, aligned with the Central Powers of Austria-Hungary and Germany against the Allied Powers of France, Great Britain, Italy, and Russia. In this war of imperial, colonial powers, the Ottoman Empire, which had failed to industrialize, offered a big territorial boon. In this view, Christianity and liberal economy are the threat that encircles the Ottomans. This much is understandable. But, the denial of the failure of the messianic, if it means necessary homogenization, fails to explain both the fact of Christian Armenians and, therefore, also their genocide as triggered by this logic of denial. For, in the first place, Armenians were converts to Christianity after they were established geographically in their lands for a good millennium. Otherwise put, a long time before they were absorbed into the Ottoman Empire. But, in the second place, Armenian Christianity had and still has its own papacy that rejects the Chalcedonian creed of the two persons of Christ. This means that when the Crusaders discovered these other Christians from Anatolia, the Western world grew infatuated with this most ancient Christian civilization bordering Mount Ararat from all sides and dating back to Noah's time. And when, in the 1800s, Protestant Christian missions were making their way into Asia Minor and the Middle East, it is these oppressed Christian Armenians that they sought to "convert." So that what must be reckoned with is the way in which conversion to Christianity, first in 301 ad, helped the Armenians preserve an identity in spite their land being at constant crossroads. The early fifth-century monk Mesrop Mashtots invented the Armenian alphabet to unify and preserve Armenian culture even outside its shrunken kingdom.

The point is that Christianity and the written word, in this case, were defensive strategies against homogenization and assimilation into invader cultures, even against Byzantine Christianity itself. In the 1800s, again, the double conversion of Christian Armenians to Western Christianity can also be seen as a defensive strategy against second-class citizen status and treatment under Ottoman rule. But, in the eyes of the Turks and circa 1915, all Armenians were decreed traitors from within: traitors for seeming Western for being Christian, traitors for seeming Western because some were economically successful. Even Christianity, with its identitarian logic founded on denial of messianic failure, is many peoples. And Islam, in spite of its identitarian logic founded on an immanent oneness in plurality, here, reduces by genocide the many to one. The secular identity embraced by the Young Turks, modeled as it might have been on the European Enlightenment ideal, demonstrates another way to understand the denial of the failure of the messianic as the denial of the failure of Islam's own idealistic creed. It demonstrates that the affirmation of its own creed can spell its negation in the denial that is called Pan Turkism.

Colonization "decivilizes" the colonizer. It is a form of contact that suspends the chameleon complex or, rather, that inverts it: from now on, the outside must look like me and fit into my God-given worldview. When I travel, I will take my own house along with my suitcase; I will have you build the roads on which I wish to travel my way. Contact on my terms: whites only, *Jude raus!* Kill the Indian, save the human being. Turkey for the Turks: "After all, who remembers today the extermination of the Armenians?" asked Adolf Hitler in August 1939.

The structural sin of whiteness is the denial of the failure to be Christian, a denial whose symptom is the equation of Western civilization with Christianity, from Constantine's conversion on, such that even Enlightenment secular ideals are viewed as the offspring of Christianity. It is in this way that one can also understand Thomas J. J. Altizer's *New Gospel of Christian Atheism*, the herald of a new theology, of a universal Christianity that stands opposed to a universal Church, "one of a universal body, a universal body which is an apocalyptic body, and thus the body of Here Comes Everybody."[42] The Christian sin is the denial of the failure to be Christian; it is the denial of the failure of the messianic; it is the denial of the death of God; it is not recognizing one's own despair, but instead reconciling any dissonance by blaming and projecting one's own sin on the Other. This sickness unto death, then, is the sick habit of identity, as it functions like an ideal that interpellates you even when you don't believe or especially when you don't believe. You'll work that much harder to disprove your disbelief. You'll equate the suffering of the Other with the dolorism of the Passion. "In the eyes of the negro," writes Jean-Paul Sartre in *Black Orpheus*, his introduction to Senghor's *Anthologie de la nouvelle poésie nègre et malgache de langue française* (1948), "[the white man's] religion wants to make him share the responsibility for a crime of which he is the victim; it wants to persuade him to see the kidnappings, the massacres, the rapes, the tortures which have covered Africa with blood, as a legitimate punishment, deserved tests."[43]

But, in the eyes of the white man, he recognizes his own sin as the black man's fault.

VIII.

During the Algerian War of Independence, Albert Camus fell out of grace from an intellectual and political standpoint for his moderate position. The *pied noir* raised in poverty by an illiterate deaf mother was shaped by French colonial education. A French Algerian by birth, he hoped France could do right by Algeria and end its discriminatory practices, that nothing French could be preserved unless justice were preserved. At root was his recognition that, though French was his mother tongue, Algeria was his homeland or, as Claire Messud suggests in her review of Camus' recently translated *Algerian Chronicles*, France was his father, Algeria his mother. He, too, was a byproduct of colonialism for whom French education offered a way out of misery.

And when Camus approached the great De Gaulle to propose the simple solution of French citizenship for all Algerians—this in March 1958, two months before the general retook power, having used, among others, the slogan "We are all Frenchmen, from Dunkirk to Tamanrasset!"—De Gaulle reportedly scoffed, "Right, and we'll have fifty niggers [*bougnoules*] in the Chamber of Deputies."[44]

Camus's "moderate" position, in this case, is that of justice for all. It is moderate because it is not the position issued of a simple alternative (a French Algerian with a subclass of natives or a Frenchless Algeria). It is a moderate position because it is an all-or-nothing position (all Algerians are French or France would not be French anymore). There is, in this way, no alternative. This was Camus's answer to the problem of French colonialism, because he refused to answer a wrong with another wrong—to answer the wrong of colonial exploitation with the wrong of forced expatriation of Algerian born French citizens.

Dwelling is the question that must be thought. It is the luxury of long lineage and the dream of pure origins that, coupled together, give the ones who belong a sense that their identity is rooted in an unadulterated yet richly cultural soil. But what gives those who have been displaced and oppressed, or enslaved by a genocidal colonial regime, the sense that they, too, are owed long lineage and the land of their origins? And, if identity is inextricably tied to land, should we stay put like a tree? Should we build fences around settlements to keep the others out? No one can own land in perpetuity save through a denial of mortality. Identity is that denial. It is a dwelling that is a building that is a thinking.

Probably the Black Forest peasant dwells there like hand in glove. A fit seemingly made in heaven. Destiny. On the contrary, the questions of a Pan-African identity or of the possibility of a Latin American philosophy or of Palestinian state are byproducts of colonial oppression. Captain Pratt might view the questions as revelatory of the silver lining of the white oppression of "savages," but the questions are not mere intellectual exercises; they are the questions that confront and inhabit those who, not unlike Camus, experience and understand that their dwelling is a building, sometimes a house of cards, and that no one chooses where and when to be born. And yet, in spite of this, one will choose to be born in that Sartrean sense that one chooses one's self. A theology of insurrection understands the bind and the burden of inheritance. One can choose like the Martinican Césaire to write Négritude in French, like the Algerian-born Jewoman Hélène Cixous to write in white ink but in French, or like Camus to write of exile and alienation in French. One can choose to do so, and in this strange way one chooses to be black in a world of white supremacy; to be a woman, and a Jewoman at that, in a man's world; to be a *pied noir*, a blackfoot, born French on Algerian soil. Oil rising to the surface, sediment settling to the bottom.

When Leopoldo Zea, the Mexican philosopher, affirms that the seed of Latin American philosophy cannot be found in pre-Columbian culture and instead argues that Latin American philosophy has to accept its European inheritance, he is refusing to live in the shadow of ideas not his own.[45] He claims them. The Americas are a product of European thought; they are utopias. In the case of North America, the experiment proves bigger and better than the European ideal. But Latin America is a result of the failure of the European ideal. The denial of the failure of the messianic is exposed once, and precisely because, its foreign and imposed cultural inheritance is recognized as a seed—a chance for a new way of life.

But, for the Peruvian thinker Augusto Bondy, Latin American philosophy is a fraud, it is the discourse of unauthentic beings who falsely see themselves in ideas that belong to different circumstances, in "the existential projects of other men."[46] "Man constructs his self-image . . . ; he is, in the words of Ortega, the novelist of himself" (236). But, as "plagiarist," he is "self-deluding" and "almost never finds himself" in this "imitated thought" (236). Unauthentic philosophies thus fail to provide a truthful image of reality and through them one only thinks one knows oneself. But this "anthropological illusion" has a "truthful side" (236–37). Unauthentic philosophies, "by lying reveal their defective existence . . . they succeed, unwittingly, as an expression of the lack of a complete and original being" (237).

A theology of insurrection recognizes the "anthropological illusion" at the heart of philosophy as part of the chameleon complex—the folding in of the outside as symptomatic of faith in language—faith as negation of loss in representation—and as Christian sin—the self-deluding self-image of interpellated subjectivity. This is its seed. With it new life springs forth. Insurrection from within.

IX.

There is in the Black Forest Heidegger's idea of a dwelling that is a building that is a thinking. Open wide a window and, in the dead of winter, this warm hearth will soon be inhospitable to mortals. Heat will escape and cold will set in.

Just as the surest way to prevent your guests from overstaying their welcome is to treat them as guests, so too we can dwell here on earth, and even build the house of our dreams, but, like nature that abhors a vacuum and heat flow that disperses energy faster, our best order of things may tend to their preservation only in waiting for the opportunity to do away with them.

This opportunity is the chance event, sin, *pistis,* the break, the miracle in the machinery of repetition, the cut of reality instantiating itself, setting itself up as a mode of repetition.[47] This is how the basic tenet of evolution, that living things must adapt or die so that adaptation commands the survival of the fittest, accords with the Second Law of Thermodynamics, namely that all things tend to equilibrium.[48] Imagine this behemoth, the earth, alive since it hatched, its energy dispersing, and dispersing faster whenever the earth produces order, that is, "whenever it gets a chance." A chance event, yesterday, is called the living cell. Today, the human being. Imagine evolution in the service of life as entropy. Imagine preservation in the service of dissipation. Imagine the space of a being at home where being at home affords comfort and security, but for the sake of intensity, the intensity of the moment when your first child leaves home; the intensity of a shared existence in love; the intensity of expenditure through works, passions, or play: intensity that burns and dissipates, that makes life worth living to the point of life's exhaustion.

Intensity, "whenever it gets a chance," is that greatest effort with minimum gain, what is also called sacrifice, a form of living that is the gesture of generosity.[49] Life that gives itself over to death only when life has nothing left to give. Not a gesture of longing for immortality, not a martyrdom or saving death, not an effort to restore or redeem the living. Not a preservation of life. Not a Christ dying for our sins. Not an atoning sacrifice. If there is a productive and creative value in suffering, it is not because suffering is some cross to bear and price to pay for our trespasses; it does not rehabilitate the offenders; it is not deserved. If there is a productive and creative value in suffering, it is only insofar as suffering is absurd, and in this "suffering carries within itself its own refusal to suffer . . . it opens onto revolt and liberty."[50] That is, sacrifice, as maximum effort with minimum gain, is also how we can "encounter the ontological break" in pain and suffering whereby the law of measure is rejected, as Job rejects it in his categorical refusal to convert to and in his existential revulsion by the transcendental vampirism of redemptive and retributive justice doled out from the eternal sky above.[51] The pain and suffering of Job is not sacrificial until he rejects it together with the "theodicy that would defend the justice of God."[52] In this theodicy, in the will to believe in a transcendental logic of suffering, the greatest effort that yields minimum gain is suffering itself. But this is a grotesque perversion of sacrifice. It is violence pitted against whatever we may call nature or the natural order, violence against the earth that is alive and deterritorialized, violence against the earth that has become a brain: violence that brings "a great chaos, a great immeasurableness."[53]

A theology of insurrection understands that earth, sky, mortals, and divinities are bound by fate. Resources are limited; death is assured. We are sojourners, not here to stay forever, but to live once and for all.

AFTERWORD

Catherine Keller

Just after the word has been so riveting, the news so new but time-deep enough to be good, one doesn't, after all, want more—words. One wants a dance, a splash of blood-red sunset with a streak of black paint, a Zen breath, a song of wordless lament and convulsive pleasure. Or perhaps just an echo of the last words of the last gospel: "Resources are limited; death is assured. We are sojourners, not here to stay forever, but to live once and for all."

Once, in the utter singularity of a life, and *fini*: not forever but "for all." Oh, there's the multiplier, already dislodging itself from any mere oneness of a once. In the face of those limited resources for mortals and perhaps for gods as well, those catastrophically and increasingly limited resources of earth and sky: that "for all" may after all call a few more words here. To live "for all"—that may be a risky, indeed terminal, practice. It sounds rather unmistakably gospel. Sounds like the golden unruliness of the impossible love. But these new gospels aren't lovey-dovey ones. They militantly exorcise the clichés, the soft self-reassurances of too many centuries of bad faith. Oh, but nonetheless, the fourth criterion, the commitment to the struggle "for an ethical-ecological vision of Life," proposes a leftist edge that "eludes dogmatic certainty" and so presents itself as trustworthily non-Stalinizing: "We side with life, with vitality, with affirmation, and with compassion, empathy, love, and care for others and ourselves." For all, indeed—and so against the power and capital that is devastating the dwelling place and the life capacity of all. But of "the least of these" first of all.

Such biblically haunted care can only annoy the cranky specters of revolutionary nostalgia. So I trust—yes, I have faith—in its insurrectionary spirit. There is something really new to its news. That means then that it is not superseding any really good news that preceded it. It does not compete for canonical status. It does not join the tacky novelty that trades its ancestors in or sells them out for the new truth—of theism or of atheism. Yet the first principle of the theology of insurrection confesses its filiation with the tradition of radical theology in its "never-ending reflection on the many and multiple 'deaths of God' of the *inherited traditions*." It is thereby cannily avoiding the modernist absolute of the news-making earlier death of God theology. In relation to the vector of the multiple deaths of God, this insurrection moves like an asymptote—ever closer, never merging: the difference between the insurrection and the death of God approaches zero as both approach infinity. But what would the death of God *mean* in infinity? An infinite dying? Would that not presuppose therefore an endless living?

Certainly in the radical corners of negative theology—a tradition unspoken in these gospels but not unknown to them—the infinite is the only proper name for God, a purely negative name. Its plasticity, its indeterminacy, its vulnerability as the *infini*, the unfinished, has still been little explored. But what if the very pressure and surge, the *surgency* of the insurgent theology, expresses that process without bounds? What if every becoming folds, bursts, or blossoms out of that incompletion, even as it then wilts or dies into unfinished business? The urgency of our finite, endlessly entangled lives comes to speech in this surging or rising up, this insurrection. Its *in* signifies negation, a rising up against the global machines of greed, which will finish off the resources it treats as unlimited if left to its own devices, but also the grammatical intensifier, the rising, the immanent surge of energy.

The surge of the Deleuzean intensity pulses in these gospels, iterating, repeating itself always differently. And its energy is recirculated in an open-system entropy, a turning in, a transformation within, an enfolding that does not merely fold down but unfolds its possibility differently. By *minding* this intensity, being bothered and provoked by it, paying attention to it, thinking it, might we energize the good of its news, a good that can yet come—the messianic event—or that imperceptibly, uncertainly, is already becoming? Do we then more mindfully materialize the intensification of becoming? If so, the *novum* comes rightly here as first gospel, as Earth, as the becoming of a new subject-earth of which we humans are a gifted and sick, sickening, part. "We are a kind of *objet petit a* for Earth, expressing its own desire, but also its neurosis and, more recently, its pathology, a psychopathology that is generating a new convulsion, and perhaps a new creation, that may happen with or without us." It may let us "seize the opportunity" of gospel 2, it may, with gospel 3, let us snatch victory out of defeat. With gospel 4 it is "the intensity that burns and dissipates, that makes life worth living to the point of life's exhaustion."

So we do not escape entropy and death—and though there ensues the endless, infinitely entangled macro- and microlife of the world, life after every death, no life in these gospels lives for the sake of its hereafter. "Life before death!" Otherwise even the most generous self-giving, the "sacrifice" honored as "the greatest effort with minimum gain," cannot give itself. It must have that intensification, that surge of life in this moment, in order to have something to pass on "once and for all."

Am I here only repeating the opening shot of this book: "we believe in the insurrection, not the resurrection"? Indeed the resurrection does "generally smack of repetition," restoration, resuscitation . . . return. Wrong direction for radicality. But what about re-volution? Oh dear, I'd better not just repeat . . . but then . . . Let me start finishing again, and fast.

I have faith in this insurrection. But I am not sure I share its "not." Indeed my mother used to cite Nietzsche's "friend of my friend, enemy of my enemy" so often that I went another way, hoping for friendships not based on common enemies. Or dead gods. I became a theologian; I befriended the writers of gospels. That didn't make *their* enemies mine either. These new insurrective evangels no doubt require their trumpet blast of opposition. But afterward, when the word has settled, I say—in friendship: why not put some insurrection into the resurrection? Rather than make of them a new antagonism, I would encourage the agonism of conflicting interpretations, multiple ethnonarratives, and potential solidarities. Indeed I would hope these new gospels would put insurgency *back* into the antique resurrections, which is to say, foment recognition of the ancestral energies of the Real and of the left, of resistance to crucifixions and lynchings, that surge quite precisely from the archival counterculture of the resurrection. But the resurrection remains mere resuscitation of a corpse, and Easter a triumphal spring parade, when it is cut off from its Jewish sources.

Easter made that doctrinal supersessionism possible, of course. Yet no contextual reading of the four (old) gospel resurrection narratives, with all their undisguised differences, permits the notion of the mere individual revivification of a dead body, come to guarantee all good

Christians a place in heaven. The notion of resurrection that Jesus and his friends could have entertained would be that of a collective arising, first of all of "Israel" or "the people" in the third Isaiah and Ezekiel, an ecopolitical "new heaven and earth" or "new Jerusalem" that in the Jewish apocalypses of Jesus' period had intensified into variously radical messianisms. Whatever imaginaries of individual life beyond death did develop, in this matrix, as among the Saducees, lived only within the Hebrew priority of socially embodied practice. The bodily resurrection of individuals would have been illegible in abstraction from this ancient materialism. I do not see how insurgency is served by any repression of what the Marxist Jew Ernst Bloch called "the Christian social utopias" and the biblical prophetic sources of all Western revolutionary movements, springing from the eschatological archive of resurrection.[1]

This is just a way of reading the resurrection against itself: stage insurrection within the resurrection! Which is all just to say: may we practice even on this doctrine deconstruction rather than destruction?

Of course there is something repetitive about any re-surrection, and the standard hope that my selfsame me will survive death and indeed maybe someday get clothed again in my body (in glorious thirty-three-year-old shape) makes the metaphor almost impossible to reclaim. But that would be pretty much true of all key theological words, wouldn't it: Jesus, Christ, Holy Spirit, salvation, redemption, love, and, oh Lord, *God.* So we do not cease to work negatively—in the way of the deconstructive negation, mindfully haunted as it comes by the ancient apophatic unsaying. If we are doing the work of the insurrection. And we find amidst our experiments *en proces* (element 5) certain haunting ancestral re-verberations—dark precursors, yes, even in those ancient gospels.

Such repetition is not just a matter of getting spooked. For does not the first gospel of the present *biblios* lovingly depend upon *Repetition and Difference,* upon the Deleuzean repetition as—far from mere recurrence of the same or even the similar—"the habitation of difference"? Is it possible, after all, that radical theology, even radical political theology, cannot do without some iteration, some re-surgence, of a reradicalized resurrection? It is noteworthy that our third insurrective gospel so powerfully re-cites James Cone, the great voice of black liberation theology, as the latter reads crucifixion as a lynching dished out to silence the voices of dissent, to stamp out the bodies of insurgence. In *The Cross and the Lynching Tree* Cone does not even name resurrection—it could undo the whole project with its triumphalism—but paraphrases it nonetheless thus, with Du Bois and the blues in mind, and no resort at all to the rationales of theodicy: "One has to be a little mad, kind of crazy, to find salvation in the cross, victory in defeat, and life in death."[2] I think our concluding gospels' minimalist sense of sacrifice has just such madness in mind. One reason I trust the insurrection staked out in these gospels is that amidst their buzz of "new networks, new solidarities, new sites of linkage and transformation" the material and just as spiritual purposes of movements of race, class, gender, and sex are not relegated to some identity-political past but move—maybe with intensified motility—within the emergent assemblage.

What about Paul? He wrote epistles, not gospels: nonetheless he has snuck deep into the present book through its second gospel. Will it do to lift up—with all those fashionably nontheist philosophers, from Agamben to Badiou to Žižek—the radical Paul, and just ignore the Corinthian figure of the resurrection? If for Paul "our faith is in vain" without the resurrection, would we then nonetheless relegate resurrection to the annals of our second gospel's "vampiric transcendence"? Might not "Paulinist partisanship *within* a vibrantly diverse first-century Judaism" allow a vibrant twenty-first-century reading of the "Body of Christ": a trope that renders the "spiritual body" of resurrection anything but a resuscitated corpse?[3] It intensifies precisely a Jewish sense of a new people, here self-assembling across previously unthinkable differences (Jew/Greek, male/female, slave/free). My students from more conservative Christian backgrounds don't want to have it rubbed in that this *ekklesia* actually constitutes the resurrected body. They want the body of Christ safely lodged in heaven, preparing their place at the table.

I sometimes blink to realize that Paul really does not only say that we are members in our diversity of a larger body, but that we are "members *one of another.*" Already an ontology of constitutive relations has come into play, unthinkable for the Hellenistic metaphysics of substance, soon thereafter to be lost. So far from individually discrete identities subject to the future life of their separable souls with or without bodies—the very meaning of this free commune of resurrection surges (in) from its entangled differences. There can be no radical Paul without them.

Or perhaps the radix of radicality is still trapping us in reactive habits. Perhaps what the Corinthian collective body of differences demonstrates is not so much radical as rhizomatic theology. As proposed early in this book, such a theology emulates the rhizome and so lacks the vertical hierarchy of the arboreal root; its tubers and bulbs, as with water lilies or grass, form "a complex knot of connections and affiliations." It will not readily hold the binary reactivities of any orthodoxies, theistic and political, however radical. Like the dichotomy of insurrection versus resurrection. Or, I cannot help noting, of rhizomatic versus arboreal. Indeed one of the great examples of the rhizome is Pando Populis, "the largest and oldest organism on the planet—a giant quaking aspen tree, spread over more than a hundred acres, thousands of years old, connected by a single root system."[4] It has lent its name to an ecological effort to intensify responsible membership in and on the body of the earth: the rhizome of rhizomes.

Our gospels have mimicked Heidegger, but warned against his "Greco-peasant fantasies" of return to a simple, crusty earth. Yet they surely do not discourage every possible experiment in economic and ecological insurgency, including local, rural, or urban, and works of recycling and restoration—is this resurrection?—that will never return us to the same willy-nilly, that will attend to the dwindling resources and the need to shift way too fast to cleaner energies. Such humble concreteness exemplifies the spirit of any new materialism that might actually be and bear good news, which will therefore repeat differently its terrestrial ancestries, its multiplicity of ways—prereligious, religious, postreligious—now inextricably entangled.

With catastrophes looming for every vulnerable population, human and otherwise, the good tidings of a rhizomatic theology may be this: to render that entangled multiplicity a source no longer of fear, loathing, and the zero-sum game, but of curiosity and an activating attraction. Unorthodox collaborations energize the creativity that crosses earth and sky, mortals, and gods. Those four registers of the real oscillate in indeterminacy; they fold into each others' vulnerability. The crossings may turn endless, just where the words end. The traumatized and resilient earth, the becoming-subject of us all, offers no escape into the silence or the stars.

NOTES

Preface

1. Slavoj Žižek, personal correspondence.

Introduction

1. Alain Badiou, *The Century*, trans. Alberto Toscano (Cambridge: Polity, 2007).
2. Peter Rollins, *Insurrection: To Believe Is Human, to Doubt, Divine* (New York: Howard, 2011).
3. See Jeffrey W. Robbins, *Radical Democracy and Political Theology* (New York: Columbia University Press, 2011).
4. Carl Schmitt, *Political Theology: Four Chapters on the Concept of Sovereignty*, trans. George Schwab (Chicago: University of Chicago Press, 1985), p. 36.
5. Antonio Negri, *Spinoza and Us: Politics and Postmodernity*, trans. William McCuaig (New York: Columbia University Press, 2013), p. 32.
6. Talal Asad, *Formations of the Secular: Christianity, Islam, Modernity* (Stanford: Stanford University Press, 2003), p. 200.
7. See John D. Caputo and Gianni Vattimo, *After the Death of God*, ed. Jeffrey W. Robbins (New York: Columbia University Press, 2007).
8. Thomas J. J. Altizer, *The Gospel of Christian Atheism* (Philadelphia: Westminster, 1966), p. 10.
9. Gilles Deleuze and Felix Guattari, *A Thousand Plateaus: Capitalism and Schizophrenia*, trans. Brian Massumi (Minneapolis: University of Minnesota Press, 1987), p. 6.
10. Carl A. Raschke, "The Deconstruction of God," in Thomas J. J. Altizer et al., *Deconstruction and Theology* (New York: Crossroad, 1982), p. 3. Raschke was the editor of this important volume, although he is not listed as such in the book.

11.   In the twenty-first century, Caputo has come to express himself in explicitly theological terms, and we want to affirm his work and its importance in *The Weakness of God: A Theology of the Event* (Bloomington: Indiana University Press, 2006) and *The Insistence of God: A Theology of Perhaps* (Bloomington: Indiana University Press, 2013). Caputo is less explicitly political in his work, but his is clearly an insurrectionist theology.

12.   Jeffrey W. Robbins, "Terror and the Postmodern Condition," in *Religion and Violence in a Secular World*, ed. Clayton Crockett (Charlottesville: University of Virginia Press, 2006), p. 201.

13.   Slavoj Žižek, *The Puppet and the Dwarf: The Perverse Core of Christianity* (Cambridge: MIT Press, 2003), p. 77 (we added in the references to masculine and feminine for the sake of clarity).

14.   See François Dosse, *Deleuze and Guattari: Intersecting Lives*, trans. Deborah Glassman (New York: Columbia University Press, 2010), pp. 183–89, 209–10. Much of the polemic stems from Lacan's rejection of Guattari in favor of Jacques-Alain Miller.

15.   François Laruelle, *The Non-Philosophy Project: Essays by François Laruelle*, ed. Gabriel Alkon and Boris Gunjevic (New York: Telos, 2012), p. 25.

16.   Ibid., p. 27.

17.   For an initial attempt to apply Laruelle's nonphilosophy to theology and religion, including the term *nontheology*, see Anthony Paul Smith, "What Can be Done with Religion?," in *After the Postsecular and the Postmodern: New Essays in Continental Philosophy of Religion*, ed. Anthony Paul Smith and Daniel Whistler (Newcastle-upon-Tyne: Cambridge Scholars, 2010), pp. 280–98.

18.   See the volume *New Materialisms: Ontology, Agency, Politics*, ed. Diana Coole and Samantha Frost (Durham: Duke University Press, 2010). See also Clayton Crockett and Jeffrey W. Robbins, *Religion, Politics and the Earth: The New Materialism* (New York: Palgrave Macmillan, 2012) and Ward Blanton, *A Materialism for the Masses: Saint Paul and the Philosophy of Undying Life* (New York: Columbia University Press, 2014).

19.   Catherine Malabou, *Plasticity at the Dusk of Writing: Dialectic, Destruction, Deconstruction*, trans. Carolyn Shread (New York: Columbia University Press, 2009), p. 57.

20.   See Catherine Malabou, *What Should We Do with Our Brain?*, trans. Marc Jeannerod (New York: Fordham University Press, 2008), p. 5.

21.   Catherine Malabou, *The New Wounded: From Neurosis to Brain Damage*, trans. Steven Miller (New York: Fordham University Press, 2012), pp. 211–12.

22.   Ibid., p. 212.

23.   Rollins, *Insurrection*, p. 156.

24.   Slavoj Žižek, "Dialectical Clarity vs. the Misty Conceit of Paradox," in John Milbank and Slavoj Žižek, *The Monstrosity of Christ: Paradox or Dialectic?*, ed. Creston Davis (Cambridge: MIT Press, 2009), p. 248.

25. See Mauricio Lazzarato, *The Making of the Indebted Man: An Essay on the Neo-liberal Tradition*, trans. Joshua David Jordan (New York: Semiotext(e), 2012).

26. Julia Kristeva, *Revolution in Poetic Language*, trans. Margaret Waller (New York: Columbia University Press, 1984), p. 22.

27. Ibid., p. 48.

28. See Bracha Ettinger, *The Matrixial Borderspace* (Minneapolis: University of Minnesota Press, 2006). Ettinger's work is resonant with Kristeva's, although Ettinger is less insistent on the need to accede to the demands of symbolic representation and the law of the Father.

29. Alain Badiou, *Being and Event*, trans. Oliver Feltham (London: Continuum, 2005), p. 1.

30. See Gianni Vattimo and Santiago Zabala, *Hermeneutic Communism: From Heidegger to Marx* (New York: Columbia University Press, 2011).

1. Earth

1. Martin Heidegger, "The Thing," in *Poetry, Language, Thought*, trans. Albert Hofstadter (New York: Harper Perennial Classics, 2001), p. 176.

2. See Bill McKibben, *Eaarth: Making a Life on a Tough New Planet* (New York: St. Martin's, 2011).

3. See Elizabeth Kolbert, *The Sixth Extinction: An Unnatural History* (New York: Holt, 2014).

4. Vandana Shiva, *Making Peace with the Earth* (London: Pluto, 2013), p. 9.

5. George Monbiot, *Heat: How to Stop the Planet from Burning* (Cambridge: South End, 2007), p. 3.

6. See Bill McKibben, "The Reckoning," published in *Rolling Stone* on August 2, 2012 (pp. 52–60) during one of the warmest periods in recorded history. According to the article, May and June 2012 "represented the largest temperature departure from average of any season on record" (p. 52).

7. Quoted in Naomi Klein, "How Science Is Telling Us to Revolt," *New Statesman*, October 29, 2013. Available online at http://www.newstatesman.com/2013/10/science-says-revolt. See also Naomi Klein, *This Changes Everything: Capitalism vs. the Climate* (New York: Simon and Schuster, 2014).

8. See the IPCC Climate Change 2014 Synthesis Report, available at http://www.ipcc.ch/pdf/assessment-report/ar5/syr/SYR_AR5_SPMcorr1.pdf.

9. Thom Hartmann, *The Last Hours of Ancient Sunlight: The Fate of the World and What We Can Do Before It's Too Late* (New York: Three Rivers, 2004).

10. See Michael T. Klare, *The Race for What's Left: The Global Scramble for the World's Last Resources* (New York: Metropolitan, 2012), p. 8.

11. Ibid., p. 11.

12. Ibid., p. 17.

13. Timothy Mitchell, *Carbon Democracy: Political Power in the Age of Oil* (London: Verso, 2013), p. 233.

14. Allan Stoekl, *Bataille's Peak: Energy, Religion, and Postsustainability* (Minneapolis: University of Minnesota Press, 2006), p. 41.

15. See Kenneth S. Deffeyes, *Beyond Oil: The View From Hubbert's Peak* (New York: Hill and Wang, 2005) and James Murray and David King, "Oil's Tipping Point Has Passed," *Nature* 481 (January 2012): 433–35.

16. For information on global oil production, see the website The Oil Drum (www .theoildrum.com). This website stopped adding new content in September 2013, but the articles and stories running from 2005–13 are archived there.

17. Mitchell, *Carbon Democracy*, pp. 259–60.

18. See John Kenneth Galbraith, *A Short History of Financial Euphoria* (New York: Penguin, 1990).

19. Christian Marazzi, *The Violence of Financial Capitalism*, trans. Kristina Lebedeva and Jason Francis McGimsey (New York: Semiotext(e), 2011), p. 113.

20. Mike Davis, *Planet of Slums* (London: Verso, 2006), p. 15.

21. Kojin Karatani, *The Structure of World History: From Modes of Production to Modes of Exchange*, trans. Michael K. Bourdaghs (Durham: Duke University Press, 2014), p. 284.

22. Ibid., pp. 17, 205.

23. David Harvey, *Seventeen Contradictions and the End of Capitalism* (Oxford: Oxford University Press, 2014), p. 247.

24. See Clayton Crockett and Jeffrey W. Robbins, *Religion, Politics, and the Earth: The New Materialism* (New York: Palgrave Macmillan, 2012).

25. See John D. Caputo, *The Prayers and Tears of Jacques Derrida: Religion Without Religion* (Bloomington: Indiana University Press, 1997).

26. Paul Tillich, *Systematic Theology*, 3 vols. (Chicago: University of Chicago Press, 1951), 1:12.

27. Ibid., p. 14.

28. Aristotle, *Metaphysics*, book 7, chapter 7, 1072b 10–11, in *The Basic Works of Aristotle*, ed. Richard McKeon (New York: Modern Library, 2001), p. 880.

29. Lynn White, "The Historical Roots of Our Ecologic Crisis," in *Ecology, Religion and History* (New York: Harper and Row, 1974), p. 5.

30. Ibid.

31. Ludwig Feuerbach, *The Essence of Christianity*, trans. George Eliot (Buffalo: Prometheus Books, 1989), p. 270.

32. See Thomas S. Kuhn, *The Structure of Scientific Revolutions*, 2d ed. (Chicago: University of Chicago Press, 1970), p. 93.

33. Ibid., p. 103.

34. Friedrich Nietzsche, *The Birth of Tragedy and The Genealogy of Morals*, trans. Francis Golffing (New York: Anchor), p. 149.

35. Slavoj Žižek, "What Rumsfeld Doesn't Know That He Knows About Abu Ghraib," *In These Times*, http://www.lacan.com/Žižekrumsfeld.htm.

36. Ian G. Barbour, *When Science Meets Religion: Enemies, Strangers, or Partners?* (New York: HarperCollins, 2000), pp. 10–38.

37. Mark I. Wallace, *Finding God in the Singing River: Christianity, Spirit, Nature* (Minneapolis: Fortress, 2005), p. 23.

38. Ibid.

39. Ibid.

40. Margaret Atwood, *Surfacing* (New York: Anchor, 1998 [1972]). For an explicit Christian theology of animals, see Andrew Linzey, *Animal Theology* (Urbana: University of Illinois Press, 1995).

41. Wallace, *Finding God in the Singing River*, p. 75.

42. Slavoj Žižek, *The Indivisible Remainder: An Essay on Schelling and Related Matters* (London: Verso, 1996), p. 63.

43. Ibid., p. 131.

44. Tim Morton, *Ecology Without Nature: Rethinking Environmental Aesthetics* (Cambridge: Harvard University Press, 2009).

45. Žižek, *The Indivisible Remainder*, p. 218.

46. Ibid., p. 220.

47. Slavoj Žižek, *The Puppet and the Dwarf: The Perverse Core of Christianity* (Cambridge: MIT Press, 2003), p. 91.

48. Ibid., p. 95.

49. Rod Swenson, "Autocatakinetics, Evolution, and the Law of Maximum Energy Production: A Principled Foundation Towards the Study of Human Ecology," *Advances in Human Ecology* 6 (1997), available online at http://www.spontaneousorder.net/humaneco2.html. See also Clayton Crockett, "Entropy," in *The Future of Continental Philosophy of Religion*, ed. Clayton Crockett, B. Keith Putt, and Jeffrey W. Robbins (Bloomington: Indiana University Press, 2014), from which this discussion partly draws.

50. Ibid.

51. Ibid.

52. Eric D. Schneider and Dorion Sagan, *Into the Cool: Energy Flow, Thermodynamics, and Life* (Chicago: University of Chicago Press, 2005), p. 6.

53. Ibid., p. 112.

54. Ibid., p. 113. Bénard's experiments took place around 1900, and they have been updated and further developed by scientists Lothar Koschmieder, Michel Assenheimer, and Victor Steinberg. Another physical experiment involves the spiral flow of a liquid between a rotating inner cylinder and a stationary outer cylinder to form complex vortices. These vortices are called Taylor vortices, after physicist G. I. Taylor. Taylor vortices are organized by pressure gradients rather than temperature differentials.

55. Ibid., p. 123.

56. Ibid., p. 129.

57. Gilles Deleuze, *Difference and Repetition*, trans. Paul Patton (New York: Columbia University Press, 1994), p. 117.

58. Ibid.

59. See Karen Barad, *Meeting the Universe Halfway: Quantum Physics and the Entanglement of Matter and Meaning* (Durham: Duke University Press, 2007), p. 72.

60. Deleuze, *Difference and Repetition*, p. 119.

61. Ray Brassier, *Nihil Unbound: Enlightenment and Extinction* (London: Palgrave Macmillan, 2007), p. 293.

62. Ibid., pp. 298–99.

63. Deleuze, *Difference and Repetition*, p. 234.

64. Ibid.

65. Ibid.

66. Lee Smolin, *Time Reborn: From the Crisis in Physics to the Future of the Universe* (New York: Houghton Mifflin, 2013), p. 218.

67. Ibid., p. 219.

68. See Roberto Mangabeira Unger and Lee Smolin, *The Singular Universe and the Reality of Time: A Proposal in Natural Philosophy* (Cambridge: Cambridge University Press, 2014).

69. Schneider and Sagan, *Into the Cool*, p. 172.

70. Ibid., p. 173.

71. Ibid.

72. Ibid., pp. 173–74.

73. Natalie Wolchover, "A New Physics of Life?," *Quanta Magazine*, January 22, 2014, https://www.quantamagazine.org/20140122-a-new-physics-theory-of-life/.

74. Actually, the really extraordinary miracle may be less the transition from inorganic organization to organic life but rather the move from single-celled prokaryotic life to multicellular complex life forms. Eukaryotic cells are defined by their possession of a nucleus, and this accidental symbiotic arrangement may have resulted from the unlikely absorption of a proteobacterium by a methanogen in a hydrogen environment prior to the production of an oxygen-rich atmosphere. In his provocative book *Power, Sex, Suicide*, Nick Lane details this "hydrogen hypothesis," and he also explains why this assemblage was so unlikely but also so crucial to the development of complex life forms. Nick Lane, *Power, Sex, Suicide: Mitochondria and the Meaning of Life* (Oxford: Oxford University Press, 2005), pp. 56–64.

75. "Solar Wind Rips Up Martian Atmosphere," *Science@NASA* (November 21 2008), http://science.nasa.gov/headlines/y2001/ast31jan%5F1.htm.

76. According to one possibility, fission reactions are directly generating magnetic moments or a quantum of magnetism as a result of nuclear decay. Next, the convection and coriolis movements of the earth's mantle and core paramagnetize

these magnetic moments. The magnetohydrodynamic fluids are being continually paramagnetized by fissile nuclear decay chain interactions. Fertile and fissile nuclear elements are thoroughly entrained in the iron-silicate mantle and core materials like yeast-leavening flour in bread dough. These interactions are doing many things at once. They are converting fertile nuclear elements into fissile ones. They are heating the magnetohydrodynamic fluids, which in turn drive density gradient structure formation. And they are continually paramagnetizing these same fluids. The self-organized efficient gradient degradation structures formed in the fluids are constructively aligning the paramagnetic moments into a global magnetic dipole field. This is an original hypothesis, as far as I can tell, based on research conducted by Kevin Mequet. See Crockett and Robbins, *Religion, Politics, and the Earth*, chapter 7, pp. 101–10 and Kevin Mequet, "A Revolutionary View to the Chronic Energy Problem" (2009), available at http://www.scribd.com/doc/33017213/KDM-Proposal-NuMEgen-Vero3-Academic-20100605-Final.

77. The plane of consistency, or the BwO, indicates what Deleuze calls the dark precursor in *Difference and Repetition*.

78. Gilles Deleuze and Félix Guattari, *A Thousand Plateaus*, trans. Brian Massumi (Minneapolis: University of Minnesota Press, 1987).

79. Ibid.

80. Deleuze and Guattari's new creation of Earth understood in terms of an absolute deterritorialization at the end of *A Thousand Plateaus* should also be read as a response to Carl Schmitt's *The Nomos of the Earth: In the International Law of the Jus Publicum Europaeum*, trans. G. L. Ulmen (New York: Telos, 2006).

81. See H. J. Morowitz, *The Beginnings of Cellular Life: Metabolism Recapitulates Biogenesis* (New Haven: Yale University Press, 1992).

82. See Lane, *Power, Sex, Suicide*, p. 86.

83. Catherine Malabou, *What Should We Do with Our Brain?*, trans. Sebastian Rand (New York: Fordham University Press, 2008), p. 5.

84. Catherine Malabou, "Darwin and the Destiny of Natural Selection," in *theory@ buffalo* 16: "Plastique: Dynamics of Catherine Malabou" (2012): 144–56, quote p. 144.

85. Eva Jablonka and Marion J. Lamb, *Evolution in Four Dimensions: Genetic, Epigenetic, Behavioral, and Symbolic Variation in the History of Life* (Cambridge: MIT Press, 2005), p. 1.

86. See ibid., p. 145.

87. See James Lovelock, *Gaia: A New Look at Life on Earth* (Oxford: Oxford University Press, 2000).

88. Bruno Latour, "Facing Gaia: Six Lessons on the Political Theology of Nature," quoted in Catherine Keller, *Cloud of the Impossible: Negative Theology and Planetary Entanglement* (New York: Columbia University Press, 2014), p. 283.

89. See the introduction to Crockett and Robbins, *Religion, Politics and the Earth*, pp. xiii–xxii.

90. Deleuze, *Difference and Repetition*, p. 24.
91. Stoekl, *Bataille's Peak*, p. 199 (emphasis mine).
92. See my discussion of theology as energy in Clayton Crockett, "The Triumph of Theology," in *Theology After Lacan*, ed. Clayton Crockett, Creston Davis, and Marcus Pound (Eugene, OR: Cascade, 2014).
93. Slavoj Žižek, *The Parallax View* (Cambridge: MIT Press, 2006), p. 4.
94. Jacques Derrida, *Margins of Philosophy*, trans. Allen Bass (Chicago: University of Chicago Press, 1982), p. 22.
95. Catherine Keller, *Face of the Deep: A Theology of Becoming* (London: Routledge, 2003), p. xvii. See also Keller's discussions of Deleuze, Whiteheadian process theology, and quantum physics in *Cloud of the Impossible*, especially chapters 4 and 5, pp. 127–95.
96. Ibid., p. 188.
97. Gilles Deleuze and Félix Guattari, *What Is Philosophy?*, trans. Hugh Tomlinson and Graham Burchell (New York: Columbia University Press, 1994), p. 201.

2. Satellite Skies

1. For exemplary discussions of call, insurrection, and friendship, here we simply point to Howard Caygill's *On Resistance: A Philosophy of Defiance* (New York: Bloomsbury, 2013), pp. 191–98, a text that I will discuss in more detail on another occasion.
2. See Martin Heidegger, "The Onto-Theological Nature of Metaphysics," in *Essays in Metaphysics: Identity and Difference*, trans. Kurt F. Leidecker (New York: Philosophical Library, 1960), pp. 33–68.
3. Kittler's Edisonian readings of Heidegger are developed above all in Friedrich Kittler, *Gramaphone, Film, Typewriter,* trans. Geoffrey Winthrop-Young (Stanford: Stanford University Press, 1999). We note, too, the way Derrida associates the end of philosophy and the emergence of "writing" with the invention of the phonograph, a media-historical argument about Heidegger that has for the most part been occluded for the sake of the history of ideas. See Jacques Derrida, *Of Grammatology* (Baltimore: Johns Hopkins University Press, 1998), p. 10.
4. Martin Heidegger. *Essays in Metaphysics: Identity and Difference,* trans. Kurt F. Leidecker (New York: Philosophical Library, 1960), p. 63.
5. Ibid., pp. 63–64.
6. Peter Sloterdijk, *God's Zeal: The Battle of the Three Monotheisms* (London: Polity, 2009); see pp. 10, 15.
7. Ibid., p. 15f.
8. Thanks to the philosophical newspaper man, Graham Harman, for the reference to the shipping merchants, even if I steer clear of Harman's own reading of the fourfold. See Harman, *Heidegger Explained: From Phenomenon to Thing* (Chicago: Open Court, 2007), p. 128.

9. Martin Heidegger, *Bremen and Freiburg Lectures: Insight Into That Which Is and Basic Principles of Thinking,* trans. Andrew J. Mitchell (Bloomington: Indiana University Press, 2012), p. 16.

10. Laurence Rickels, *The Vampire Lectures* (Minneapolis: University of Minnesota Press, 1999), p. 26.

11. See Lisa Parks. *Cultures in Orbit: Satellites and the Televisual* (Durham, NC: Duke University Press, 2005), pp. 2–3; John Naughton. *A Brief History of the Future: The Origins of the Internet* (London: W&N, 2000), pp. 77ff.

12. Martin Heidegger. *The Event* (Bloomington: Indiana University Press, 2013), p. 69.

13. Lisa Parks, *Cultures in Orbit: Satellites and the Televisual* (Durham, NC: Duke University Press, 2005), p. 3.

14. Carl Schmitt, *Writings on War* (London: Polity, 2011), p. 91.

15. Ibid., pp. 94–95.

16. Ibid., p. 95.

17. Ernst Junger, *Storm of Steel* (New York: Penguin, 2004), p. 214.

18. Bram Stoker, *Dracula* (London: Vintage, 2007), p. 119.

19. Heidegger, *Bremen and Freiburg Lectures,* 17.

20. Jeremy Carrette and Richard King, *Selling Spirituality: The Silent Takeover of Religion* (London: Routledge, 2004).

21. Heidegger, *Bremen and Freiburg Lectures,* 90.

22. Stoker, *Dracula,* p. 238.

23. See, for example, Martin Heidegger. *Being and Time,* trans. Joan Stambaugh (Albany: SUNY Press, 1996), p. 45.

24. Heidegger, *Essays in Metaphysics,* pp. 64–65.

25. Cf. Luke 1:1–4.

26. Brett Buchanan, *Onto-Ethologies: The Animal Environments of Uexküll, Heidegger, Merleau-Ponty, and Deleuze* (Albany: SUNY Press, 2009), p. 152.

27. Ibid.

28. Gilles Deleuze and Leopold von Sacher-Masoch, *Masochism: Coldness and Cruelty and Venus in Furs* (New York: Zone, 1991), pp. 85, 87.

29. See Paola Marrati, *Gilles Deleuze: Cinema and Philosophy* (Baltimore: Johns Hopkins University Press, 2012); Clayton Crockett, *Deleuze Beyond Badiou: Ontology, Multiplicity, and Event* (New York: Columbia University Press, 2013).

30. Gilles Deleuze. *Cinema 2: The Time Image* (London: Continuum, 2005), p. 166.

31. See Clayton Crockett, "Saint Paul with Deleuze" in Ward Blanton and Hent de Vries, eds., *Paul and the Philosophers* (New York: Fordham University Press, 2013), pp. 210–23.

32. While they disagree profoundly about the way Paul interacts with Hellenistic philosophical traditions, several crucial touchstones must be mentioned here: Stanley Stowers, *A Rereading of Romans: Justice, Jews, and Gentiles* (New Haven: Yale University Press, 1997); Dale B. Martin, *The Corinthian Body* (New

Haven: Yale University Press, 1999); Troels Engberg-Pedersen, *Paul and the Stoics* (London: T&T Clark, 2000) and *Cosmology and Self in the Apostle Paul* (Oxford: Oxford University Press, 2010); Emma Wasserman, *The Death of the Soul in Romans 7: Sin, Death, and the Law in Light of Hellenistic Moral Psychology* (Tübingen: Mohr Siebeck, 2008); George Van Kooten, *Paul's Anthropology in Context* (Tübingen: Mohr Siebeck, 2008); Niko Huttunen, *Paul and Epictetus on Law: A Comparison* (London: T&T Clark, 2009); Runar Thorsteinsson, *Roman Christianity and Roman Stoicism: A Comparative Study of Ancient Morality* (Oxford: Oxford University Press, 2010).

33. We should note immediately that discourses about *nomos* in ancient Mediterranean contexts afforded a panoply of modes by which to double, and effectively to circumvent, sublimate, or negate the value of a particular instance of *nomos*. Philosophers, of course, regularly switched codes from ethnic to natural law, often precisely in order to allow the doubling and displacement of *nomos* as a mode of escaping the effective operation of the local or the allegedly general. Jewish traditions from Josephus to Philo to the texts of the Dead Sea Scrolls perform similar operations, sometimes adding additional tricks about the (oral or written) media of nomological discourse. In a word, in moments like these Paul inhabits, rather than subtracts himself from, Jewish and philosophical traditions alike. Two very important efforts to locate Pauline discussions of *nomos* within their general Greco-Roman environments are Brigitte Kahl, *Galatians Re-imagined: Reading with the Eyes of the Vanquished* (Minneapolis: Fortress, 2010) and Davina Lopez, *Apostle to the Conquered: Re-imagining Paul's Mission* (Minneapolis: Fortress, 2010).

34. Josephus, *Antiquities* 2.239.1, in *Jewish Antiquities,* vol. 5. Loeb Classical Library 242 (Cambridge: Harvard University Press, 1930).

35. See, e.g., the "discussion on sin" in Georges Bataille, *The Unfinished System of Nonknowledge* (Minneapolis: University of Minnesota Press, 2004); and the reference to hyperbolic sin in the lecture "On the Moral Law" in Jacques Lacan, *The Seminar of Jacques Lacan. Book VII: The Ethics of Psychoanalysis* (1959–60), trans. Dennis Porter (New York: Norton, 1992), p. 84.

36. Sextus Empiricus, *Against Physicists, Against Ethicists,* vol 3. Loeb Classical Library 311. Trans. R. G. Bury (Cambridge: Harvard University Press, 1936).

37. For an excellent discussion of Schmittian exceptionalism, with an accompanying genealogy of Schmitt's precursors, see Marc de Wilde's excellent essay, "Politics Between Times: Theologico-Political Interpretations of the Restraining Force (*katechon*) in Paul's Second Letter to the Thessalonians" in Ward Blanton and Hent de Vries, eds., *Paul and the Philosophers* (New York: Fordham University Press, 2013). See also Massimo Cacciari, *The Witholding Power: An Essay on Political Theology* (London: Bloomsbury, 2015).

38. Philo of Alexandria, *On the Special Laws,* vol. 7. Loeb Classical Library 320 (Cambridge: Harvard University Press, 1937).

39. Philo of Alexandria, *On the Special Laws, On the Virtues. On Rewards and Punishments*. Loeb Classical Library 341 (Cambridge: Harvard University Press, 1939).

40. Ancient discussions assumed that the fund of *aphormē* could be borrowed, saved, and the origination of new enterprises (cf. Xenophon, *Memorabilia* 2.7.12, 3.12.4), or even the distributed fund of the state itself (cf. Aristotle, *Politics* 6.1320a39).

41. For an excellent discussion of the role of Joyce as exemplar of a quasi-emancipatory fidelity to one's (singular) symptom, see Lorenzo Chiesa, *Subjectivity and Otherness: A Philosophical Reading of Lacan* (Cambridge: MIT Press, 2007), pp. 188ff.

42. Henri Bergson, *Laughter: An Essay on the Meaning of the Comic* (New York: DigiReads, 2010), p. 1.

43. Christopher Watkin brings together nicely Nancy's criticisms of recent philosophies of the death of God to Nancy's criticisms of Badiou's ahistoricism in *A Difficult Atheism: Post-theological Thinking in Alain Badiou, Jean-Luc Nancy, and Quentin Meillassoux* (Edinburgh: Edinburgh University Press, 2011), pp. 37f.

44. See the discussions of Pauline calling and Epicurean "swerve" in Ward Blanton, *A Materialism for the Masses: Saint Paul and the Philosophy of Undying Life* (New York: Columbia University Press, 2014).

45. Jonathan Edwards, *The Works of Jonathan Edwards*, 2:9. Edinburgh: Banner of Truth Trust, 1834.

46. See "Tony Blair: A Conversation at Yale University," at minute 2.50, https://www.youtube.com/watch?v=jfle-pflirI (accessed July 11, 2013). The blurb on YouTube reads as follows: "the former British Prime Minister and Howland Distinguished Professor, Tony Blair, sits down to talk with Richard Levin, Yale University President, Paul Kennedy, J. Richardson Dilworth Professor of History, and Lita Tandon, Yale College Class of 2010, at a 'Fireside Chat' in Woolsey Hall on September 19, 2008."

47. Cf. Mark C. Taylor, *Confidence Games: Money and Markets in a World Without Redemption* (Chicago: University of Chicago Press, 2008).

3. A Theory of Insurrection

1. See Giorgio Agamben, *Remnants of Auschwitz: The Witness and the Archive*, trans. Daniel Heller-Roazen (New York: Zone, 1999).

2. See Richard L. Rubenstein, *After Auschwitz: History, Theology, and Contemporary Judaism* (Baltimore: Johns Hopkins University Press, 1992).

3. Martin Heidegger, "Letter on 'Humanism,'" in *Pathmarks*, ed. William McNeil (Cambridge: Cambridge University Press, 1998), pp. 245, 250.

4. James Cone, *The Cross and the Lynching Tree* (New York: Orbis, 2011), pp. xv–xvi, xvii.

5. Ibid., p. 31.

6. Ibid., p. 6.

7. See George M. Fredrickson, *Racism: A Short History* (Princeton: Princeton University Press, 2002), p. 110.

8. Cone, *The Cross and the Lynching Tree*, p. 9, 166.

9. My gratitude to co-author Clayton Crockett for helping to illuminate the importance of the time-image in Deleuze's thought. See Clayton Crockett, *Deleuze Beyond Badiou: Ontology, Multiplicity, and Event* (New York: Columbia University Press, 2013).

10. Gilles Deleuze, *Cinema 2: The Time-Image*, trans. Hugh Tomlinson and Robert Galeta (Minneapolis: University of Minnesota Press, 1989), p. 155.

11. David Mitchell, "Cloud Atlas: Time to Say Goodbye to Your Characters," in the *Independent* (January 30, 2013), http://www.independent.co.uk/arts-entertainment/films/features/cloud-atlas-time-to-say-goodbye-to-your-characters-8471754.html.

12. Andrew A'Hehir, "The Overblown, Funny, Romantic 'Cloud Atlas,'" *Salon*, October 25, 2012, http://www.salon.com/2012/10/25/pick_of_the_week_the_overblown_funny_romantic_cloud_atlas/.

13. Mitchell, "Cloud Atlas."

14. For instance, in "The Time Is Out of Joint," Derrida consents to the definition of deconstruction as "more than one language." In *Deconstruction Is/in America: A New Sense of the Political*, ed. Anselm Haverkamp (New York: New York University Press, 1995), 27. See also Jacques Derrida, *Monolingualism of the Other, or The Prothesis of Origin*, trans. Patrick Mensah (Stanford: Stanford University Press, 1998), p. 51, where he writes of his early deconstructive impulse, "the dream, which must have started to be dreamt, at the time, was perhaps to make something happen to this language . . . forcing the language then to speak itself by itself, in another way, in his language."

15. Catherine Malabou, *The Future of Hegel: Plasticity, Temporality, and Dialectic*, trans. Lisabeth During (New York: Routledge, 2005), p. 6.

16. On this point regarding an insurrectionist theology as a theology of life as opposed to death, J. Kameron Carter provides a provocative and helpful reminder that this is as much a racial problem as it is a theological one when he writes in the epilogue of *Race: A Theological Account* (Oxford: Oxford University Press, 2008), p. 377: "The tragedy is that whiteness continues to reign as the inner architecture of modern theology, and a fortiori theology continues to function as a discourse of death."

17. Michel Foucault, *"Society Must Be Defended": Lectures at the Collège de France, 1975-1976* (London: Picador, 2003), pp. 46–47.

18. Delores S. Williams, "Black Theology and Womanist Theology," in *The Cambridge Companion to Black Theology*, ed. Dwight N. Hopkins and Edward P. Antonio (Cambridge: Cambridge University Press, 2012), pp. 65, 68.

19. Ibid., p. 67.

20. Antonio Negri, *The Labor of Job: The Biblical Text as a Parable of Human Labor*, trans. Matteo Mandarini (Durham, NC: Duke University Press, 2009), p. xix.

21. Ibid., p. 7.

22. Ibid., p. xviii.

23. Ibid., p. xvii.

24. Franco Berardi, *The Soul at Work: From Alienation to Autonomy*, trans. Francesca Cadel and Giuseppina Mecchia (Los Angeles: Semiotext(e), 2009).

25. Negri, *The Labor of Job*, pp. 10 and 11.

26. Ibid., p. 12.

27. Ibid., p. xx.

28. Walter Brueggemann, *An Introduction to the Old Testament: The Canon and Christian Imagination* (Louisville, KY: Westminster John Knox, 2003), p. 295.

29. Negri, *The Labor of Job*, p. 36.

30. Catherine Malabou, *What Should We Do with Our Brain?*, trans. Sebastian Rand (New York: Fordham University Press, 2008), p. 12.

31. Fredrickson, *Racism*, p. 137 and 140 (emphasis mine).

32. W. E. B. Du Bois, *Dusk of Dawn* (New York: Harcourt, Brace, 1940), p. 58.

33. Catherine Malabou, *Changing Difference: The Feminine and the Question of Philosophy*, trans. Carolyn Shread (Cambridge: Polity, 2011), p. 3.

34. Ibid., p. 38.

35. Ibid., p. 98.

36. For an elaboration of this materialist critique of Butler, see Manuel A. Vasquez, *More Than Belief: A Materialist Theory of Religion* (Oxford: Oxford University Press, 2011), pp. 143–47.

37. Malabou, *Changing Difference*, p. 102.

38. Ibid, p. 111.

39. Ibid., p. 112.

40. Ibid., p. 99.

4. The Gospel of the Word Made Flesh

1. These introductory remarks on Heidegger's *Beiträge* hark back to Clayton Crockett's "On God and Being: A Review of Martin Heidegger's *Contributions to Philosophy*," *Journal for Cultural and Religious Theory* 2, no. 3 (Fall 2001), http:/// www.jcrt.org/archives/02.3/crockett.shtml (accessed June 26, 2015).

2. "Metaphysics always supposes, somehow, a solid earth-crust, from which a construction may be raised. . . . So long as Heidegger does not leave the earth, he does not leave metaphysics. Metaphysics does not inscribe itself either on/ in water, on/in air, on/in fire . . . and its abysses, both above and below, doubtless find their interpretation in the forgetting of the elements which don't have the same density." Luce Irigaray, *L'Oubli de l'air*, p. 10, from Naomi Schor, "This Essentialism Which Is Not One: Coming to Grips With Irigaray," in *Engaging*

with Irigaray: Feminist Philosophy and Modern European Thought, ed. Carolyn Burke, Naomi Schor, and Margaret Whitford (New York: Columbia University Press, 1994), p. 72.

3. See Catherine Malabou, *Plasticity at the Dusk of Writing: Dialectic, Destruction, Deconstruction*, trans. Carolyn Shread (New York: Columbia University Press, 2010), p. 44.

4. On this very concept of the "motor scheme," see ibid., p. 12–17. In particular, in referring to Derrida, Malabou writes that, "for example, the act of conferring an enlarged meaning on writing has nothing at all to do with an arbitrary decision or 'word play.' All thought needs a *scheme*, that is, a *motive*, produced by a rational imagination, enabling it to force open the door to an epoch and open up exegetical perspectives suited to it." Ibid., p. 13. Or again, of this new meaning of writing: "it is also an invention born of a productive philosophical imagination." Catherine Malabou. *Changing Difference: The Feminine and the Question of Philosophy*, trans. Carolyn Shread (Malden, MA: Polity, 2011), p. 54.

5. Naomi Schor, "This Essentialism Which Is Not One," p. 66. On plasticity as the new motor scheme, see Malabou, *Plasticity at the Dusk of Writing*, pp. 57–62 and *Changing Difference*, pp. 55–66.

6. Schor, "This Essentialism Which Is Not One," p. 67.

7. Charlotte Perkins Gilman, in her 1898 work, *Women and Economics*, argues that woman is the product of civilization and custom rather than natural selection, the direct action from which men have cut her off, such that her condition is that of "exaggerated sex-development." In sum, woman develops according to the skills and character that help her retain [her] status as a dependent and parasitical being—a "gypsy moth." Charlotte Perkins Gilman, *Women and Economics*, in *The American Intellectual Tradition*, vol. 2: *1865 to the Present*, ed. David Hollinger and Charles Capper (New York: Oxford University Press, 2011), pp. 96–102, p. 97 and p. 99, respectively.

8. Schor, "This Essentialism Which Is Not One," p. 67.

9. Ibid., p. 67. "But there is yet another aspect of mimesis . . . that has largely been misread, and even repressed, because it involves a far more controversial and riskier operation, a transvaluation rather than a repudiation of the discourse of misogyny, an effort to hold onto the baby while draining out the bathwater."

10. This point is developed and argued in Jeffrey W. Robbins, "Changing Ontotheology: Paul Tillich, Catherine Malabou, and the Plastic God," in *Retrieving the Radical Tillich: His Legacy and Contemporary Importance*, ed. Russell Re Manning (New York: Palgrave Macmillan, 2015), chapter 9.

11. Ibid.

12. See Jeffrey W. Robbins, *Between Faith and Thought: An Essay on the Ontotheological Condition* (Charlottesville: University of Virginia Press, 2003).

13. Irigaray, *L'Oubli de l'air*.

14. Catherine Malabou, *The Heidegger Change*, trans. Peter Skafish (New York: SUNY Press, 2011).

15. Robbins, "Changing Ontotheology."

16. Malabou, *Changing Difference*, p. 99.

17. See Karen Barad, "Getting Real: Technoscientific Practices and the Materialization of Reality," in *Differences: A Journal of Feminist Cultural Studies* 10, no. 2 (1998): 87–128.

18. Ibid., p. 112.

19. Interview with Bob Simon, "Hollywood's Villain: Kim Dotcom," *60 Minutes*, January 5, 2014, http://www.cbsnews.com/news/kim-dotcom-60-minutes/ (accessed on January 6, 2014).

20. See USA v. Dotcom et al, 1:12-cr-00003, No. 1 (E.D.Va. Jan. 5, 2012), p. 2, https://www.docketalarm.com/cases/Virginia_Eastern_District_Court/1--12-cr-00003/USA_v._Dotcom_et_al/1/ (accessed June 15, 2014), http://www.immagic.com/eLibrary/ARCHIVES/GENERAL/USCOURTS/V120105U.pdf(accessed June 25, 2015).

21. *Official Report of the Nineteenth Annual Conference of Charities and Correction* (1892), pp. 46–59, rpt. Richard H. Pratt, "The Advantages of Mingling Indians with Whites," *Americanizing the American Indians: Writings by the "Friends of the Indian," 1880–1900* (Cambridge: Harvard University Press, 1973), pp. 260–71, http://historymatters.gmu.edu/d/4929/ (accessed on January 3, 2014).

22. Ibid.

23. Ibid.

24. Ibid.

25. Ibid.

26. From the German *Lebensunwertes Leben*. The phrase gained currency within the context of the Nazi euthanasia program that ran from 1939 and was supposedly disbanded in 1941, though, in other words, it was expanded through extermination camps. At its inception, the euthanasia program aimed to do away with the incurably ill, the mentally and physically disabled, and the elderly. It operated through "psychiatric institutions, hospitals, and homes for chronically ill patients." The point was to be disburdened from the charge of caring for, and then of living with, those deemed "inferior." See *Encyclopaedia Britannica Online*, s.v. "T4 Program," http://www.britannica.com/EBchecked/topic/714411/T4-Program (accessed May 23, 2014).

27. While the dictum may be used by anti-Semites and Christian apologists, the sentiment it evokes is found in Rashi's interpretation of the Talmudic maxim "the Jew, though he has sinned, remains a Jew" (Sanhedrin 44a), as he applied it to the apostate (whether he converted willfully or was forced into conversion). This is Jacob Katz's contention as evidenced in the following: "By using [the maxim] in this striking manner [in reference to the apostate], Rashi ensured the almost uncontested adoption of his definition. Behind this clear-cut statement lies an

emphasis on the unchangeable character of the Jew, an emphasis that would contest any possible justification for obliterating Judaism by baptism. Jacob Katz. *Exclusiveness and Tolerance: Studies in Jewish-Gentile Relations in Medieval and Modern Times* (Springfield, NJ.: Behrman House, 1961), p. 71. The racialization of Judaism thus ontologizes a definition that was a response to the hostile or hegemonic milieu of medieval Europe. But it does this in spite of the fact that, as Daniel Boyarin writes:

> There are significant differences between Jewishness and the modern socio-political senses of race. The primary dissimilarity involves the fact that people can convert to Judaism. . . . More revealingly, however, the convert's name is changed to "ben Avraham" or "bas Avraham," son or daughter of Abraham. The convert is adopted into the family and assigned a new genealogical identity, but also, since Abraham is the first convert in Jewish tradition, converts are his descendants in that sense as well. . . . On the other hand, Jews do not sense of themselves that their association is confessional, that it is based on common religion, for many people whom both religious and secular Jews call Jewish neither believe nor practice the religion at all. This kind of "racialism" is built into the formal cultural system.

Daniel Boyarin, *A Radical Jew: Paul and the Politics of Identity* (Berkeley: University of California Press, 1997), p. 241.

28. J. Kameron Carter, in *Race: A Theological Account* (New York: Oxford University Press, 2008), argues quite strikingly that, well before the Spanish Inquisition and *limpieza de sangre*, Christianity's efforts to separate itself from its Jewish origins is what led to the racialization of Judaism, to the becoming white (as universal) of Christianity, and to the ensuing relegation of Jews to an inferior status together with the inception of white supremacy. Thus, for Carter, race consciousness clearly precedes race as color. In other words, in order for whiteness to be supreme, Jews cannot be "white," not even through conversion, as that would negate the distinction between Christianity and its Jewish roots, without which the myth of white supremacy could not be. In this sense then, Jews are "too white"—they "have the *wrong* religion"—to be mingled with whites without risk of corruption: collapse of Christianity with its Jewish roots = collapse of white supremacy.

29. Daniel Colucciello Barber, "The Immanent Refusal of Conversion," in *Journal for Cultural and Religious Theory* 13, no. 1 (Winter 2014), pp. 142–50, http://www.jcrt.org/archives/13.1/barber.pdf (accessed June 25, 2015).

30. Ibid., p. 145.

31. Luc Ferry and Pierre Jerphagnon, *La tentation du Christianisme* (Paris: Livre de poche, 2010). The temptation of Christianity is its personal God who defies the rules of finitude—it is the internal dialogue it offers.

32. Barber, "The Immanent Refusal of Conversion," p. 150.

33. W. C. Harris, *E Pluribus Unum: Nineteenth-Century American Literature and the Constitutional Paradox* (Iowa City: University of Iowa Press, 2005), p. 196.

34. The Stanford Prison Experiment was part of a larger research project sponsored by the Office of Naval Research to understand the psychological mechanics underlying human aggression. The experiment simulated a prison environment or "total institution." See Craig Haney, Curtis Banks, and Philip Zimbardo, "A Study of Prisoners and Guards in a Simulated Prison," *Naval Research Reviews* 26, no. 9 (1973): 1–17. The 1973 issues can be accessed online at http://hdl.handle.net/2027/ucl.$b672035 (accessed June 25, 2015).

35. Aimé Césaire, "Discourse on Colonialism," trans. Joan Pinkham, in *Discourse on Colonialism* (New York: Monthly Review Press, 2000), p. 33. .

36. Ibid, p. 37.

37. Ibid.

38. See Charles Mills, *The Racial Contract* (Ithaca: Cornell University Press, 1997), p. 24; and Frances Gardiner Davenport, ed., *European Treaties Bearing on the History of the United States and Its Dependencies to 1648* (Washington, DC: Carnegie Institution of Washington, 1917), pp. 20–26 (Google books).

39. Eric Weitz, *A Century of Genocides: Utopias of Race and Nation* (Princeton: Princeton University Press, 2003), p. 64.

40. Ibid., p. 97.

41. For more on this point, see Weitz, *A Century of Genocides*, especially chapter 2, pp. 53–101.

42. Thomas J. J. Altizer, *The New Gospel of Christian Atheism* (Aurora, CA: Davies, 2002), p. 8.

43. Jean-Paul Sartre, *Black Orpheus*, trans. John MacCombie, *Massachusetts Review* 6, no. 1 (Autumn 1964–Winter 1965): 13–52, 45, http://www.jstor.org/stable/25087216 (accessed August 24, 2013).

44. Claire Messud, "Camus and Algeria: The Moral Question," *New York Review of Books,* November 7, 2013, http://www.nybooks.com/articles/archives/2013/nov/07/camus-and-algeria-moral-question/ (accessed on January 3, 2014).

45. Leopoldo Zea, *Essays on Philosophy in History*, in *Latin American Philosophy in the Twentieth Century*, ed. Jorge J. E. Gracia (New York: Prometheus, 1986), pp. 219–30.

46. Augusto Salazar Bondy, *The Meaning and Problem of Hispanic American Thought*, ibid., p. 236.

47. See Ward Blanton's Gospel. I borrow, steal, and plagiarize his words.

48. See Clayton Crockett's Gospel. I borrow, steal, and plagiarize his words, and I believe, self-deluding me, that they do reflect my becoming.

49. It is Antonio Caso who defines sacrifice this way, in contrast to what he calls life as economy, namely living as the least effort with the maximum gain. See *Existence as Economy, Disinterest, and Charity* in *Latin American Philosophy in the Twentieth Century*, ed. Jorge J. E. Gracia (New York: Prometheus, 1986), pp. 48–52.

50. Sartre, *Black Orpheus*, p. 46.
51. See Jeffrey Robbins's Gospel.
52. Ibid.
53. Ibid.

Afterword

1. See the discussion of Ernst Bloch's 1959 *Principle of Hope* in Catherine Keller, *Apocalypse Now and Then: A Feminist Guide to the End of the World* (Boston: Beacon, 1996; rpt. Minneapolis: Fortress, 2005), especially chapter 3.
2. James H. Cone, *The Cross and the Lynching Tree* (Maryknoll: Orbis, 2011), p. 25. Cone here discusses the designation by W. E. B. Du Bois of black faith as a "pythian madness"—sprung from the African forests "mad with supernatural joy."
3. Ward Blanton's radical reading of Paul offers a "spiritual materialism" not apparent in the current spread of (post)secular infatuation with Paul. Ward Blanton, *A Materialism for the Masses: Saint Paul and the Philosophy of Undying Life* (New York: Columbia University Press), 2014.
4. "Seizing an Alternative" was the name of a major conference in Claremont, CA, in June 2015; see http://www.pandopopulus.com.

INDEX

INSURRECTIONS:

Critical Studies in Religion, Politics, and Culture

Slavoj Žižek, Clayton Crockett, Creston Davis,
Jeffrey W. Robbins, Editors

The intersection of religion, politics, and culture is one of the most discussed areas in theory today. It also has the deepest and most wide-ranging impact on the world. Insurrections: Critical Studies in Religion, Politics, and Culture will bring the tools of philosophy and critical theory to the political implications of the religious turn. The series will address a range of religious traditions and political viewpoints in the United States, Europe, and other parts of the world. Without advocating any specific religious or theological stance, the series aims nonetheless to be faithful to the radical emancipatory potential of religion.